BLOOMSBURY
PORTRAITS

BLOOMSBURY PORTRAITS

Vanessa Bell, Duncan Grant,
and their circle

RICHARD SHONE

PHAIDON

for Richard and Sally Morphet

Phaidon Press Limited, Littlegate House
St Ebbe's Street, Oxford

Published in the United States of America
by E. P. Dutton & Co., Inc.

First published 1976
© 1976 by Phaidon Press Limited
All rights reserved

ISBN 0 7148 1628 0

Library of Congress Catalog Card Number: 76–5354

Printed in Great Britain by Jolly & Barber Ltd., Rugby

Contents

List of Illustrations

8

The frontispiece is *The Hookah Smoker, c.* 1924, Duncan Grant, 8 × 5 in. Private Collection, London.

The two designs used at the beginning of chapters have been adapted from drawings by Vanessa Bell.

The boards on this book are adapted from a design by Duncan Grant, 1968.

Acknowledgements

I wish to express my gratitude to the following people who helped me in various ways while I was writing this book:

Mrs Benita Armstrong; Mrs Barbara Bagenal; Dr Wendy Baron; Professor and Mrs Quentin Bell; Dr David Brown of the Tate Gallery; Miss Judith Collins; Miss Elizabeth Cuthbert; the late Mr Harry Daley; Mr Angus Davidson; Mrs Pamela Diamand (for arranging a memorable visit to *Durbins*, her father Roger Fry's house); the Marchioness of Dufferin and Ava; Mr Leigh Farnell; Mrs David Garnett (particularly for an invaluable memoir of her parents' studios); Mrs Barbara Halpern; Sir Rupert Hart-Davis; Mr Michael Holroyd; the Lady Keynes (Mme Lydia Lopokova, who even danced for me); Sir Geoffrey Keynes; Dr W. M. Keynes; Mr Eardley Knollys; Dr Richard Le Page; Mme Charles Mauron of St Rémy; Mr Robert Medley; the late Mr Michael MacCarthy; Miss Yvonne Mitchell; Mr Raymond Mortimer; Miss Lucy Norton; Mrs Ralph Partridge; Mrs Henrietta Partridge; Mrs Frances Spalding; Miss Velda Sprott; Mr Simon Watney; Mr Edward Wolfe.

I would particularly like to thank Mr Duncan Grant who, while remaining admirably disinterested throughout, readily answered many questions, made fruitful suggestions and gave me stimulating, not to say startling, information about his friends and his early life, including irreversible evidence as to the date of his birth. He generously put into my hands his many letters to his mother, letters to him from Jacques Copeau, Virginia Woolf and others and some autobiographical writings. Mr Keith Baynes has been extremely helpful in a number of ways, not least in showing me letters to him from Vanessa Bell. Miss Diana Holman Hunt has been a constant source of encouragement and information from when I first began writing this book and I am grateful for her keen comments on several of its earlier chapters. To Mr Richard Morphet I owe much, not least the many discussions we have had in which he shared with me his information and inspiring enthusiasm. His attentive reading of my manuscript saved me from several errors.

A note on the unpublished sources used in this book appears after the bibliography. For permission to read and make quotations from them I gratefully acknowledge Professor Quentin Bell, Mrs Pamela Diamand, Mrs David Garnett, Mr Duncan Grant and Sir Geoffrey Keynes. I would also like to thank here all those people who have allowed me to reproduce pictures and photographs in their possession, especially Mr Anthony d'Offay.

I take pleasure in recording the kindness I received from the late

Dr A. N. L. Munby of King's College Library, Cambridge, and from his most helpful assistants; the Fawcett Society for allowing me access to certain Strachey papers; the Library of the Victoria and Albert Museum; the Witt Collection at the Courtauld Institute; and the Westminster Public Reference Library. I gratefully record my debt to Miss Daphne Roddick of the Lefevre Gallery, to the Mayor Gallery, to Thomas Agnew & Sons, to the Gallery Edward Harvane and above all to the Anthony d'Offay Gallery for photographs, information and encouragement on so many occasions.

I wish to thank Mr John Calmann, late of the Phaidon Press, for all his interest and industry on my behalf, his severe criticisms and firm but understanding help throughout the writing of this book; to the staff and photographers of my publisher and to my vigilant editor Mrs Diana Davies. She made an heroic effort with my manuscript and her numerous suggestions were always to the point and have only been to its betterment.

1. *Vanessa Bell*, 1942, by Duncan Grant. 40 × 24 in. The Tate Gallery, London. Painted at Charleston during the Second World War, this is one of Grant's most penetrating portraits of Vanessa Bell

Introduction

Since I began writing this book four years ago (1971) the two painters who are my subjects have become better known to a wider public not only through exhibitions of their work but by much writing about the circle with which they were intimately connected – 'Bloomsbury'. Bearing in mind this increase in knowledge I have altered the original conception of this book. A more general work on Bloomsbury as a whole illustrated by paintings by Duncan Grant and Vanessa Bell composed the initial plan. I then realized that in fact little was known beyond some generalities and a few often repeated anecdotes about the lives of these painters. Duncan Grant's appearance in the biography of Lytton Strachey threw little light on his activities as a painter, and similarly little is known about Vanessa Bell save her important role in the life of her sister Virginia Woolf. This was only to be expected. While the painters were an absolutely essential element in their group of friends, they led relatively quiet lives. They were rarely embroiled in art politics as were Roger Fry or Clive Bell; polemics and propaganda were of little interest to them and generated no enthusiasm. They were essentially private and immensely hard-working. The tremendous social life enjoyed by Clive Bell or Virginia Woolf, for example, was not for them and though they could never be called unsociable their activities as painters came before all else. Thus I have chosen to narrate their lives in terms of their painting, keeping away, at one extreme, from a too personal narrative and at the other, from an almost entirely critical book.

Because of the accessibility of the writings of Virginia Woolf, of Strachey and Forster, and the widespread influence of Keynes and Fry, the two painters in Bloomsbury have not received the recognition they deserve. As one commentator has written of Vanessa Bell, referring to her later years (she died in 1961):

> Art world tastes of the period and the preponderance on public display of more recent works combined to render almost or actually invisible the bold pioneering work she did between the ages of 30 and 40. This in turn led both to an undervaluing, perhaps – even when it was praised – of her later work . . . and to an exaggerated distinction being made between her easel painting and her decorative work.[1]

Much the same could be said of Duncan Grant. His fame was at its greatest between the two World Wars, his work entered galleries the world over, from Vancouver to Cape Town, and he was one of the few English artists with any reputation in France. During the second War and afterwards this position was reversed and he became one of the most neglected painters in England and his reputation abroad dwindled rapidly.

So varied is Grant's style and subject matter, so disarmingly indifferent has he been to wordly preoccupations and prevailing tastes, that neglect and hostility were only too inevitable. The exhibition of much bad work (he is a prolific artist) has resulted in an easy dismissal and to his critics his weapons seem ludicrously modest and self-effacing. The lyricism of his best work becomes the plodding realism of his least good and the lyric is often despised in favour of weightier concepts. Only recently, through a variety of circumstances, has the richness of his early achievement been revealed and though it would be dangerous to isolate it within his whole output, it is conspicuously adventurous beyond the confines of English modernism. In his work as decorator, Grant has a more spontaneous and inventive style of design in two dimensions than any of his contemporaries. His work appears increasingly substantial, as it continues to be 'rediscovered', in its sensuous and humane contemplation of the natural world.

The lengthiest and most detailed part of the book – the whole central section – deals with the years from 1910 to 1920. They were baffling, exciting, continually changing years in the private lives and in the painting of Duncan Grant and Vanessa Bell. There is a large cast of characters, much changing of houses and studios, influential visits abroad, the two Post-Impressionist Exhibitions, the founding and running of the Omega Workshops and of course, sandwiched in the decade, the Great War. From all these changes and new experiences and experiments, certain themes emerge and roots are put down which I have tried to develop in the less detailed later sections of the book. In the 1920s and '30s, their lives were more fluent and rhythmic, with a solid background of work in Sussex, in London and the South of France.

I must say something here with regard to 'Bloomsbury' for I have not felt the necessity in this book for a lengthy discussion of the subject. I know this will please some people and others will perhaps be disappointed, so insatiable is the present appetite for anything touching on that subject. That there was such a thing as Bloomsbury I have never doubted though most of the so-called members have been reluctant to assert its existence. But much of what I have read about Bloomsbury over several years seems to me to be rubbish. It would be tedious to cite examples of the misconceptions, the absence or abuse of the facts and the resulting mistakes in judgement. Frequently a mantle of common philosophical or aesthetic agreement is thrown over this highly varied group of friends as an explanation for their intimacy, swamping individuality of temperament and expression. That somewhat drab garment *Principia Ethica* of George E. Moore is usually the garb for such concealment. Undoubtedly it was influential and had also an indirect effect on those in Bloomsbury who did not read it. The cultivation and value of personal relationships which it extols must not however be taken too earnestly as a motivating force behind the group's continued existence. Accidents of geography, of family, marriage, love, and similarity of work are equally important. Of course this is true of any group of friends but at the risk of stating the obvious, it must be stressed. There was personal antagonism and uneasiness between 'members' of the group. Rows, jealousies and sharp differences of opinions add a lively counterpoint to the generally smooth melody of friendship. Invariably, such upsets were caused by the introduction of a new element – a new activity or a new friend – which threatened the established pattern of life. An unspoken frame of reference guided each person's response to this novelty. It was pitted against assumptions and ideas about conduct which were adaptable but which could hardly be ignored. This applied more to the earlier days of Bloomsbury; later on such conscious rigour was relaxed.

This brings me to that other much discussed point of when Bloomsbury began and when it ceased to exist. Some say that the outbreak of the First World War brought it to a rapid end; others that it survived the War and that the true Bloomsbury only really flourished in the 1920s and '30s. Some take the death in 1932 of Lytton Strachey as the end of Bloomsbury and others the death nine years later of Virginia Woolf. For myself I prefer to think of the beginning of Bloomsbury as around 1910 for reasons which will become obvious in the narrative, a date rather later than the majority of writers. The First War was a testing time for those Bloomsbury friendships owing to the overwhelmingly pacifist feelings of the group. The friendships survived and after the War there was a public and a private Bloomsbury. In the 1920s it hit the headlines, the name was used in the newspapers and in books. As early as 1922 we find an article in an American periodical called 'Bloomsbury and Clive Bell' introducing American readers to Lytton Strachey, Virginia Woolf, Vanessa Bell, Maynard Keynes and Duncan Grant. Surprisingly the names mentioned can be said to be of Bloomsbury. So often all sorts of people, some most improbable, have been made members of the group – Max Beerbohm for example and George Bernard Shaw. In this book I have not attempted to bring in everyone usually called Bloomsbury – there is little reference to E. M. Forster or Desmond MacCarthy. In a study from a literary angle they would appear prominently. Figures come forward or recede as is natural in a group of friends and I have tried to show as far as possible the Bloomsbury painters' relationships with others of their own profession; such names as Sickert or Derain, Nina Hamnett, Segonzac or Marchand might not be mentioned in other discussions of the group. But the charge of exclusiveness and snobbery in their personal relations cannot I feel be levelled at the painters.

As I have gone further into the relationships within Bloomsbury, Vanessa Bell emerges as the pivotal figure and not, as some would have it, Lytton Strachey or Virginia Woolf. She was essentially unworldly and an absolutely dedicated painter. She liked to, and usually did, get what she wanted for herself and her immediate circle, and in that circle was, under a seemingly mild and silent surface, demanding almost to the point of ruthlessness. In circumstances beyond her range of personal influence, she was reasonableness itself. Her maternal instincts were exceptionally strong. She was psychologically complicated, but could be maddeningly simple, untroubled

2. Vanessa Bell at Cassis,
c. 1929

by others' motivations and sometimes blind to their feelings. Increasingly in her later life the prospect of a visitor, an old friend even, could shatter her nerve completely, she could not paint, the clouds gathered, life was intolerable. The threat of invasion hung over her, the charmed circle was in danger. 'You give one a sense of security of something solid and real in a shifting world,' wrote Roger Fry to her. To keep and tend this security and maintain her confidence (for she neurotically deprecated her gifts), she would go to great lengths in establishing a familiar and protected territory around her, staking out the ground with determination.

One of the constant features of the relationship between Vanessa Bell and Duncan Grant was her unbounded admiration for his painting. She was prepared to play second fiddle and this became the public view of her work, that she was a pale imitator. To anyone looking at the illustrations in this book, the differences between the two painters are soon apparent and in the text I have further developed this theme. The similarity of their subject matter – the landscapes in Sussex and France, the Venetian views, interiors of Charleston, and the same models for portraits and figure compositions – it is this which often confuses and blurs the distinction between their approach and style. In their decorative work their personalities are distinctive, particularly when they are working on a small scale – painting pottery or designing a book jacket for example. Vanessa Bell does not have that large

3. Virginia Woolf at a picnic, *c.* 1939

imaginative conception of composition which is Duncan Grant's. But she can be extraordinarily resourceful with a few basic forms when designing a fabric or painting a tile, whereas Duncan Grant is inclined to be over-elaborate. In decorative work of a larger scale, he is exuberant, often fantastic, and attempts more ambitious schemes. She is altogether graver, less restless, less concerned with her actual subject matter. 'Mr Grant taps', wrote Virginia Woolf, whereas Mrs Bell is as 'mute as mackerel'.

In later years her subject matter narrowed even more in her easel painting. 'I don't think I'm nearly as enterprising as you (or Duncan),' she wrote to Roger Fry, 'about painting anything I don't find at my door.'[2] But her responses were fresh despite the familiarity of her surroundings. Duncan Grant was always more willing to make forays into new circles or discover new landscapes. His sympathies were wider and his prejudices much less rigid. One of the delights of his character was his fondness for out of the way facts and a peculiarly magical response to seemingly ordinary sights and situations. Roger Fry conveys some of this in a letter to Vanessa Bell: 'I think I'd felt, going about London with Duncan, more than ever how wonderful his visual life is, how infinitely quick he is in his reaction to sight, how he misses the point of nothing. He can look at every face in the street and never miss one that has something in it, and all the time be seeing the whole effect and all with such a curious imaginative intensity.'[3] It is to his credit as well as to his friends' that he emerges virtually unscathed from all the memoirs and letters, published and unpublished, that I have read during the writing of this book. One of the reasons for this unblotted copybook is perhaps the one matter for criticism – his secretiveness. Even Virginia Woolf found this rather an obstacle when probing for information or for gossip.

I have chosen to end the book with the death of Vanessa Bell's son Julian in 1937 in Spain and the approach of the Second World War. There began then a process of withdrawal, only in part brought about by physical circumstances. In 1939 Vanessa Bell's house in the South of France was given up and in 1940 her London studio was bombed along with Duncan Grant's in Fitzroy Street. A few months later in 1941 her sister Virginia committed suicide.

Life after the War was considerably different for Vanessa Bell and Duncan Grant and belongs to another kind of book. In my attempt to convey the variety of their work and the sort of lives they led in the twenties and thirties, I am conscious of omissions of fact and circumstance. Of the careers of Vanessa Bell's children, of the deaths of Roger Fry and Lytton Strachey, for example, there is little or no mention. It seemed to me more urgent to record events and friendships which as yet have gone unrecorded, which exist only in people's memories or in tattered press-cuttings. This is particularly true of the decorative work of the two painters, most of which perished in the War or has since been variously destroyed.

The life style they embraced was a complex mixture of inheritance and personal preference. There was a touch of camping out, a happy domestic improvisation which comically clashed with sturdy middle-class comfort and fastidious culture. There was nothing precious about it, though aesthetic enjoyment of one's surroundings was often placed before other considerations. To some it seemed intolerably Bohemian and haphazard, to others, too ample and not Bohemian enough.

Against such a background went hard work and constant occupation. A chance visitor arriving at Charleston, Vanessa Bell's home for many years, might reasonably have thought the house empty until one by one the inhabitants emerged from studio or library, from the pottery or a corner of the garden, to meet for an unhurried lunch or lingering tea. Then it was back to a History of the Roman Empire in French, to a still life in the studio or an evening landscape, to proof-reading or writing a review, to weeding or sewing or sitting in a deckchair to talk, cigarette smoke curling blue against the flint wall of the garden and floating over it with drifts of conversation and laughter.

London
January 1975

[1] Richard Morphet, 'Vanessa Bell', catalogue introduction to exhibition, Anthony d'Offay Gallery, 1973, p.5.

[2] 16 September 1921.

[3] 24 November 1918.

Of the numerous portraits and drawings of Vanessa Bell by Duncan Grant there is one which is better known than all others (plate 1). It shows her at the age of sixty-three, seated on a high-backed chair, eyes gazing from under heavy lids at the spectator. A long brown cloak covers her shoulders and falls either side to the floor revealing as it does so its rich red lining. A screen behind her with purple draperies on top emphasizes the formal nature of the portrait's conception. Seen here as almost a late Victorian of consequence, she appears regal in bearing 'sensitive but uncompromising', an individual viewing the world on her own terms and yet a figure whose roots go back into the nineteenth century. Her life consciously and unconsciously was a re-action against that nineteenth-century youth, a building up of elaborate barricades·against a siege which remained an ever-vivid possibility. In so doing she exercised some of those qualities inherited from her father which paradoxically had made her early years at times so unhappy for her.

Born on 30 May 1879 Vanessa was the oldest child of Sir Leslie Stephen and his second wife Julia Duckworth (*née* Jackson). Julia brought to the Stephen household at 22 Hyde Park Gate her three children by her first husband Herbert Duckworth, George, Stella and Gerald, who were alto-gether more conventional than her four children by Sir Leslie. In 1880 when she was thirty-four Thoby was born; Adeline Virginia followed in 1882 and Adrian, the last, in 1883. In temperament and looks Vanessa was closer to her mother than was Virginia who tended to sympathize with their father, the author, critic, and editor of the *Dictionary of National Biography*. Their mother was a daughter of one of the Pattle sisters, famous for their beauty and their accomplishments in the world of Society. Sarah Pattle had married Thoby Prinsep and settled at Little Holland House which became a focal point for the Pre-Raphaelites, and where Holman-Hunt and Woolner became enamoured of the Prinseps' daughter Julia, and where the guests, informally but lavishly entertained, included Tennyson, Gladstone, Dis-raeli and Thackeray. G. F. Watts had a studio in the house and conceived a passion for a sixteen-year-old actress, Ellen Terry, whom he disastrously married. Val Prinsep, Julia's cousin, became a painter under the encourage-ment of Watts, studied in Paris where Whistler and du Maurier were fellow students and associated with the Pre-Raphaelites. He became an R.A. and died in 1904. His *Home from Gleaning* (shown at the Fine Art Society, London, in 1973) shows four robustly-limbed girls with suspiciously Pattle-like faces, carrying their loads, like bundles of accumulated sin and guilt, through a melancholy landscape lit by a harvest moon. Another remarkable artist-relation of Vanessa's was her great-aunt Julia Margaret Cameron who late in an eccentric life took to photography with brilliant results. It is from her camera that we can appreciate not only the awe-inspiring looks of Tennyson and the nervous profile of Carlyle but also the dreamy, heavy-lidded, long-necked beauty of Julia Stephen as a young woman.

In spite of these connections with an earlier generation of artists, the Stephen family were conspicuously literary and frequent guests to the house were James Russell Lowell (Virginia's godfather), Thackeray's daughter Aunt Anny Ritchie (the novelist sister of Sir Leslie's first wife), George Meredith, Thomas Hardy and Henry James. Painters to be sure were visitors – Burne-Jones, Watts, Charles Furse, their neighbour Arthur Studd, and the very young William Rothenstein – but they were not so intimate with the family as were the writers. However when Vanessa started drawing lessons under Sir Arthur Cope and later attended the Royal Academy Schools there were stimulating if not always sympathetic visits to Watts and encouragement from Furse.[1] The latter's portrait of Vanessa was exhibited at the New English Art Club in 1902. Furse had studied under Legros at the Slade and in Paris. He was very much in favour of the French Impressionists, particularly Degas, and was also influenced by Whistler. His appreciations must have encouraged Vanessa in her own admiration of Whistler and in her distaste for the Royal Academicians. Furse was by all accounts a most delightful man and no doubt Vanessa regarded him, such was her ignorance at that time of contemporary French painting, as very progressive, a member of the New English Art Club and an exhibitor at the Paris Salon. In his last years, he became extremely friendly with Sargent and painted under his influence.[2]

After the death of Julia Stephen in 1885, her daughter Stella Duckworth took charge of the young Stephens but this arrangement was not to last for Stella married shortly afterwards and a year later she died. Vanessa's responsibilities therefore were onerously increased. She had to care for the unstable Virginia, adminster to the blackmailing moods and demands of her shattered father, and attend to the daily running of the household and such domestic trivia as the entertaining of old friends and relations, the tea-table duties of a young Victorian woman. We can get some idea of this life from Virginia's novel *Night and Day* through the character of Katherine Hilbery. The book is dedicated appropriately to Vanessa and is a monument to her courage, care and suffering. Although Virginia felt it was not a picture of their 'particular Hell' it apparently gave Vanessa 'the horrors'. Katherine Hilbery secretly studies mathematics which is paralleled by Vanessa's study of painting.

In 1899 Thoby went up to Trinity, Cambridge, and a new element and new friends entered the Stephens' lives. There were weekend visits, May Balls, friendships with the Darwin girls and talk of Thoby's new friends – Strachey, Woolf, Sydney Turner and Clive Bell. Thoby, the adored brother with his splendid figure and disarmingly truthful eyes in his handsome face was surrounded by admirers but unspoilt it seems. He was a natural law-giver, upright, tending towards the conservative, a fine though not brilliant

mind, with Johnsonian opinions, slightly pedantic but with an elegant sense
of humour. Yet despite his letters and the accounts we have of him, he
remains curiously out of focus, unlike the chiselled features of his photograph. His goodness and his beauty were enhanced, indeed almost petrified,
by his early death. His influence was profound on his friends and family. He
was the inspiration for the hero in *Jacob's Room* and for Percival in *The
Waves*.

Towards the end of her apprenticeship under Arthur Cope, Vanessa
decided to try for the Royal Academy Schools, and drawings from the
antique had to be submitted for judgement. 'I have been at the studio all
today where I am drawing my Academy figure. It's very dull and I'm doing it
very badly so I don't expect I shall even get my first drawings accepted – I
don't know where I shall hide my head then.'[3] In spite of this characteristic
modesty, her drawings were accepted and for the next three years Vanessa
attended the Academy Schools. Among her teachers were MacBey and
Sargent. Though in later years she deprecated the School as hopelessly out of
touch, for Sargent as teacher she retained great admiration and found his
criticisms helpful in a way no others were. 'Sargent is teaching most extraordinarily well at the R.A. How I wish you were there,' she told a friend.[4] 'He
gives lessons as you said he did that would apply to any painting. . . . He
generally tells me that my things are too gray. The one thing he is down upon
is when he thinks anyone is trying for an effect regardless of truth.' While this
last stricture may seem surprising coming from Sargent, it was certainly
something he could not apply to Vanessa. In fact he was 'a splendid teacher
and very kind to her' reported Virginia to Thoby. Three days a week were
spent at the Academy and three days at home, often working from nude
models or at the monthly composition.

'How many females tried for Paris' apples? and where can I read about it in
English?' she appealed to her scholarly brother. 'It's the subject for this
month's composition at the R.A. and I want to do it as Sargent will criticize.
You might send me a card with all information as soon as possible. The rest of
my family is grossly ignorant.'[5] The family helped in other respects with
gifts of paints and books – Fra Angelico and Botticelli were two she
particularly wanted.[6]

Vanessa's closest friend at this time was a young art student, Margery
Snowdon, and it is in her letters to Margery that we get some idea of her
preoccupations, her views on technique, painting and painters, and on the
difficulties of working and running a family at the same time, particularly
since her father was becoming increasingly ill and her sister subject to
alarming periods of depression and insanity. Margery was, according to
Vanessa, 'a wise, sensible and consoling old animal' and had the advantage of
coming from a very different background. Among Vanessa's other friends
were Mary Creighton, daughter of the famous Bishop Creighton, and a
rather up-to-date girl called Sylvia Milman who later on, much to Vanessa
and Margery's horror, exhibited at the Royal Academy, an institution regarded by them with the utmost distaste. But they all generally agreed that
the French Impressionists were enormously interesting and all that was

modern, and that Whistler was preferable to Watts. There are very few paintings by Vanessa done before 1907 in existence, but certainly the influence of Whistler is evident, especially in the general low tone of her painting, the grayness to which Sargent referred.[7]

In March 1903, Vanessa visited Watts in his Surrey studio: 'Mr Watts is painting a huge tree trunk covered with ivy. "That's going to be sent to the Academy as a protest against Impressionism. You see every leaf is clearly painted. There's no smearing and cleanness is a great quality".' He continued in this vein – anti-Impressionist, Rubens having no style, Rossetti as the greatest of the great men he had known, anecdotes of Millais, praise of Sargent and Shannon. '"When I paint a picture I want to give a message and I care comparatively little about how good the art is. . . . "' Vanessa makes no comment in her report to Margery Snowdon but she must have found such views questionable. A year or two later, Watts's work struck her as 'rather beastly'. But at the time of this visit, Watts was still venerated by the Stephen family. He had painted both Leslie and Julia.[8]

On the surface Vanessa was very much part of the late Victorian scene. 'She looked as though she might have walked among the fair women of Burne-Jones's *Golden Stairs*; but she spoke with the voice of Gauguin.' Rothenstein's implication is clear though it is doubtful whether Gauguin meant anything to Vanessa in 1903.[9] With the death of her father on 22 February 1904, the Victorian scene, Watts, and much else went out of the window as it opened, gradually but firmly, onto a different landscape. While Sir Leslie's relationship with his children had become more affectionate in his last years, his death was a liberation for Vanessa in a way that the grieving Virginia did not comprehend until years later. It brought a sense of freedom and time to work, above all an independence which before had seemed impossible; nothing need be taken for granted or accepted for purely conventional reasons. There was no longer the weekly agony of taking the household books for Sir Leslie's groaning, horrified inspection, where a characteristic silence was her only self-protection; no need to dress for fashionable parties with George Duckworth or to pour tea and listen to the rambling of critical relations and family friends.

A holiday in Italy was planned and on 1 April the four Stephens and Gerald Duckworth went to Venice. Vanessa spent most of the time looking at pictures and found Tintoretto 'an absolute revelation', an enthusiasm she shared with Thoby who wrote in the Venetian's praise to his Cambridge friend Clive Bell, attempting to convert him from his antipathy. Vanessa discovered for herself that Ruskin's aesthetic found little place in her own experiences in Venice. 'He never cares for anything unless it is a symbol or has several deep meanings which doesn't seem to me to be what one wants.'[10]

After a fortnight in Venice, the Stephens travelled to Florence to join Violet Dickinson, then Virginia's closest friend. Vanessa had been in Florence two years before – 'the loveliest place I had ever seen and still think so'. There were numerous English visitors bringing an unwelcome whiff of Hyde Park Gate; but pictures came first, mainly the earlier Italians such as Cimabue, Giotto, Filippo Lippi and Botticelli. Her appreciation of these painters was not at all conventional and we find a parallel independence in Duncan Grant's discoveries when he came to Florence the following year.

As an exhilarating finale to the holiday, there was a week in Paris where Vanessa with Virginia, chaperoned by Violet Dickinson, rejoined Thoby who had been on a walking tour. It was in Paris that they were entertained by Thoby's close friend Clive Bell who was beginning to appear more frequently in the sisters' lives. Bell introduced them to the young Gerald Kelly and the painter Roderick O'Conor; they visited Rodin's studio and at the Salon Vanessa particularly admired Whistler and Sargent. They dined with Bell at the Café de la Régence. For Virginia, while the holiday had its pleasurable moments, it was made painful by Vanessa's eager absorption, so soon after their father's death, in the pictures she saw and the people she met, her excitement in Italy and the sympathetic café life to which she had been introduced, the closest she had yet come to Bohemianism. She hoped, she wrote after returning home, that Clive Bell and 'Mr Kelly' would 'continue those arguments' one day in London.

It is as well to say something here of Clive Bell and doubtless at the time the Stephens were saying a great deal about him. He was born in 1881 into a wealthy family who had made their fortune from coal and occupied a place in Wiltshire society as conspicuous as it was dull. They owned a large Victorian gothic mansion, Cleeve House, a philistine establishment where country pursuits occupied pride of place and where 'animals dominated the conversation, yielding only occasionally to lawn tennis, hockey and the weather.'[11] There were two daughters and three sons, Clive being the youngest and as able as any young county gentleman to hold his own in the traditional country sports. He was educated at Marlborough, a time on which he looked back, though rarely, with a distaste and even bitterness. There was something which prevented him from following the herd, from being moulded into the typical rich young gentleman his parents presumed they were rearing. In fact, Clive was saved by his intelligence and capacity for scholarliness and hard work, and a sensitivity which in a less robust person, one with a less greedy delight in life, would perhaps have proved fatal or at least atrophying.

Clive went up to Trinity College, Cambridge, in the autumn of 1899 and within a month or so he met Thoby Stephen (whom he later called his 'first real friend'), Leonard Woolf and Lytton Strachey – all introduced to him by Saxon Sydney Turner – the remarkable nucleus of what was to become Bloomsbury. Along with another undergraduate A. J. Robertson, they formed the 'Midnight Society', 'which met at midnight because another – the X – of which some of us were members, met earlier on Saturday evening, assembled in my rooms in the New Court, and having strengthened itself with whisky or punch and one of those gloomy beef-steak pies which it was the fashion to order for Sunday lunch, proceeded to read aloud some such trifle as *Prometheus Unbound*, *The Cenci*, *The Return of the Druses*, *Bartholomew Fair* or *Comus*.'[12]

Clive and Thoby tended to pair off through their interest in sport (though not competitive College sports), Thoby finding Clive an admirable companion, a relief from the sterner stuff of Woolf and the eccentricities of Sydney Turner and Strachey. In Thoby, Clive found a worldly friend – they hunted, smoked cigars and went together to the best London restaurants – and also an escort, as it were, into the late-Victorian intellectual world of the Stephens and Stracheys, and a fellow explorer, though less adventurous than himself, of contemporary literature and ideas. Thoby was one of the earliest of Clive's friends to discuss painting with him and though his appreciation was erratic and conservative, it was stimulating. It is in a letter from Thoby to Clive (February 1906) that there occurs a mention for the first time of Cézanne whose work was on view at the International Society Exhibition among various 'dead or dying froggies' who included Degas, Manet and Monet. Soon after the Paris holiday of 1904 Thoby noticed and admired two paintings at the New Gallery by Jacques-Emile Blanche, later Duncan Grant's master at 'La Palette', his school in Paris.

After some desultory research for a dissertation on the Congress of Verona and an autumn spent big-game shooting with his father in British Columbia, Clive decided to continue his research in Paris. And there he went for a year in January 1904, finding the attractions of a daily visit to the Louvre infinitely more pressing than pouring over documents in the 'Archives'. His friends and acquaintances in Paris were mainly young writers and painters and the society at the 'Chat Blanc' – Roderick O'Conor, Gerald Kelly, J. W. Morrice, Arnold Bennett and Aleister Crowley (who was married to Kelly's sister). Through O'Conor (whom he met in October 1904)[13] and to a lesser extent Morrice, Clive was early introduced to the painting of the Post-Impressionists and the Nabis. Photographs of Cézanne's work littered O'Conor's studio and there were Gauguin drawings, gifts to O'Conor from the painter, on his walls. There was talk of Bonnard, Vuillard and Matisse. Early visits to the Caillebotte collection of Impressionist painting had bowled him over. Clive's initiation into French contemporary painting left an indelible impression; he accepted it at once so that on his return to England he found things very tame when people still talked of Monet and Manet with amazement, flocked to the huge Watts exhibition at the R.A. and to Whistler at the New Gallery, and discussed the latest watercolours by Arthur Melville in rapt admiration. But among the Stephens and friends like Saxon Sydney Turner, he could discuss what he had seen without fear of a complete lack of recognition or of animosity. This certainly endeared him to Vanessa and he wooed her not only with pheasants and grouse but with the ranging gaiety of his conversation and the novelty of his style of living, this strange mixture of cartridges and turpentine, the country club and Paris studio.

The four Stephen children were eager to leave Hyde Park Gate and had discussed the project even before Sir Leslie's death. They were not wealthy but had sufficient money to move into 46 Gordon Square on the Bedford estate in unfashionable Bloomsbury. The square in the nineteenth century had certainly been well-to-do, with admirably respectable inhabitants such as the Rev. Christopher Heath, responsible for the erection of the Catholic Apostolic Church, Victorian thirteenth century (adjoining the late Gothic University Hall of Residence), surgeons (Sir Frederick Treves of appendicitis fame), theologians, barristers, journalists, and Sir Charles Whetham, Chairman of the London and Blackwall Railway Company. When the Stephen brothers and sisters went to live there in 1904 it was dowdy with widows, poor students and a characteristic sprinkling of minor aristocracy. Most important, it was far away from Kensington.

Of Thoby's friends, Lytton was at Cambridge forming a fruitful alliance with Maynard Keynes and holding sway over the Apostles Society, Saxon Sydney Turner was at the Treasury, Clive divided his time between Paris and his Temple chambers, Leonard Woolf was just leaving for Ceylon as a member of the Colonial Civil Service, and others were variously employed in London.[14] As a way of keeping in touch with these friends, Thoby decided to be 'at home' one evening a week, rather in the manner of his friends Charles and Dora Sanger who entertained in their rooms on Fridays, opposite the ABC café in the Strand.[15]

Thoby had hardly considered the introduction of his sisters at these evenings but Vanessa with her insatiable curiosity and a mind as independent if less 'educated' than Thoby's and his friends' could scarcely be excluded. Virginia however was more reluctant, being then fiercely anti-male, especially the Cambridge variety. They could not possibly come up to the standard of her father, for instance, or to Meredith, those awesome giants of the previous century. Who could doubt her, seeing the short pale Saxon Sydney Turner lighting his pipe silently on a sofa? How could it be otherwise,

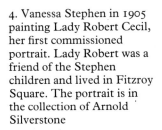

4. Vanessa Stephen in 1905 painting Lady Robert Cecil, her first commissioned portrait. Lady Robert was a friend of the Stephen children and lived in Fitzroy Square. The portrait is in the collection of Arnold Silverstone

seeing Lytton Strachey giggling in a chair, his legs as convoluted as his conversation?

They were at home from 9 o'clock in the evening in the large ground floor sitting-room, Gurth, Vanessa's sheep dog, in attendance and Thoby letting people in. Saxon was a regular, sometimes coming in late after the Opera and Clive was a frequent guest; among other visitors were Hilton Young, Charles Tennyson and Jack Pollock; occasionally Gerald Duckworth came, rather condescending towards these friends, unable to see, as Thoby did, a future for the writings of Clive Bell or Lytton Strachey. Naturally some people brought relations and friends, most notably Lytton whose sisters would sometimes come, especially Marjorie, Pippa and Pernel. Then there might be Edward Marsh, recently appointed Private Secretary to Winston Churchill, and his painter friend Neville Lytton.[16]

In the autumn of 1905, Vanessa decided to form a Club. The Club was to be concerned with painting, a place where artists could talk shop, listen to lectures, discuss their work and even from time to time hold exhibitions. Friday was the chosen day for these meetings, generally held at Gordon Square. There were 'lay' members such as Saxon, and of course Virginia and Adrian. There were Vanessa's female painter friends such as Mary Creighton, Sylvia Milman and Gwen Darwin (later Gwen Raverat).[17] By the time the younger painters came to exhibit (just a year or two before the outbreak of the First War) the Club had ceased to function as a meeting place and only the exhibitions continued, coming to a halt at some time in the early twenties. By then, Vanessa had nothing to do with it; it had, as she said 'gone to the bad', like many such ventures, but in its first seven or eight years it was a useful and in some ways important organization for the progressive painters. Catalogues of the exhibitions are virtually untraceable and references in the press scattered and infrequent. But there was certainly a show in 1907 at Clifford's Inn Hall and another in 1908 (26 June to 23 July) at the Baillie Gallery in Baker Street. In this latter exhibition works by Renoir and Pissarro were also shown and one of Vanessa's earliest works, a small portrait of Saxon Sydney Turner seated at the piano. There were four paintings by J. D. Innes who at the time was painting under Steer's influence, his teacher at the Slade (which Innes had left that summer). Another interesting exhibitor was Bernard Leach, not yet launched into the career of potter. Further exhibitions of which there are records such as those in 1910, 1912 and 1913 are mentioned later.

Vanessa prospered enormously with this new way of life at Gordon Square and she quickly seized any opportunity for fresh experiences. There was for instance the arrival of Henry Lamb, with his rather cruel and beautiful face and his bewitching freedom from conventions, exemplified above all in his mistress Nina Forrest.[18] He had come to London from Manchester where under parental pressure he had studied medicine. On winning an art prize, he hurried off to London with Nina Forrest and studied for a short time at Orpen and John's Chelsea school. His introduction to the Stephen family came through his older brother Walter. Vanessa took up with Lamb and he visited the Friday Club where at one meeting Nina Forrest, such were the

5. *Clive Bell*, c. 1907, by
Vanessa Bell. 9 × 7 in.
Gallery Edward Harvane,
London. Portraits of Clive
Bell are rare. This sketch
was painted soon after the
Bells' marriage

conventions, had to be concealed behind a curtain. Unluckily she was discovered, much to the indignation of the more strait-laced members. There was a plan to share a studio in Chelsea, and Lamb and Vanessa met to discuss the matter. 'Then he asked me to come and have tea with him at a shop and I agreed – so we went to a shop in the King's Road and there we sat for about an hour – Lamb in his corduroys, smoking a pipe – and I thought with joy of how shocked all my friends and relations would be if they could only come in and see us! But our conversation was most innocent and all about Miss Forrest.'[19] Almost certainly Thoby would have scowled at such liberal behaviour and at those pale grey corduroys. Bohemianism was all right with that good fellow Bell but rather unforgivable in his sister.

In the following summer, an ambitious expedition to Greece was planned by the Stephens. Thoby and Adrian went ahead to be joined later by Vanessa, Virginia and the faithful Violet Dickinson, at Olympia. But in Athens Vanessa's health gave way and grew worse as they went on by sea from the Peloponnese to Constantinople. Although Vanessa's condition gave rise to anxiety, it was felt that Thoby might safely travel back early to England. But once back in London he too fell ill. It was thought he had malaria and the alarming diagnosis of typhoid fever came too late. He died on 20 November. The news of his death horrified his friends, particularly that original Cambridge nucleus, Saxon, Leonard Woolf, Lytton and Clive. Clive had been at Gordon Square at the time; two days later Vanessa and Clive became engaged.

The announcement of the engagement was not entirely unexpected among the family and close friends. Clive had proposed to Vanessa in July 1905 but had been turned down. 'It really seems to matter so very little to oneself what one does. I should be quite happy living with anyone whom I didn't dislike if I could paint and lead the kind of life I like – yet for some mysterious reason one has to refuse to do what someone else very much wants one to.'[20] She liked him but was not in love with him and felt it was 'utterly degrading and horrible' to marry for anything but love. She had again turned him down before going to Greece; she had done so with much thought and, in some respects, regret. On his part, Clive was passionate, gallant and pressing; he was positively invigorated by these refusals. By the time of Thoby's death, Vanessa was ready to re-consider his offer. Her feelings were clarified by Clive's grief over Thoby and his concern for herself. She capitulated and after a visit to her future family-in-law which was nearly as distasteful as all her subsequent visits, they were married on 7 February 1907 at the St. Pancras Registry Office, the scene of several of Bloomsbury's excursions into officialdom. They honeymooned first of all in Wales and later, while alterations were carried out at Gordon Square, they went to Paris. There they renewed their slight acquaintance with Duncan Grant (accompanied by Adrian and Virginia), sat talking in the Café de Versailles, met Clive's friends, bought clothes for Vanessa, much to Clive's pleasure for he enjoyed a well-dressed woman, and found themselves enchanted with Paris and each other.

[1] Charles Wellington Furse had married in 1900 Katherine Symonds, daughter of John Addington Symonds and sister to Madge who married a cousin of the Stephens, William Wyamar Vaughan. He died in 1904, aged 36.

[2] The Furse portrait was left to Vanessa Bell by Gerald Duckworth in 1937. It was destroyed by fire, 1940.

[3] VS to J. Thoby Stephen, 6 February 1901.

[4] VS to M. K. Snowdon, *c.* 1902

[5] VS to JTS, December 1901.

[6] A little book on Gainsborough bought at this time was in her studio when she died.

[7] Many of Vanessa Bell's early and student works were destroyed by fire in her studio at 8 Fitzroy Street in 1940. She also destroyed many herself in later years.

[8] In January 1905, she was decidedly 'against' and she told Clive Bell that she had succeeded in persuading Virginia that 'there was nothing to be said "for that family idol, G. F. Watts." ' Quentin Bell, *Virginia Woolf*, Vol. 1, 1972, p.95.

[9] W. Rothenstein, *Men and Memories*, Vol. II, 1934, p.53.

[10] VS to M. K. Snowdon, 9 April 1904.

[11] Quentin Bell, *Virginia Woolf*, Vol. I, 1972, p.113.

[12] Clive Bell, *Old Friends*, p.26

[13] Somerset Maugham told Clive Bell that it was O'Conor rather than Gauguin of whom he was thinking when he wrote *The Moon and Sixpence*.

[14] Ralph Hawtrey, Robin Mayor, Theodore Llewelyn Davies (at the Treasury with Sydney Turner) and Walter Lamb, a friend of Adrian and Clive and brother of the painter Henry Lamb.

[15] For a 'fictional' picture of such an evening see Chapter 4 of *Night and Day* by Virginia Woolf.

[16] It was over Marsh's purchase of Duncan Grant's *Parrot Tulips* in 1911 that Marsh's friendship with Neville Lytton, who could not condone such a 'slovenly piece of work', virtually ended. But in those pre-Post-Impressionist days Neville Lytton found himself able to exhibit with Vanessa Bell's new Friday Club. *Parrot Tulips* is now in Southampton Art Gallery.

[17] The Slade School provided another stratum – Innes, Albert Rutherston (né Rothenstein), Henry Lamb and Edna Clarke Hall (née Waugh) of the older generation, and of the younger ones who later on exhibited with the Club there were Edward Wadsworth, David Bomberg, Gertler, Nevinson and the Nash brothers.

[18] Later to leave Lamb and live with J. D. Innes.

[19] VS to M. K. Snowdon, 21 December 1905.

[20] VS to M. K. Snowdon, 14 August 1905.

Soon after Clive and Vanessa's marriage, it was decided that Adrian and Virginia should move from Gordon Square and leave it to the privacy of the Bells. And so, crossing the Tottenham Court Road, they took 29 Fitzroy Square, an early nineteenth-century house on the west side of the square formerly occupied by, among others, George Bernard Shaw. Later in the year they rather timidly began asking friends on Thursdays. Clive and Vanessa often had two or three people to dine at Gordon Square and would walk over afterwards to join the rest in Adrian's book-lined study on the ground floor looking out to the trees and garden. The company was much the same as the previous 'Thursdays' – Saxon of course, Lytton, Charles Sanger, Hilton Young and Charles Tennyson. But Virginia often asked unexpected friends from Hyde Park Gate days – Janet Case and Clara Pater, Imogen Booth, Katherine Horner (Mrs Raymond Asquith), Lady Beatrice Thynne, and many others whose names remain obscure or later found their ways into very different (and usually more conventional) circles.[1]

It was in these years 1907 and 1908 that Vanessa began to exhibit, very sparingly, some of her work – at the New English Art Club, the more progressive if less select Allied Artists Association, as well as the Friday Club exhibitions. After the birth of her first son Julian on 4 February 1908 and the necessary convalescence, she started painting with greater regularity and disciplined her day. She would see Julian for an hour before 10.30 in the morning and then work for three hours until lunch. After lunch and after tea she would see the baby again for half an hour. In the afternoon she would either paint or attend to household business, shop etc. In the evenings, there was often someone for dinner, there were the Thursdays and the Fridays. In September she and Clive, having rather reluctantly, on her part at any rate, deposited Julian with the Bells at Cleeve House, set out for Italy with Virginia, spending time in Siena and Perugia. Clive's enthusiasm for the early Sienese was infectious and in Perugia Vanessa's main discovery seems to have been the Peruginos in the Galleria Nazionale and his frescoes in the Collegio del Cambio. But the English tourists were a nuisance in their large and luxurious Grand Hotel and encounters in the street were dreaded by Vanessa. The Fletchers, for example, were London acquaintances met constantly at the Booths, the Pollocks and other family friends. 'Hoping to avoid them for ever,' Vanessa 'turned suddenly . . . and gazed into the nearest shop window. Unluckily it was a tallow-chandler's and so the device was obvious.'

6. *Iceland Poppies*, 1908, by Vanessa Bell. 22 × 18 in. Collection Duncan Grant. This still life is one of the few works by Vanessa Bell from before 1910 still in existence. 'Nessa has a picture in the New English, and all her friends are envious,' wrote Virginia Stephen to Violet Dickinson. The painting was commended by Duncan Grant in one of his rare reviews (*Spectator*, 19 June 1909)

Similar stories of Vanessa's unsuccessful attempts to hide from old 'friends' abound in the mythology that arose about her. Clive and Vanessa finished the holiday with a week in Paris where there was further admiration of French clothes and many purchases.

On a visit to Italy the following year Vanessa wrote to Margery that 'Clive is an extraordinarily good person to travel with. He is very deliberate and never loses his head and seems to get one corner seats and food and all other comforts quite easily without any fuss.'[2] It also meant a great deal to her to look at pictures with someone so acutely sensitive and knowledgeable and with tastes that so often coincided with her own and gave her confidence – though Titian was still a stumbling-block with Clive while Vanessa rated him 'higher than anyone'.[3]

7. *Hotel Garden, Florence*, 1909, by Vanessa Bell. 9 × 7 in. Collection Duncan Grant. Painted in May during a visit to Italy with Clive Bell and Virginia Stephen. An early work unusual for its luminosity of colour

During this 1909 visit Vanessa painted in Florence – there is a small, very luminous little painting of the Hotel Garden near the Pitti in the Via Romana (plate 7). She also started a portrait of an old Stephen friend Rezia Corsini (*née* Rasponi) who had stayed on her honeymoon with the Stephens in Hampshire in 1901. Erratic morning sittings were arranged in the Palazzo Corsini but genial family interruptions rather impeded her progress. There were lazy, hot days when they did nothing at all, a visit to the Berensons, a glimpse of Violet Meynell, and quarrels with Virginia who left early in a truculent and unhappy frame of mind.

In 1908 several portraits had occupied Vanessa. The year before, Francis Dodd, who lived in Fitzroy Square and had encouraged Henry Lamb in Manchester, had persuaded Virginia to sit to him for portrait drawings which

8. *Julian Bell and Nanny,*
c. 1909–10, by Vanessa Bell.
11 × 20½ in. Private Collection,
London

he used later for etchings. Vanessa took the opportunity to paint Virginia in a green and yellow dress against a dark blue background. There is no record of this picture and it probably remained unfinished. Two years later, Duncan Grant persuaded Virginia to sit in the spotless first-floor drawing room in Fitzroy Square. But nothing came of it beyond an ink drawing of the composition, though the figure is most recognizably that of Virginia. Clive, another elusive subject for his painter friends, sat briefly to Vanessa and there were small heads of Julian asleep. In the autumn she began an ambitious portrait of Lytton's sister Marjorie who was becoming a regular visitor in Fitzroy and Gordon Square. Marjorie was a large, plain rather ungainly young woman, tremendously high-spirited, rather overshadowed by her brothers and sisters (her historical novels are excruciating), with an under-current of frustration and unhappiness that her giggling, her lewd jokes, her zestful performances in amateur theatricals were intended to disguise. But at this time, aged twenty-seven, little of this was apparent even to herself and for the next ten years or so she was very much part of Bloomsbury. She sat to Vanessa in a black dress and a large black hat that shaded her face, her body thrust forward slightly on a green sofa with a vase of flowers behind her. Only a thumbnail sketch of the picture exists in a letter to Margery Snowdon but it does indicate the conservative nature of Vanessa's work at this time, fitting in perfectly with the New English Art Club and in close accord with what some of her contemporaries like Harold Gilman, Duncan Grant or, though less flamboyant, Augustus John and Henry Lamb, were doing.

9. *Portrait of Virginia Woolf*, 1911, by Duncan Grant. 22 × 16 in. Private Collection. Painted in the Stephens' house at 46 Gordon Square

Lamb and John both turned up in her life again at this period. Virginia had commissioned Lamb to make one of his very clever, clear, finished Slade portrait drawings of Vanessa, who found him charming and delightful once more and they had further talks about painting – materials and techniques especially. Lamb lived in a huge old house at 8 Fitzroy Street where Augustus John also had a studio in a large room at the back on the first floor. (In the 1890s it had been Whistler's studio and during the War Sickert took it over and kept his school there. In 1920 it became Duncan Grant's studio and the large room backing on to it was Vanessa's London studio from 1928.) John was already a considerable figure, in the first flush of success but still with enough novelty and shine to his rising star to attract a lot of attention. His whole personality coloured these early years of the century – impoverished and extravagant, wildly dressed in cloaks, earings and black Carlyle hats, a noted womanizer, a party-goer and -giver with secret mistresses and numberless children, a man who was at home in elegant evening-dress at smart dinner parties and who might be found a couple of days later, scruffy and begrimed, smoking a pipe on the steps of a caravan in some gypsy encampment in Wales. In his paintings of gypsies and tramps, his large idylls of bare-footed children with lovely unkempt hair as they run amidst females languorously draped and abstracted, he exemplified that romantic Celticism which was so much a part of Edwardian literature. He swept people along, carried them off; he was magnetic, a genius, the saviour of English painting. Enforcing this reputation were his magnificent looks, his pale perceptive eyes, his hair 'cut like a Renaissance prince', and the rather withdrawn, sometimes fierce, expression that preceded any change into gaiety and friendliness.

One late afternoon, some time in early 1909, William Rothenstein took Clive and Vanessa to see Augustus John in Fitzroy Street. He was standing in the huge studio lit only by a gas lamp and some candles and with him was an equally tall and magnificent lady with masses of dark red hair, ropes of pearls, and strong scent. This was, of course, Lady Ottoline Morrell. She asked the Bells soon afterwards to her house in Bedford Square to see other works by John. She has left her own account of the meeting in her Memoirs: 'Before we left, Clive Bell and his wife Vanessa arrived. I looked at them with a certain amount of awe. I had already heard of her and her sister, Virginia . . . "Do you know the Stephens?" I had been asked. "Who are they?" "They sit round the fire in a dark room and say nothing, except occasionally, after a long silence, one of them makes a very clever remark. Virginia and Vanessa are both beautiful, and like their father, very intellectual." I was thus very interested to see with my own eyes one of these wonderful remote beings, who lived in a world of intellect and art. Vanessa had the beauty of an early Watts portrait, melancholy and dreamy. They stood in front of the picture of the lake, Clive Bell gesticulating in an excited way, showering speechless admiration, Vanessa, head bent, approving.'[4]

Ottoline Morrell and her husband Philip had moved to 44 Bedford Square soon after the Stephens came to Bloomsbury. In 1906 Ottoline decorated and furnished the house in a luxurious and, for the time, novel way, partly

10. *Lady Ottoline Morrell,* *c.* 1910, by Henry Lamb. 14 × 12 in. Private Collection, London. One of a series of studies of Lady Ottoline by Lamb, this shows perhaps more than most his indebtedness to Augustus John

inspired in its colour scheme by a dance studio painted by Degas. From then until 1915 Bedford Square was a restless social hot-house for painters, writers, and politicians. Ottoline has been singled out as Bloomsbury's official hostess. It is true that in time she came to know most of what is called Bloomsbury, some of them intimately, and during the First War she was extremely helpful to those who were conscientious objectors. She was an early patron of Duncan Grant and of Vanessa and she considerably increased the clientele of Roger Fry's Omega Workshops. But she cannot be called Bloomsbury in the strict sense; she was intimate with people of whom Bloomsbury disapproved or did not know and with circles – such as that around D. H. Lawrence – who were considerably anti-Bloomsbury. She was more worldly and more generally gregarious; she was wealthier, she was aristocratic, and she was creative only in the sense that her entertaining and patronage were catalysts for other people's creativity, her house a place where people might fruitfully meet. Number 44 Bedford Square had much higher standards of comfort and in its chintzes, down cushions, its objets d'art, and pervading scent of pot-pourri and incense, it showed a fastidiousness that found no place in the more ramshackle appearance of the rooms at Gordon or Fitzroy Square. Though Vanessa and Virginia often dressed with distinction and originality, if somewhat untidily (pins in strange places might catch the light at odd moments – Virginia's drawers fell down at the Opera), they never aspired to Ottoline's sartorial extravagances, the veils, brocades, enormous hats which, with the coming of Bakst and the Ballets Russes, burst into an amazing conflagration of colours and styles. She became the Brighton Pavilion of fashion. But it was her face that was unforgettable, her deep red hair that occasionally changed its hue, the white cheeks, the long gap between her nose and lip and the jutting Velasquez chin; a face with deep-set eyes and hawkish nose and a voice that gurgled, moaned and seduced.

Ottoline knew 'everyone'. At her Thursday evening parties, the most unlikely people would come together. She was a great hostess and her qualities of inquisitiveness, curiosity and personal attention, which in other circumstances led her into trouble, here held her in good stead. She certainly had an eye for painting by the younger English artists; she was widely read with a genuine if over-romantic love of poetry and had a highly subjective appreciation of music. She was a romantic through and through and there was an aura of disillusion about her and a vein of melancholy. This, combined with her infinitely aristocratic presence and attitudes ('I love the people. I married into the people' she is reputed to have said in a political speech) made her a strikingly original figure at that time. Polite society was shocked by her, she was a terrible and artistic woman who had disgraced her family – her brother was the sixth Duke of Portland. In later years she believed that she had had a harder struggle to break with her background than had her friend D. H. Lawrence to break with his. It was in part this independence, spirited yet never entirely complete, which drew Bloomsbury to her and from about 1908 onwards she gradually came to know all of them, particularly Virginia, Clive and Vanessa, and Roger Fry.[5] That curiosity which added to her success as a hostess prevented her from becoming an integral part of Bloomsbury. They could not feel entirely at ease with her. She was a confidante at one's own risk; though not a calculating scandal-monger, she might drop remarks unthinkingly, sometimes with the best of intentions, which when they had worked through the groups around her, made her seem the fountainhead of intrigue and malice. But in 1908 she was welcomed at Virginia and Adrian's Thursday evenings as an enlightened and remarkable woman, often bringing with her no less remarkable attendants.

In 1910, a figure of great importance in Vanessa's life came occasionally to the Thursday evenings and was invited to lecture to the Friday Club. This was Roger Fry who in that year, aged forty-four, had left his position as European Adviser to the Metropolitan Museum of New York. He was well known as an authority and writer on the old masters and becoming known as a painter through his own one-man exhibitions (1903, 1907 and 1909) and his contributions to the spring shows at the Whitechapel (*Tivoli*, owned by Lady Ottoline Morrell was shown in 1910) and general shows at the Goupil Gallery and elsewhere. On paper he seemed to be an intelligent and sensitive connoisseur, a man of wide sympathies and a rather reactionary member of the New English Art Club. But already he was causing a disturbance by his enthusiasm for the 'old masters' of the modern movement, Cézanne, Van Gogh and Gauguin. His conversion was slow and thoughtful. He had been impressed and puzzled by Cézanne in Paris in 1906; in the following year he described him as a 'great and original genius' and in 1908 he was writing of Cézanne with praise in the *Burlington Magazine*, and of Gauguin, Signac, Maurice Denis, Bussy and Matisse. His friendship with Simon Bussy whom he had met some years before at the Stracheys, certainly aided his growing appreciation of modern French painting, but in England he knew little of the younger painters' work and tended to reserve his admiration for Steer, John and Rothenstein. Thus his friendship with Clive and Vanessa and soon afterwards with Duncan Grant greatly helped him as he plunged into the sea of modernism. They were his supporters, his allies and above all his friends. In his turn, Fry could assist Vanessa and Duncan in his official capacity by helping them to exhibit their work and introduce it to likely patrons. He was somewhat older than the rest of Bloomsbury and this gave him a less parochial, less cliquish attitude to life while at the same time he felt completely at ease in the unworldly but not unsophisticated gatherings in Fitzroy or Gordon Square. His friendship with several Cambridge people facilitated his entry into these houses – it was at Desmond MacCarthy's house, for instance, that he and Vanessa first met. With his appearance on the scene, Bloomsbury greatly expanded its contacts and its interests, becoming a definite social and intellectual force in the years before the First War.

In her memoir of Fry and their early friendship, written years later, Vanessa makes abundantly clear his importance in her life. It was not simply a matter of his greater contacts and experience or his ability to fire other people's enthusiasms. There was a deep personal sympathy between them which matured during the autumn of 1910 and the early months of 1911. 'It was then,' she wrote,[6] seeing him every day – most of the day sitting near him, reading, talking, looking, that I first realized fully what an absolutely enthralling companion had come into one's life. Our feelings jumped together at each new sight but for the first time here was someone who could convey his feelings and show that he understood mine. Such sympathy was so delightful, so complete, so quick that in itself it gave one as it were new senses and apprehensions. Not only that however, but also such fascinating speculations and trains of thought, such imaginings seemed to spring continually from some inexhaustible source that one felt here was a prospect of endless delight ahead.

[1] One of Adrian's friends who played so important a role in the Dreadnought Hoax, is only otherwise remembered for his name – Tudor Castle.

[2] 1 May 1909.

[3] VS to M. K. Snowdon from Florence, 18 May 1909.

[4] *Ottoline*, ed. R. Gathorne-Hardy, 1963, p.157.

[5] She was a founder member with Roger Fry of the Contemporary Art Society in the spring of 1909.

[6] 'Roger Fry', memoir in manuscript by Vanessa Bell, 1934.

Duncan Grant comes from a large and in many respects distinguished Scottish family. John Grant, Chief of the clan who married Lady Marjorie Stewart in 1539, had two sons, Duncan (d. 1582) who became Chief of Grant, and Patrick (d. 1617) from whom the Grants of Rothiemurchus were descended. The Doune, the Grant's house in Inverness-shire, had long been in the possession of the family but it was not until the early years of the nineteenth century that the house became a little less remote and comfortless and that the estate began to realize a substantial income from its timber. It was difficult to reach 'cut off by the rapid Spey from every neighbour', a plain house 'in the bosom of the Grampians' surrounded by fir trees. The loveliness of the country was dear to all the Grants and Duncan's visits to Rothiemurchus were an important ingredient in his visual memory. He inherited other qualities from his Grant forebears, particularly the poetic and practical sides of his character.

Each Laird of Rothiemurchus was continually involved in practical affairs whether in Scotland or India. Duncan's father, Major Bartle Grant, though

11. Major Bartle Grant (1860–1924) and Ethel Grant (1863–1948); Duncan Grant's parents at about the time of their marriage

38

never the Laird, shared this characteristic; he was a cook, a botanist, a writer of drawing-room songs and a knowledgeable gardener. Duncan however took this inheritance into creativity of a different order, if no less practical in approach. But it must also be stressed that Bartle Grant was a military man even if not entirely committed to military values and life-styles. Organizing concerts and theatrical performances was more to his taste than the conventional duties of an Anglo-Indian major. He was well educated, a wide reader all his life, especially of history, poetry, French literature and the natural sciences. He was often withdrawn, somewhat taciturn, and later in life only his wife could coax him from periods of depression and inactivity into his former spriteliness and gaiety of manner.

Bartle Grant had married Ethel MacNeil of Scotch and English ancestry, whose beauty, manners and sympathetic understanding impressed all those who knew her.[1] She was not an intellectual woman and had nothing like her husband's range of interests. But she created a charming, easy atmosphere around her, was devoted to her family and to her two unmarried sisters, Daisy and Violet. In later years she was looked upon as a fairy-godmother by some of the more woebegone female relations inevitable in large families at that time. She nursed, visited, housed and helped but never with condescension or virtuousness. Where human beings were concerned she was unsuspicious, unsentimental and always ready to give the benefit of the doubt. Her contribution to Duncan's life as a painter was in her superb execution in cross-stitch and embroidery of his designs for chair-covers, fire-screens and decorative panels. From the 1920s to her death in 1948 she was constantly at work, not only on her son's designs but on those by Vanessa Bell and Roger Fry. She was always demanding more work, and asking about wools and types of canvas. Luckily her work was preserved and there remain several examples (some in the Victoria and Albert Museum) which testify to her sensitive interpretive skill and taste. It was an occupation which increased her circle of friends and involved her in Duncan's life in a way that was satisfactory to both of them. She gained the admiration and devotion of many of his friends including Vanessa Bell, Maynard and Lydia Keynes, and Angus Davidson. Virginia Woolf is thought to have had her in mind when she wrote the opening pages of *Jacob's Room* and describes Mrs Flanders.

Duncan James Corrowr Grant was born at The Doune on 21 January 1885. His parents had returned on leave from India so that their child could be born in the family home. Bartle Grant was originally in the 8th Hussars but later joined a much inferior regiment and returned to England every two years. Duncan's early life was spent mainly in India and the colour and excitement of life there, the temples and palaces, bazars and processions made a lasting impression on him. In fact his earliest memories are mainly visual ones – of sitting on a fence in the Himalayas in a blue and white striped jersey, of Rangoon and Burmese elephants, of putting in at Valetta Harbour, Malta, where the houses and churches seemed to tumble over each other down to the water-front. His holidays were spent with his cousins the Stracheys[2] and other relations at Rothiemurchus and elsewhere. James, youngest of all the Strachey children, became a particular friend among all the variety of cousins

12. Duncan Grant, *c.* 1897, at Hillbrow Preparatory School, Rugby

– Rowes, Ridpaths, Ewebanks, Plowdens and Grants. Duncan was a sociable child among those he knew, and especially enjoyed going to the theatre and taking part in plays and charades at Rothiemurchus. He inclined to illustrating his letters, almost to the exclusion of writing, with oriental palaces, Scottish scenes and eighteenth-century characters in full evening-dress. And when he went to school, art lessons were the main feature of the timetable, with English and French coming next.

At Hillbrow Preparatory School, Rugby, James Strachey and Rupert Brooke were among his fellow students. From there Duncan passed to St. Paul's, West Kensington, in the spring of 1899. Not being a classical scholar, he was placed on the army and history side, later going up to the History VIII. By that time, the art master, a Mr Harris, was encouraging his talent for drawing and painting and he was awarded a prize for his work – Chevreul's *On Colour* was one of the three books he was given.[3] After two terms of boarding, Duncan began to attend St. Paul's as a day boy, living with the Stracheys, or with his parents when they were on leave in England – as they were in 1900 when his father was stationed in Malta during the Boer War. Duncan enjoyed this arrangement, for he was able to be with his cousins, go to the theatre or concerts with them, or to picture galleries with his father, which compensated for the rigours of mathematics at school.

Life at 69 Lancaster Gate where the Stracheys lived – that Italianate Palace with its seven storeys and one bathroom, its preposterous butlers and in the drawing-room the inescapable sound of the lavatory flushing above – has been fully described, particularly by Lytton Strachey in his memoir of the house and its occupants. He stresses that though certainly not Bohemian it was rather dowdy and makeshift, with the cutlery from the Army and Navy stores and the port and claret from the neighbouring grocer. The dominant figure, Lady Strachey, while giving all her children great attention and love, was never particularly committed to the smooth and economic running of the household. She was infinitely more interested in French Literature or Elizabethan drama, in talk of Darwin or Huxley, in arranging concerts in the drawing-room. She sacrificed comfort and luxury for the things of the mind and such a view of life certainly fell on eager and receptive soil. Nearly all her children wrote in one form or another and some were extremely musical, particularly James and Oliver. Duncan's musical taste, which he shared with his father, was greatly encouraged by the concert-parties and family music-making. He would go through Gilbert and Sullivan operas by the hour with James and Marjorie around the piano in the drawing-room. He also learnt to dance, particularly Scottish reels and the sword-dance. It was not until he was seventeen or eighteen that Lytton began to influence his thinking and reading and became with Pippa, thirteen years Duncan's senior, his particular friend in the family. At this time James was his closest companion among his cousins though their difference in age tended to separate them at St. Paul's, as it had at Hillbrow.

Lady Strachey was not always perceptive about her children and much that concerned their feelings deeply passed her by. But she had seen that Duncan was not particularly happy studying mathematics and realized that

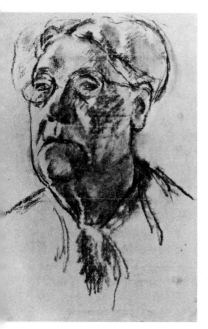

13. *Lady Strachey*, 1921, by Vanessa Bell. 12 × 8 in. Private Collection. A preparatory drawing for a portrait in Duncan Grant's collection. Jane Maria Strachey was an important figure in Duncan's early life and was responsible for his leaving St. Paul's to go to the Westminster School of Art

art training of some kind would be more fitting and agreeable. So she took steps to remedy the situation.

Someone who was soon to become part of the family, and who was to influence Duncan in his desire to paint, was the French artist Simon Bussy. Born in 1870, the son of a cobbler, he had studied under Moreau in Paris where Matisse was a fellow student and became a life-long friend. In 1899 he had met Pernel Strachey while she was studying for her doctorate in Paris and Sir Richard Strachey had bought one of his pictures. He came over to London where the Stracheys were hospitable, and made portraits of Dorothy, Pernel and Sir Richard, all in his chosen medium of pastel. He had a great admiration for Piero della Francesca; other influences on his work included Degas, Whistler, Japanese prints and Oriental art. His portraits were usually extraordinarily accurate and showed a delicate feeling for the placing of the figure, often seen from an unusual angle, from above or in profile. He took a studio in Kensington and opened a small school there. He did not mix easily with the English and his work was thought rather outlandish though William Rothenstein was quickly and helpfully appreciative.

In the early spring of 1903 Dorothy Strachey, then aged thirty-seven, announced her engagement to the French painter, much to her family's consternation. In April they married and went to live at a small house, La Souco, at Cabbé Roquebrune near Menton, bought for them by Dorothy's father. Bussy continued to exhibit in England and had one-man shows of pastels at the Carfax Gallery in 1903 and at Leighton House in 1907. He visited England with Dorothy and worked at Rothiemurchus where he made some pastels of the landscape there.[4] He gave Duncan much advice about painting, emphasizing particularly the benefits of copying the old masters. His influence is easily discernible in Duncan's early portraits – compare for example Bussy's pastel of Sir Richard Strachey (plate 14) and Duncan's painting of Lytton (plate 15). He was obviously a bracing master with uncompromising views and a severe dedication to his work. One of his most useful lessons was his insistence on the necessity of regular working hours, of getting into the habit of painting every day even if one did not particularly want to. It was worth occasionally turning out rather mechanical work to have the advantages of such a discipline. Bussy took pains to help his wife's cousin, gave him introductions, recommended a teacher in Paris and brought about Duncan's later visit to Matisse.

Duncan's parents were persuaded by Lady Strachey to let their son study painting. While his father was naturally disappointed that his son was not going into the army, he was not hostile to the new plan and in September 1902 Duncan entered the Westminster School of Art where he remained until 1905. The principal was an ex-Slade student Mouat Loudan, an elegant Scotsman of French extraction who ran the 'Drawing and Painting from the Life' class and appears to be of little consequence. Duncan learnt much more from a group of talented and spirited fellow students chief among whom was Marius Forestier, son of an Anglicized French illustrator who worked on the *Illustrated London News*. Forestier was already an admirer of the French

14. *Sir Richard Strachey*, 1902, by Simon Bussy. Formerly Collection James Strachey. Duncan Grant's familiarity with Bussy's work goes back to his schooldays when he lived at the Stracheys' home in Lancaster Gate. This portrait hung there along with Bussy's portraits of Sir Richard's daughter Pernel, his son Lytton, and Bussy's future wife Dorothy Strachey

15. *Lytton Strachey*, 1909, by Duncan Grant. 21 × 26 in. The Tate Gallery, London. Painted at the Stracheys' home in Belsize Park Gardens. Flowers against a patterned background such as the floral chintz seen here have continued to be a favourite motif in Grant's painting. The limp gloves add a slightly sinister touch to an otherwise serious, discreet composition

16. *The Kitchen*, 1902, by Duncan Grant. 20 × 16 in. The Tate Gallery, London. One of Grant's earliest surviving paintings (there is a 1901 landscape of Rothiemurchus in a private collection, London), *The Kitchen* was painted at Streatley-on-Thames and already embodies several of Grant's later preoccupations, notably the delight in the patterned wallpaper, the view from one room through to another (plate 87, *Interior at Gordon Square*) and the homely still life on the table

Impressionists, particularly Monet and Sisley. He and Duncan were happy companions and both continued their studies in Paris.[5] Another student was Norman Gould who later became a Royal Academician, 'an amiable, clever, weak character' who made perfect drawings – 'there seemed nothing further to say if one could say it so well'. Gould admired Whistler and Degas but it was difficult to see the latter's work. A third friend was Ballard, a countryman and a conscientious student.

In 1904 the Art School moved from the Royal Architectural Museum to the Westminster Technical Institute in Vincent Square. At the end of the autumn term in the new quarters, Duncan and his mother went to Florence for the winter. There was plenty of society [6] and Duncan made friends with a young girl, Helen Maitland, and her mother. He was to know them better in Paris two years later when they lived in a little house in the Place St. Sulpice, Mrs Maitland having taken up painting under a quack who made his students dance in the sun on the studio roof before starting work; her lovely, round-faced daughter studied music under d'Indy at the 'Scuola Cantorum'. [7]

Copying in the Uffizi took up the greater part of Duncan's days that winter and it was on the advice of Simon Bussy that he copied Piero della Francesca's portrait of Federigo da Montefeltro and visited Arezzo to see the Pieros there. Another copy that engaged him during these three months was of part of the Masaccio frescoes in the Brancacci Chapel in the Carmine, a commission from Harry Strachey. Enthusiasm for such early Italian painters was unusual at that time and showed Duncan's youthful independence.

One of Duncan's aunts, Elinor, Lady Colvile, a wealthy, leisured and artistic woman had put aside £100 for Duncan's twenty-first birthday. When the sum was duly made available it was decided that Duncan should go to Paris, accompanied by Lytton, who would then go on alone to Lady Colvile's villa at Menton. They set off on 18 February 1906 and made their way to the 'Hotel de l'Univers et du Portugal' where Lytton stayed one night before taking his train south. Duncan rented an attic room near Marius Forestier and his friend Urquart, another Scotsman, both of whom were already in Paris studying at the Académie Julian. Also lodging in the hotel was Ballard, another of the Westminster students. The hotel was cheap, convenient and run by a sympathetic Balzacian woman, Madame Troulet, with 'a miraculous and elevated toupé, fine bust and ringed fingers'. As concierge there was Rosalie, an old peasant woman from the Vosges who regaled Duncan with terrifying stories of the German atrocities of 1870.

At first Duncan was undecided as to what course of instruction he should follow. Eventually Simon Bussy suggested a newly-founded school 'La Palette' near Les Invalides, run by Jacques-Emile Blanche. Blanche was a highly cultured man and a tremendous anglophile who counted English writers and painters among his friends. He was also on intimate terms with some of the older Impressionists such as Degas and Manet, whose pupil he had been. But there was another side to Blanche, the witty figure of French society, launched by Robert de Montesquiou, and the cosmopolitan portrait-painter on the edge of that Edwardian circle which included Lavery, Tissot, Boldini, Sargent and Helleu. Blanche could in fact be an interesting painter and was never entirely seduced by purely worldly success or the exigencies of fashionable men and women. Some of his landscapes in Normandy and sketches of Dieppe testify to his merits, modest though they are. But his fame rests on such portraits as Proust in evening-dress, the large double-portrait of Colette and Willy, Karsavina in the *Firebird* ballet, and portraits of Thomas Hardy and Sargent. But of the new generation of Post-Impressionists he was often absurdly critical and tetchy in his comments, though in fact in age and training he was much nearer to them than the older painters whom he venerated. Thus there was little knowledge at Blanche's school of what the young painters in Paris were doing. The Louvre and the Impressionists were the fare and though Vuillard and Bonnard were advertised as visiting teachers, they rarely appeared. Blanche came in at least twice a week, was amiable and conscientious, and seemed to take pleasure in his teaching. He could be at times 'a stimulating and exciting "professor"'. Particularly valuable were the days when he accompanied his students to the Louvre at the times set aside for copying. He was very pleased with Duncan's copy of a still life by Chardin, an unusual choice it seems at that period. '*C'est bien émouvant. C'est le drame de la lumière,*' he commented. The modesty of approach and unrhetorical nature of Chardin's work, and his ability to take the most ordinary or commonplace objects and render them with such vitality and depth, impressed themselves on the young student.[8]

Three years earlier than this stay in Paris, Duncan had spent a summer painting at Streatley-on-Thames, where his parents had taken a house. While painting a landscape he experienced there what he has called a vision, which took the form of an advisory inner voice. 'You must go out into the world to learn all that there is to know and be seen in the world of painting. The Impressionists you must see and learn from and there are other things going on at this very moment of which you know nothing.' By the time he went to Paris his visual education was certainly more advanced and sophisticated than it had been at the moment of that vision in an Edwardian English village.[9] He knew of the older Impressionists and their work could be seen at some London galleries – Manet, Degas and Monet in particular – although Impressionism was still slightly shocking to some of his English contemporaries. The Caillebotte Collection in the Luxembourg provided a revelation, especially of those painters who were still unfamiliar to him in London such as Pissarro and Sisley. As for the younger painters, he saw occasional canvases at dealers' shops but they seem to have made no great impression at the time. Certainly the name of Matisse was known to him, mainly through Simon Bussy. But the furore caused by Matisse's work at the Salon des Indépendants in 1906 and the Salon d'Automne seems to have passed him by. It was difficult for the young English student to find out what was going on especially as Duncan's circle was mainly restricted to English friends. The painter Segonzac, his friend in later years, was attending La Palette in 1906 but they did not meet.

Duncan worked extremely hard: he was at La Palette, after a brief breakfast, from eight until midday; the afternoons were usually spent at the Louvre, copying, looking and noting, and in the evenings after dinner, he invariably went to the library of the Ecole des Beaux Arts and studied drawings and anatomy. Of course there were diversions. Bussy introduced him to the sculptor Auguste Bréal whose little book on Velasquez had appeared in England the year before, translated by Dorothy Bussy. In later years when they were both in the South of France Duncan was to know Bréal much better.

Another friendship which began at this time and continued for years afterwards was with Constance Lloyd, a spirited girl from a well-known Birmingham family of Quakers. She had left the Slade School, disliking

Professor Tonks' teaching, and entered Simon Bussy's classes in Kensington. She spent much of her painting life in Paris but her agreeable, francophile pictures appeared from time to time in London exhibitions. She also designed for French textile companies and her fabrics were on sale at Heal's in 1914.

At the end of the summer term, Duncan spent a week at Versailles and then returned home to his parents at 143 Fellows Road in Hampstead, his base until going back to Paris after Christmas. He saw a good deal of Forestier, meeting him at the National Gallery or spending an evening at his home in Dulwich. He also saw something of Maynard Keynes, and became very attached to Arthur Hobhouse a Cambridge undergraduate noted for his looks and athleticism, a friend of Keynes and Lytton and their circle. A rather irksome commission came his way from his cousin John Peter Grant, to copy Watts' picture of their grandfather for The Doune family portraits. In August Duncan went to Rothiemurchus with Hobhouse for several weeks of painting, bicycling and walking; they read Milton and *King Lear* aloud and witnessed the annual summer festivities of the clan Grant.

Duncan's next year in Paris was enriched by the visits of friends from England, by an expansiveness towards the French, and by the continuing helpfulness and admiration of Blanche for his work. Marius Forestier had left Paris and Duncan decided to move from the Hotel Portugal. In April 1907 after a short stay in the rue Delambre he moved to 45 rue Campagne Première, Montparnasse. It was in a large block of studios with dingy passages and vast windows. His days were much the same, though he now spent more time painting on his own in his studio, particularly still lifes (plate 18) which show his indebtedness to Chardin and the seriousness of his purpose and of his approach to work. In the Louvre, he tended to make copies in watercolour, in particular of Rubens and Rembrandt, but his great discovery, as he told Lytton, was Poussin. 'I have developed a passion for Poussin – his drawings. I really think they suggest everything that's heavenly in this world. And they are so grand and splendid and at the same time so intimate in some curious way.' With this study of Poussin began his interest in larger compositions, often with a mythological basis and depicting sporting gods and goddesses. His sketch books are filled with gatherings, bachanalias, *concerts champêtres*, scenes of bathing, and amorous, pastoral gambollings. They are the imaginative fruit of the long series of careful studies of the nude which occupied him in Blanche's Life classes (plate 17).

Breaking into this studious, very regular existence came a figure in the shape of a rather theatrical looking art student, who was to play a dramatic role in Duncan's life and that of his friends a few years later. This was Wyndham Lewis. A little older than Duncan and also living in a studio in the rue Delambre, Lewis would appear among the marble-topped tables of the Café du Dôme – not at that time the celebrated café it was to become, in fact it was decidedly shabby and quiet. 'I have begun to have depressing intervals,' wrote Duncan to Lytton,[(10)]

17. *Standing Male Nude*, 1906, by Duncan Grant. $12\frac{1}{8} \times 9\frac{1}{2}$ in. Private Collection. A life drawing done at Blanche's school, La Palette, Paris

18. *Still Life on Table*, 1907, by Duncan Grant. 24 × 15 in. Private Collection, London. Painted in the rue Delambre in early 1907 shortly after Grant resumed his second year at La Palette. Chardin, whom Grant copied in the Louvre, is an obvious influence

not because I have no one to talk to but because on the contrary there's someone turned up to whom I have to talk. He's a poet-painter called Lewis who always feeds at the same places as I do and my gorge simply rises when ever I see him. And just because he talks about interesting things I have to answer and so I suppose he thinks I like him. But really it's too awful – I simply descend into the depths of despair and gloom after seeing him and I cannot decide whether my feelings are absurd and silly, but I certainly think all his hopelessly 'mesquin' and putrid. You will think all this is mere hysterics – perhaps it is, but it's very odd that any one should have the power of making one go into them.

Duncan was not to see much of Wyndham Lewis again until about 1911 when Lewis was already in the ascendant as a figure of power and originality and when they were both members of the Camden Town Group. This earlier meeting does point to Duncan's initial hostility to Lewis, but later, against his earlier unsympathetic impressions, he became more friendly towards Lewis when the latter joined the Grafton Group of painters and the Omega Workshops.

A more satisfactory encounter was the appearance of Henry Lamb. Duncan had known Walter Lamb, Henry's older brother, at Cambridge, though very slightly, and had followed Lamb's fluctuating fortunes with regard to election to the Apostles, in which quarter he was in fact unsuccessful. Henry had recently married his first wife Euphemia and moved to Paris where, under the influence of Augustus John, he continued his studies and attended La Palette. Lamb introduced Duncan to Augustus John who was living in Paris with his mistress Dorelia while his first wife Ida was dying in a nearby hospital. During the upheavals in the Lamb and John ménages, Duncan befriended Euphemia for a time. Ida John was a friend of Constance Lloyd; it was with the latter that Duncan went to visit Gwen John 'living with her cats on the old fortifications', not yet the recluse she was to become, and ready to join the party for a picnic tea and talk a little of her new friendship with Rodin.

There were many visitors in the spring, some of whom were to become Duncan's closest friends when he returned to London. Maynard Keynes arrived with Harry Norton. Duncan had met Keynes with Lytton on a few occasions but in Paris he took to him more and was amused by Keynes's enthusiasm for the fountains at Versailles. Pippa Strachey arrived and James who was then at Cambridge. In April 'early Bloomsbury' appeared in the shape of Clive and Vanessa Bell, now honeymooning in Paris, Virginia and Adrian Stephen. They all dined together; 'What a quartet! I seem to like them all so, so much,' Duncan told Lytton.[11] 'As for Virginia, I think she's probably extremely witty and amazingly beautiful.' Vanessa he had met in the autumn of 1905 when he was introduced to her by Pippa at a meeting of the Friday Club in Gordon Square. Clive he had met in 1903 when he paid his first visit to Lytton at Cambridge. Lytton had disappeared for a Saturday meeting of the Apostles, leaving his nervous, most amiable and rather wide-

19. *J. M. Keynes*, 1908–9, by
Duncan Grant. Collection
W. M. Keynes. In 1908
Grant painted a full-length
portrait of Keynes when
they were together in the
Orkney Islands. An amusing
study of Keynes's shoes and
hat dating from about 1909
is in the artist's possession

eyed cousin in the care of Thoby Stephen. Thoby had taken him to a party in
Trinity where Clive, among others, was friendly and kind. Vanessa wrote to
Margery Snowden that 'We have asked a young artist called Duncan Grant
to dine with us. We both knew him before we came here as he is a cousin of the
Stracheys. He is clever and very nice and I hope we shall see him in London
quite often when he goes back there.' Thus the pattern of later friendships
was assembling. The familiar names with tentative epithets attached of
appreciation, amusement or positive liking begin to appear in Duncan's
letters to his mother and to his confidant, Lytton. His letters to Lytton are
full of lively descriptions of people and events, comments on the books he is
reading (often from Lytton's recommendations), lewd witticisms and sly
French phrases, a little about painting and his activities and occasional hints
as to his feelings and state of mind. In his love for his cousin Lytton created a
role for him that was romantic and heroic, a role which both distorted
Duncan's character and blackened Lytton's vision of the family house as a
prison of unmitigated gloom and confinement. Duncan's exclamations such as
'I am perfectly happy and absolutely intoxicated' or 'at present I feel very ambitious' made Lytton's own fog-bound existence seem even more intolerable.

Another new friend was the painter Maxwell Armfield, older than
Duncan, effeminately good-looking and already with something of a reputation in Paris. One of his pictures had been bought from the Salon and was
in the Luxembourg Collection. They had originally met in the National Gallery in London in February 1906 when Armfield introduced himself to Duncan who was copying the angels in Piero della Francesca's *Nativity*. Armfield
wrote in his diary: 'Have seen a most thrilling person at the National Gallery
copying Piero della Francesca's Madonna. He is exactly like a Piero person. I ac-
costed him today and he appears quite delightful – Scotch. His name is . . . Duncan Grant . . . his eyes are extraordinarily grey and liquid, very pale, with huge
irises and long lashes.' Armfield himself belonged to a somewhat earlier,
ninetiesish aestheticism executing immaculate, decorative pictures in 'spotless tempera'. The masters of past painting whom he admired were not
particularly sympathetic to Duncan who was not inclined to go into raptures
about Terbourg or Memlinc when he was discovering Poussin and the
Impressionists. But they met from time to time in 1906 and saw more of each
other in 1907. They made a short visit to Chartres in mid-May where
Armfield drew and made pastels and *pochades* of the small streets around the
Cathedral. But Duncan finally decided that Armfield was a somewhat dreary
and affected character and their friendship petered out in London soon
afterwards. For his part, Armfield felt that Duncan was being ruined by the
influence of the Impressionists and an aesthetic checkmate ensued.

When the term at La Palette ended – Duncan's last – in June, he went to
Florence and stayed with his cousins, the Ewebanks, in an apartment overlooking the Arno, on the Lungarno Amerigo Vespucci. Once again there
were the delights and curiosities of the English community to savour and,
most memorably, visits to the Berenson household at I Tatti.[12] Princesses
and countesses flowed in at tea-time, Berenson was grumbling about being a
failure; among the party were Ray Costelloe, Mrs Berenson's daughter by her

20. *Portrait of John Peter Grant*, 1907, by Duncan Grant. 29 × 24 in. National Galleries of Scotland. John Peter Grant (1859–1927), Laird of Rothiemurchus and cousin of the painter, commissioned this portrait of, in his own words, his 'ugly features', in the summer of 1907

first husband and later the wife of Oliver Strachey, and Leo Stein, Gertrude's brother. Duncan was well acquainted with Berenson's writings; they had helped him to see the disadvantages and sentimentalities of Ruskin. 'Tactile values', 'ideated space' and 'life-enhancing', all these phrases meant something to him and were generally influential in his responses to painting and the Tuscan landscape. A later and more prolonged stay at I Tatti in the company of Maynard Keynes and Vanessa Bell left more mixed feelings about Berenson and the visit nearly ended in disaster.

From Florence, Duncan went on to Il Castello at Certaldo, near Siena. He also visited San Gimignano, 'a great discovery', and finally spent a week in

Siena where he watched the famous *Palio* and spent hours at the Pinacoteca. He returned to Paris and joined Lytton for a week at Versailles which was mostly spent in the gardens of the Grand Trianon. They had one excursion to Paris where, after looking at immense numbers of paintings in the Louvre, they ended the day with 'a farce in the Boulevard Montmartre'.[13] In mid-July Duncan returned for good to England and after seeing his parents set off for Rothiemurchus to paint a portrait of the laird, John Peter Grant (plate 20).

[1] 'Staggeringly beautiful', 'tremendous charm', 'one of the most distinguished women I've met', are some of the descriptions from those who knew her.

[2] Bartle Grant's sister, Jane Maria, married Sir Richard Strachey, as he became, in 1859. For further details of the Grants, see *Memoirs of a Highland Lady* by Elizabeth Grant of Rothiemurchus, edited by Angus Davidson, 1950. The Grant-Strachey connection is well amplified in *Two Victorian Families* by Betty Askwith, 1971.

[3] At this time *c.* 1900, Duncan attended drawing classes under the painter Louise Jopling (1844–1933), friend and model to Millais and Whistler, who had married George Rowe, a distant relation of the Grants. Her amusing autobiography *Twenty Years of My Life* was published in 1925.

[4] *Fir Trees*, Collection Duncan Grant.

[5] Duncan later heard that Forestier committed suicide. In his last years he worked in North Italy, particularly in the region of Lake Como.

[6] Another visitor to Italy was Harry Strachey (1863–1940) son of Sir Edward Strachey and a cousin to Lytton. He devoted his life to painting, playing the violin, and the Boy Scout Movement. For over thirty years he was art critic to the *Spectator* and made valiant attempts to write appreciatively of the Post-Impressionists. He held Whistler, Manet and Degas in high regard but was puzzled by Duncan's admiration of Piero. He and Duncan visited Rome for a few days, mainly to see the Vatican, at the end of February.

[7] She was to marry, some years later, the Russian mosaicist Boris Anrep and later lived with Roger Fry. It was in the Maitlands' Paris home that Duncan came across Anrep and his friends Lamb and John. Dorelia MacNeil (later Mrs Augustus John) was a particular friend of Helen Maitland.

[8] Curiously enough it had been the sight of a painting by Chardin in 1902 that had set Roger Fry thinking so that 'he became aware that his views on the primary importance of content might be mistaken', Quentin Bell, 'Roger Fry', p. 10, Inaugural Lecture, Leeds University, 1964.

[9] Among Grant's juvenilia are drawings in the style of Burne-Jones and Beardsley. He had been impressed with the latter's 'Yellow Book' illustrations in 1900.

[10] 18 February 1907.

[11] 7 April 1907.

[12] A few days before, Roger Fry had visited the Berensons while staying in Florence with Hubert Horne.

[13] M. Holroyd, *Lytton Strachey*, Vol. I, 1967, p.324.

Few modern English painters have been so well grounded as Duncan in the French and Italian schools of the past. His study of them was neither unselective nor academic. We have seen his early preferences – Masaccio, Piero della Francesca, the Sienese and early Florentine painters, Poussin and Chardin. He showed a marked preference for elegance, sobriety and formal values in art – Racine, Bach, Mozart, Jane Austen and eighteenth-century French writers were among his early loves. Such admiration was not of course exclusive but it was abundant and profound. Not only was this preference a natural expression of his temperament but also, it appears, a reaction to the predominant culture of his youth, especially the great popularity of German symbolist art and music: *The Ring* seemed constantly to be at Covent Garden. The direction of his taste, above all in literature, was stimulated by Lytton Strachey's classical sympathies and perceptions, transmitted to Duncan through a romantic imagination. Thus one sees in some of Duncan's early figure compositions such as *The Dancers* (plate 32), *Idyll* or *The Lemon Gatherers* (plate 26) with their definite Italian overtones, especially of Piero, a poetic imagination though without emphatic symbolism. It is no great jump from Burne-Jones's paintings of flowingly-draped females to that circle of stately movement in *The Dancers*.

Beside this knowledge of past painting, we must place the technical accomplishment he had then attained, seen in the 1908 *Portrait of Maynard Keynes* and better still in the *Portrait of James Strachey*.[1] Simon Bussy's advice to copy paintings had been fully and conscientiously followed. This often invigorating, always illuminating habit has continued all his life, sometimes faithful to the original, sometimes freely adapted (as in, for example, the still life *After Zurburan*, 1928, in the collection of Lord Clark). His technical versatility is evident in his treatment of textures and surfaces in still life and interiors. His portraits (before about 1910) present us with an extraordinarily solid world, comfortable and quiet, an air of scholarly reflection enveloping his figures. There is Lytton Strachey deep in State Trials (plate 15), long pale hands on the large pages; James Strachey (plate 22), looking up for a moment from the book on his lap; their sister Marjorie (plate 23), her face hidden in her hands, a copy of *Crime and Punishment* lying on the sofa beside her.[2] His delight in pattern is very much in evidence in the wallpaper, the scrolled and colourful carpets, the chintz on Lytton's chair, the rhythm of the screen behind James. It is in these passages that one sees Duncan the decorator, whose musical swirls and flourishes emerged a

52

21. *Portrait of Cecil Taylor*,
1909, by Duncan Grant.
31 × 32½. Collection the late
Dr A. N. L. Munby. Cecil
Taylor (1886–1955) went in
1912 to Clifton College
where for many years he was
an inspiring teacher of
classics. The setting and
position of the figure once
again show the influence of
Simon Bussy

22. *Portrait of James
Strachey*, 1909, by Duncan
Grant. 25 × 30 in. The Tate
Gallery, London. Probably
begun in late 1908 this
portrait of the artist's cousin
James (1887–1967) was
exhibited at the New English
Art Club in December 1909.
This 'famous picture
of James' legs' as Rupert
Brooke called it, is perhaps
the most notable
achievement of Grant's
'apprenticeship'

few years later from his early 'discreet realism' with its respect for appearances and almost excavatory attitude to the objects in front of him. This long series of careful, sturdy pictures[3] seemed to work as a necessary discipline to set against his more imaginative and experimental compositions. Naturally they were part of the same occupation, a drive to focus his gifts, to come to terms with what was possible in combining this modest and searching view of reality and an imagination of a lyrical and exuberant nature. In these difficult years immediately after his return from Paris – there was an abortive attempt in 1908 to study at the Slade which lasted a few weeks – he must have felt isolated from the painters of his own generation (few in fact were known to him); he was often depressed by his work and though some was exhibited (two studies were shown at the United Arts Club in 1907) he was at first rejected from exhibiting at the New English Art Club, the most progressive group of painters, for want of anything more advanced, in London at that time. There is an interesting letter to William Rothenstein from Duncan after this rejection in the former's *Men and Memoirs:*[4]

> My dear Rothenstein,
>
> I do not know how I am to thank you enough for your kind letter about my pictures at the Alpine Club [Friday Club exhibition]. You accuse me of never showing you any of my work, but it has never been because I doubted your power of judgement, but that I considered there could be no two opinions about the many faults in my production.
>
> It was therefore an extremely pleasant surprise that someone whose opinion I value as highly as I do yours should see some merit in my work or rather would consider that on the whole the merit exceeds the faults (in these particular ones).
>
> You also cannot know how encouraging your criticism and sympathy are to me. I work, I feel, too much in the dark, so to speak, as regards getting opinions about my work, and I find yours both stimulating and illuminating.
>
> I feel very strongly the need for simplicity, so that my failure to reach it is the more marked, but objects to me have a most deceptive way of *looking* simple, in spite of their details, and I only realize my mistake when I try to make them. . . .

During this period Maynard Keynes became Duncan's greatest friend and in spite of many changes in both their lives remained so until Keynes's death in 1946. Maynard's deepest regard was reserved for the creative artist, and his patronage, both private and public, was greatly inspired and renewed by a friendship which gave him insight into the artist's mind. Over the next few years, they were together not only in London and Cambridge but in the country during the summer and on holidays abroad. In the summer of 1908, they holidayed together in the Orkneys where some millionaire friends of Duncan's Aunt Daisy MacNeil owned the island of Hoy. Duncan set off alone in late July. From Stromness on the largest of the Orkneys he went to Melsetter on Hoy, across rough seas sighting cormorants and seals through the spray from a tiny motor launch. On arrival at the Middlemore's house all

23. *Le Crime et le Châtiment*, 1909, by Duncan Grant. 21 × 26 in. The Tate Gallery, London. Painted on the reverse of the *Lytton Strachey* (plate 15) this shows Lytton's sister Marjorie (1882–1964) at Belsize Park Gardens. She has just finished Dostoevsky's novel and, head in hands, is overcome by its gloom

was comfortable with Burne-Jones drawings, Morlands and Coxes, plenty of food and warmth and delightful walks round about, a calm bay in front of the house and a view of the rocky Pentland Firth from a hill behind. Painting, reading, sleeping, eating, and long walks were the days' occupations with the occasional bonus of a cattle show or a fishing regatta. A village further up the coast aroused Duncan's interest in that its population were said to be crazy from too much incest and the blood of the remnants of the Spanish Armada did not mingle well with that of the settling heroes of the Icelandic Sagas; there was no church and no policeman. It was obviously an ideal place to take rooms when Maynard arrived. However, none could be found and the two spent six weeks on Orkney, Maynard working on his *Treatise on Probability* while Duncan painted a large portrait of him. The holiday also resulted in numerous small landscapes of that austere scenery.

In October, Keynes returned to London, shut up his flat near St. James's and went to Cambridge where he had been given a lectureship in Economics.[5] Duncan travelled south to Rothiemurchus and in spite of his enthusiasm for the colours of the Orkney landscape and the cobalt blue sea, the beauty of Rothiemurchus seemed to blot out those visual delights. It was late autumn with the birches by the Ord pale green and gold and deer moving about among them. There was a family party at The Doune which included Anna Alma-Tadema, the painter's elderly daughter, and a large, energetic American lady whom Duncan came across one day excitedly flushed from watching with lascivious glee the rutting of the stags through a pair of opera-glasses.

Through Maynard, Duncan renewed his contact with The Apostles, the important and formative *conversazione* society. Maynard remained 'Apostolic' in London in that he did not discuss the secret society's affairs in general company and the same was true of James Strachey, a later Apostle. Others were more lax; Roger Fry was always eager to talk of it and Desmond MacCarthy saw nothing unusual in doing so. Above all, it was Vanessa who was downright inquisitive and her desire to know the truth of the society's proceedings, which involved friends and acquaintances, was sometimes embarrassing for Duncan who, though an outsider, was told much by Maynard.

Compared to Maynard and his Cambridge friends, Duncan was virtually uneducated but of his innate intelligence there was no question. His point of view might be different, unacademic, even exasperatingly original but to someone like Maynard it was refreshing, coming as it did from a person whose natural process of thought was unclouded by dogma and disarmingly logical in its personal way. Though he was not given to philosophical or abstract argument, Duncan's presence during discussions on these topics was uninhibiting. He was not, as it were, fighting for his life in such arguments; his battles were fought on quite other grounds, silently and solitarily.

Among Duncan's new friends in Cambridge were the economist Gerald Shove, Arthur Cole, with whom Maynard had founded a bibliophile's club, and J. T. Sheppard, all of King's; and two graduates of Emmanuel College introduced by Sheppard, Gordon Hannington Luce, a poet and teacher of English for many years at Rangoon University, and Cecil Taylor who in 1912 went as a classics teacher to Clifton School. All five sat to Duncan for paintings and drawings – from the large sombre portrait of Cole (early 1909) to the brighter, less finished picture of Luce, painted under the first influence of the Post-Impressionists, with its broken and spotted colour (plate 33). Cole and Sheppard sat in the early months of 1909 when Duncan was also painting a still life of tulips, a composition of *The Adoration* in greens and blacks, and a model and her son who sat regularly for drawings. The evenings were set aside for dinner with the Stracheys, recently installed at Belsize Park Gardens, visits to the theatre – Galsworthy's *Strife* was very interesting but Irving in *Hamlet* 'rather poor'. Two exhibitions were visited regularly, 'The International' and 'Fair Women'; at the latter Duncan particularly admired Manet's portrait of his mother and Augustus John's *Smiling Woman*, the hit of the exhibition. Duncan also attended some of the Thursday evenings at Fitzroy Square – Henry Lamb, Saxon Sydney Turner and Clive and Vanessa were among those he frequently saw there.

In April 1909, Maynard and Duncan spent a fortnight in Versailles. There were visits to the Louvre and the Indépendants as well as a performance by Sarah Bernhardt in *L'Aiglon*. In August and September, Maynard took a house in the village of Burford near Oxford and Duncan had a room made over as a studio. He painted still life in the morning and landscapes in the afternoon until dusk made it too difficult to see. And he continued his portrait of Cecil Taylor who sat again for him during his stay (plate 21). James Strachey, another guest, was at that time involved with the Fabian Society which had recently held a summer school in Wales. Duncan had attended two of Sidney Webb's lectures when staying nearby with relations. He was 'much interested' he told his mother in 'socialism as it's called'. In the same letter[6] there is an interesting postscript: 'Please tell Daddy that Keynes who knows about these things thinks india-rubber a most unsafe investment.'

Keynes did know about these things and with the money he began to make he bought pictures and books and took ambitious holidays. In the Easter of 1910 he and Duncan were in Greece and Constantinople, and in 1911 in Sicily and Tunis. The former holiday included a stop in Senegal – where the colours, cries, camels, the mysteries and beauties were '*d'un tout autre genre même*'[7] – a special journey to Troy, painting on the Acropolis and a visit to the Hagia Sophia; it was the mosaics there and in the Kariye Camii that were particularly impressive and Duncan felt that the Hagia Sophia was the greatest building he had seen. Enthusiasm for things Byzantine was increasing in the West but still rare. An article on Byzantine Art written by W. R. Lethaby[8] appeared for the first time that year in the *Encyclopaedia Britannica*. The impact of these mosaics made itself apparent in Duncan's paintings though the full force of Byzantine decoration did not appear until after his visit to Ravenna in 1913. His enthusiasm was shared by his friends, and Clive Bell in his book *Art* (1914) went as far as to say that since the Byzantine achievements of the sixth century, European art had been one long decline. The Byzantine emphasis on linear vitality at the expense of organization in depth, the rich colour and overall decorative effect can certainly be seen in Duncan's murals *Football* and *Bathing* (plates 36, 34), in *The Queen of Sheba* (plate 46) and the murals at Fry's house Durbins, where a mosaic of badminton players was also attempted.

Towards the end of 1910 Maynard and Duncan moved from Belgrave Road into Bloomsbury, to 21 Fitzroy Square where on the first floor Duncan had his studio and Maynard a room for his use on visits from Cambridge. Adrian and Virginia Stephen lived further along the same side of the square and Duncan became a frequent visitor.[9] He was especially friendly with Adrian and there are three portraits (plate 25) and numerous drawings of him done at Fitzroy Square.[10] The year 1911 was extremely productive: several self-portraits (plate 24), studies of Virginia Stephen (plate 9) and Fry's daughter Pamela, the *Bathing* and *Football* murals, two versions of *The Dancers, Man with Greyhound*, and an ambitious decoration in Maynard's rooms in Cambridge. The variety of style and subject are partly accounted for by the stimulating exhibition organized by Fry of the Post-Impressionists and other new painters in 1910. While Duncan was already familiar with much of the work shown, to see it in bulk and often,[11] to be able at last to discuss it with fellow-enthusiasts brought about a varied and intoxicating reappraisal of his talents.

In 1909 Duncan armed with an introduction from Simon Bussy had visited Matisse at his home at Issy-les-Moulineaux outside Paris. Matisse was painting a still life of nasturtiums, which flowers, much to Duncan's surprise, Matisse cultivated in a greenhouse like some rare orchid. The large, unstretched canvas for *La Danse* was also in the studio. Matisse was amiable though reserved. In the same year Duncan went to see Leo and Gertrude

24. *Self Portrait, c.* 1908, by Duncan Grant. 21½ × 16½ in. Private Collection, London. This picture has been dated as late as the autumn of 1909 but its handling and sombre colour suggest a slightly earlier date

25. *Portrait of Adrian Stephen*, 1910, by Duncan Grant. 13½ × 10 in. Collection the artist

26. *Lemon Gatherers*, 1910, by
Duncan Grant. $22\frac{1}{4} \times 32$ in.
The Tate Gallery, London.
Inspired by the Sicilian Players
who performed tragedies of
peasant life at the Shaftesbury
Theatre, London, in February
and March 1908. In a review,
Lytton Strachey wrote of their
overwhelming visual and
expressive use of gesture
(*Spectator*, 29 February 1908)

27. *46 Gordon Square*,
c. 1908–9, by Vanessa Bell.
29×20 in. Collection Duncan
Grant. Exhibited as *Apples* in
the February-March Friday
Club Exhibition 1911 (no. 138)
this picture already announces
several characteristics of
Vanessa Bell's later work,
notably the strong vertical
emphasis and the theme of a
still life by a window

Stein's collection in the rue du Fleurus in Paris and probably met Picasso. Before 1911 his painting had been surprisingly little affected by these new contacts and the work he had seen, but from that year on he entered into several years of restless experiment, and became a leading contributor to the English Post-Impressionist movement. His long and accomplished apprenticeship was over.

(1) At King's College, Cambridge, and the Tate Gallery respectively.

(2) This painting is unique in Duncan Grant's work and the artist insists on his title *Le Crime et le Châtiment*. I mention it here for its technical accomplishment for it is atmospherically far from the scholarly reflection of the portraits of her brothers.

(3) It also includes a portrait of his cousin Pernel (winter 1908–9: untraced), another of Pernel and Naomi Foster over a tea table (early 1909: untraced), and portraits of Cambridge friends such as Arthur Cole (1908–9: Collection John Cole) and Cecil Taylor (1909: Collection the late Dr A. N. L. Munby).

(4) *Men and Memoirs*, Vol II, 1934, pp.180–1.

(5) The following March, Keynes was elected a Fellow of King's.

(6) 18 August 1909.

(7) DG to Lytton Strachey, 15 April 1910.

(8) Architect and designer who had built the house in the Orkneys where Duncan Grant had stayed in 1908.

(9) His account of this time appears as a contribution on 'Virginia Woolf' in *Horizon* Magazine, June 1941, Vol. III, no. 18; reprinted in *Recollections of Virginia Woolf*, ed. Joan Russell Noble, 1972.

(10) Two heads are in the artist's collection and a larger portrait is owned by Mrs R. Synge, the sitter's daughter.

(11) There is a sketch of the Matisse room at the Second Post-Impressionist Exhibition by Vanessa Bell with Duncan Grant seated on a sofa, Musée d'Art Moderne, Paris.

The two Post-Impressionist exhibitions arranged by Roger Fry in London in 1910 and 1912 created an enormous furore. Fry's position as a leading connoisseur of the old masters was temporarily halted; he was slanged and dismissed as a sensationalist and madman. The jeers aimed at the artists were savage enough, and unknown foreign names were an easy target for journalists. But a real, personal animosity was directed against Fry; he was socially ostracized, lampooned and accused of charlatanism. On the surface he had seemed very much part of that establishment art world which the exhibitions so disarmingly threatened. As he soon realized, social rather than aesthetic reasons lay behind some of the indignant anger. Though the reception of the two exhibitions confirmed all his worst suspicions about the British public's attitude towards painting, he was not embittered by the experience. In fact he greatly enjoyed the outraged comments of the press and the venomous controversies that ensued in the letter pages of papers and respectable journals. There had been nothing quite like it. His conviction as to the merits of the painters he had chosen never wavered; he was happy in their defence, flags flying and guns blazing.

What did upset him perhaps, or rather puzzle him, was the attitude of certain painters with whom previously he had felt in some degree sympathetic, particularly William Rothenstein and his old friend Walter Sickert. The disgusted comments of Royal Academicians were totally expected but from supposedly enlightened men such as these two, it was depressing. Sickert's long account of the first exhibition[1] contains much praise and it is obvious that he had been familiar for many years with some of the work shown. Fry was in fact a late-comer to an appreciation of Cézanne and Gauguin. Sickert could not abide Matisse who was full of 'the worst art-school tricks' and Picasso was 'a *faux fauve*'. But some of his remarks about Gauguin and Cézanne were extremely perceptive and he saw that Vlaminck, for example, was hardly capable of really interesting development, as indeed proved true. With Fry's increasingly passionate advocacy of Cézanne, Sickert became more adversely critical of that painter and later remarks descended into unthinking abuse: Cézanne would be 'remembered as a curious and pathetic by-product of the Impressionist group. . . .'

The older painters, however, must look after themselves; what Fry found most satisfactory was the support of the younger artists. From this emerged several schemes which occupied him over the next few years and made him the spokesman and apologist (with Clive Bell) of the new movement in

28. Walter Sickert and Roger Fry at Newington, 1912. Fry and Sickert had been friends as young men and Fry enormously admired Sickert's painting. Sickert however was suspicious of Fry's relatively late championship of the Post-Impressionists and took every opportunity to make gentle fun of him in his writings. Newington, near Oxford, was the home of the Painters Ethel Sands and Nan Hudson

England. Being a painter himself he saw some of the problems confronting his juniors. He was responsible for the decoration with five other painters of the dining-room of the London Borough Polytechnic. He included himself and ten others in the English section of the Second Post-Impressionist Exhibition and organized an exhibition in Paris (1912) of younger British painters. In 1913 he formed the Grafton Group and started the Omega Workshops. His energy was amazing and inspiring.

Under his influence, Bloomsbury buzzed with schemes and plans. He organized visits to see mosaics in Turkey, early Italian painting and the Ravenna mosaics, and arranged a bicycling tour in France to look at Romanesque churches. His own life was equally energetic. There was his painting, undergoing a strenuous conversion, his writing and editorial activities, lecturing at the Slade, his two children, Julian and Pamela, to care for, and the running of his house Durbins at Guildford (plate 29).

The First Post-Impressionist show, held at the spacious Grafton Galleries at the invitation of the directors, ran from 8 November 1910 to 15 January 1911. Manet, who prefaced the fireworks to come, was already appreciated in London; the *Bar at the Folies-Bergère* (Courtauld Institute) was among his pictures shown. There were twenty-one Cézannes, thirty-seven Gauguins, and among the twenty Van Goghs were *The Postman,* one of the *Sunflowers, Orchard under Rain,* and *Dr Gachet.* Desmond MacCarthy, the show's secretary and Fry's right-hand man has given an amusing account of how these pictures were selected. He and Fry had gone to Paris to choose pictures from the collections of the dealers Bernheim-Jeune, Vollard and Drouet. Afterwards, a small bicycling tour was planned before Desmond MacCarthy was sent off to choose more pictures in Holland and Munich, notably the Van Goghs from the artist's sister Mme Gosschalk-Bonger in Amsterdam. Roger was a very capable traveller and a great one for organization. But there was one drawback. He wanted to bicycle too fast and too far at one stretch. To mitigate that, MacCarthy would subtly draw Roger's attention to a distant barn or the charm of a line of hills; 'By Jove' Roger

29. 'Durbins', near Guildford, Surrey, the house Roger Fry designed for himself in 1910 on his return from America. He had hoped to live a family life here with his wife Helen who suffered from a mental illness; Helen did not recover sufficiently and Fry moved back to London in 1919. Nikolaus Pevsner has described 'Durbins' as 'one of the landmarks in the evolution of an independent contemporary style in English architecture'

would cry taking out his sketch-book; MacCarthy meanwhile would restfully smoke a pipe. They spent a night at Meaux where the Cathedral struck Roger as being a monster, visited a very good circus and went on the next day to Château Thierry. Among other painters they finally chose were Matisse, Picasso, Derain, Rouault and Maurice Denis. For two months the exhibition was visited by flocks of uncomprehending visitors. But there were others who were appreciative.[2] Some favourable criticism came from Arthur Clutton-Brock, Charles Holmes and Lewis Hind.[3] Hugh Blaker, the inspirer of the Davies collection of modern painting at Cardiff, wrote in his diary:[4] 'The Press, headed of course, by the ponderous stupidity of *The Times*, makes fun of it – derides it . . . society . . . is enthusiastic over the "jokes" . . . thus proving that cultured London is composed of clowns, who will, by the way, be thoroughly ashamed in twenty years time and pay large sums to possess these things. How insular we are still.'

The publicity was naturally a very good draw and in the end the exhibition proved 'a prodigious success', wrote Clive Bell.[5] 'It set all England talking about contemporary painting and sent the more alert not only to Paris but to museums and collections where they could have a look at primitive, Oriental, and savage art. The attendance was a record for the gallery; the sales were more than satisfactory; the Yorkshire Penny Bank, which held the Grafton Galleries in mortgage, made a pretty penny. . . .' Clive Bell made a bid for a Cézanne of Mont Ste-Victoire at £400 but it was beyond his pocket and went to the National Gallery of Finland. Instead the Bells bought a large Vlaminck landscape, *Poissy-le-Pont*, to hang by the Picasso still life they already possessed, and Roger bought a Derain landscape, *Trees by a Lake* (Fry Collection, Courtauld Institute).

The most immediate impact of the exhibition could be seen in the work of some of the younger painters in England who had gathered around Walter Sickert as the most progressive and interesting painter of the older generation. The young were dissatisfied with the afternoon impressionism of the New English Art Club; yet it was one of the few places where their work might be accepted. In 1908 the Allied Artists Association had come into being organized along the lines of the French Salon des Indépendants and held exhibitions annually at the Albert Hall. The first exhibition was enormous and run on the no-jury system with a hanging committee selected alphabetically from the exhibitors. It found support from Sickert and his circle.

Harold Gilman, Spencer Gore and, from early 1910, Charles Ginner were notable among that group. Gore had already looked appreciatively at Matisse; Ginner was even more cognizant of the Post-Impressionists and had received contemptuous treatment at his art school in Paris for admiring Van Gogh. But their own work was not startlingly indicative of their knowledge of French developments. There was not such a wide gap between the conservative New English and the committed progressives until 1911. But the group who met in Sickert's studio at 19 Fitzroy Street on Saturday afternoons did represent the vigorous left of British painting at that time.

30. *Peaches, c.* 1910, by Duncan Grant. 12¾ × 16¾ in. Courtauld Institute Galleries, Fry Collection. Painted at about the time of the First Post-Impressionist Exhibition, this still life shows the impact of Cézanne

Most of the artists lived or had studios around Fitzroy Street. Gore was at number twenty-one and Albert Rutherston at number eighteen. Lamb and John were at number eight, Derwent Lees for a time in Gore's house, and Sickert at number nineteen and all over the place up to Camden Town. Sickert and Lucien Pissarro were the older hosts at these afternoons. 'There was an appetising smell of tea and pigment as you ascended to a glorious afternoon of pictures and of talk. Easels and chairs faced the fireplace with a serried stack of canvases against the wall. Six works or more of an individual painter were extricated in turn, each Fitzroyalist displaying his quota or having it displayed for him by the untiring Gore.'[6] Other painters who went were Innes, Bevan, Lightfoot, and Wyndham Lewis. There was also a different element added by such figures as Ambrose MacEvoy and Edna Clarke Hall.[7]

The history of the various small groups over the next two or three years is complicated by internal schisms, overlapping membership and divergence of opinion. The most significant however was the Camden Town Group formed in 1911 when it held two shows, another following in 1912. Duncan Grant was a member in 1911 and at the December show exhibited his *Parrot Tulips* which Edward Marsh bought, the first modern picture of his collection.

With the advent of the Post-Impressionists, a much firmer line can be drawn among the English painters. On one side was the Royal Academy and the New English Art Club, Sickert in the middle, and on the other side the Camden Towers, some of the Friday Club and recent Slade School students like Spencer and Bomberg. Such compartmentalizing is intended only as a guideline; it does not convey the fluidity that in fact existed nor the tremendous excitement and rapid change that ensued.

Neither Duncan nor Vanessa were eager exhibitors. Sickert who knew and liked Vanessa did not know she was a painter until he saw her *Iceland Poppies* (plate 6) at the 1909 New English exhibition. '*Continuez!*,' he told her enthusiastically. Nor were they eager participants in groups but with Roger Fry in their midst they became much more involved in exhibiting and came to know a wider circle of painters. They were launched into the movement.

Before discussing some of the results of their association, such as the Borough Polytechnic murals and the Omega Workshops, it is necessary to mention the love affair between Roger Fry and Vanessa which began during a visit to Turkey in April 1911 with Clive and Harry Norton, a Cambridge friend and mathematician devoted to Vanessa. At Broussa, Vanessa fell seriously ill and Roger took charge of the invalid under difficult circumstances. On their return to England, Vanessa convalesced in the summer months at a cottage near Durbins and Roger was constantly in attendance. By then they knew they were in love. Roger's great passion for Vanessa lasted several years, causing much pain and frustration when Vanessa extricated herself in favour of Duncan. While the love affair lasted it was an incredible source of joy and happiness to Fry after the dreadful years of his wife's increasing madness. He loved domesticity and the sharing of intimacies and Vanessa helped satisfy this side of his nature. He was devoted to her children. There was also the pleasure of discussing painting with a painter he respected and they often worked together. It was a relationship which was to effect them both for the rest of their lives.

Durbins, Guildford.
June 19th 1911

My dear Duncan Grant,

Can you come at 3.45 p.m. instead of in the morning on the 30th to the Borough Polytechnic as Basil Williams wants to meet us. I hope you'll have got something to show him as we shall get the whole thing passed then I expect.   Yours very sincerely, Roger Fry.

Basil Williams, a friend of Roger's from Cambridge days, was Chairman of the House Committee of the Borough Polytechnic near the Elephant and Castle. He had suggested that the students' dining-room might be decorated by Fry and some young painters of Post-Impressionist persuasion. Fry eagerly accepted. Here was a real chance to put into practice his ideas about the decorative possibilities of the new movement, to enliven drab environments and Victorian rooms with all the colour and freedom that it had released. He recruited Albert Rutherston, Bernard Adeney and a young painter who became increasingly friendly with the painters in Bloomsbury, Frederick Etchells. Etchells, who was born in Newcastle upon Tyne in 1886, had studied at the Royal College of Art and had been impressed by the

31. Detail of a mural at King's College, Cambridge, *c.* 1910–11, by Duncan Grant. From a contemporary photograph. The mural, representing grape-pickers, was commissioned by Maynard Keynes for his rooms in Webb's Court. It remained unfinished and is preserved behind later panels by Vanessa Bell and Duncan Grant. In subject and treatment the mural is closely related to the 1910 *Lemon Gatherers* (plate 26)

32. *The Dancers*, 1910–11, by Duncan Grant. 21 × 26 in. The Tate Gallery, London. Another larger and less finished version of this picture was in the Second Post-Impressionist Exhibition. Grant was particularly interested in figure-groups at this time and the work of Maurice Denis has been suggested as an influence

Grafton exhibition. He and his sister Jessie, also a painter, were members of
the Friday Club. After the Borough Polytechnic scheme Etchells divided
his time between London and Paris and exhibited in the Second Post-
Impressionist exhibition and with the Grafton Group.[8] The painters took
to him and found his work sympathetic and it was with Etchells that Duncan
discussed the manner in which they should carry out the decorations to give
them some form of unity.[9]

The subject chosen for the decorations was 'London on Holiday'. Duncan
chose *Football* and *Bathing* (representing the Serpentine, Hyde Park),
Etchell's *The Fair*, Roger Fry *The Zoo* and Adeney *Sailing Boats* (The
Round Pond, Hampstead). Later two more panels were added, Rutherston's
Paddlers and Macdonald Gill's *Punch and Judy*.[10] The paintings were done
in oil on casein on canvas, separated and surrounded by a decorative border.
In the autumn the scheme was finished, though not without a great deal of
discussion and criticism. Vanessa was most enthusiastic about Duncan's and
Etchells' panels – 'it's extraordinary how indistinguishable they become. I
suppose their general colour schemes have a great deal in common.'[11]
Duncan was somewhat critical of Roger's and Roger at one point was
disgusted with his. The students were not particularly pleased with the
results but a talk given by Roger about modern painting and its possibilities
with regard to murals and interior design roused interest and Roger thought
conversion to his views had followed. The press widely covered the venture.
The critic in the *Spectator* was guardedly enthusiastic, distinguishing
between work conceived from within the new movement and that simply
given 'a Fitzroy twist', as he wrote of Rutherston's *Paddlers*. 'Mr R. Fry's
cartoon,' he continued, 'may contain an inner symbolism as it presents a child
(of light) offering a Post-Impressionist bun to a dubious elephant, who might
be the British Public. A meditative giraffe rears its head unconcernedly into
the heavens, and quite in the background is an Italian old master tree.' He
reserved his praise for *Bathing* (plate 34). 'If the Signorelli figures arching
themselves like great bows in the foreground are contrary to nature, the
figure scrambling into the boat in the distance is a noble piece of draughtsmanship, and when all is said the effect of the whole gives an extraordinary impression of the joys of lean athletic life. It makes one want to swim – even in water
like an early Christian mosaic.'[12] *The Times* writer was pleased and amused,
particularly by Etchells' *The Fair* (plate 35). But it was *Bathing* which
again received the laurels. 'Mr Grant has used all his remarkable powers of
draughtsmanship to represent the act of swimming rather than any individual swimmers. . . . They are lost, as it were, in the act of swimming. They
seem, rather than Cockney bathers in the Serpentine, to be primitive Medi-
terraneans in the morning of the world. All the colour of the painting, arbitrary
as it appears, is equally expressive and conveys the same feeling.'[13]

Not all the reviews, however, were so tolerant or interested and 'A Post-
Impressionist Scribbler' in the *National Review*[14] thought the whole thing
a hideous and clumsy nightmare. He imagines his own edifying version of the
chosen topics and the effect 'painting could have on the poor sunless children
of the East End working classes'. Etchells contributed 'the most repellent

33. *Portrait of G. H. Luce*,
1910–11, by Duncan Grant.
20 × 15¾ in. Collection the
late Dr A. N. L. Munby. G.
H. Luce (b. 1889) was a poet
and teacher of English at the
University of Rangoon. His
Poems (Macmillan, 1920)
was financed by Maynard
Keynes and a later edition
with decorations by Duncan
Grant was published by the
Hogarth Press (1923)

34. *Bathing*, 1911,
by Duncan Grant.
90 × 120½ in. The
Tate Gallery,
London. Mural for
the dining-room of
the Borough
Polytechnic, South
London, purchased
by the Tate Gallery
in 1931. Duncan
Grant's murals in
c. 1911 were
considerably more
advanced than his
easel painting at
that time. The
opportunity to
design on a large
scale released a
formal inventive-
ness which had
previously been con-
fined to sketches
and drawings of
figures in the manner
of Poussin and
Rubens

35. *The Fair*
(detail), 1911, by
Frederick Etchells.
98¾ × 242 in.
The Tate Gallery,
London. Etchells
and Grant worked
in close collaboration
over the Borough
Polytechnic murals

36. *Football*, 1911, by
Duncan Grant. $89\frac{1}{2} \times 77\frac{1}{2}$ in.
The Tate Gallery,
London. It was through
these two murals for the
Borough Polytechnic that
Grant first became known to
a wider public. He was
invariably singled out as the
most promising of the
English Post-Impressionists

and fruitless attempt . . . which does not contain one quality or possibility of
distinction' and while 'the least feeble in intention is *Swimming*', its artist if
'he shook off his attachment to his "ego" and would learn to paint and draw
with some reverence and modesty, might in time do interesting work.' The
work could only have the most degenerate influence on the children of the
working classes and 'the perpetrators of these travesties of decoration are
more to be pitied than blamed.' One can imagine Fry's delighted reaction on
reading this.

As an overall scheme the paintings are not particularly successful but for
reasons quite different from the outraged morality of the 'Post-Impressionist
Scribbler'. Unity is arrived at neither stylistically nor in the artists' varied
approach to their subject matter. Duncan's contribution and that of Etchells

however are distinctive. The former's *Bathing* is a moving and forceful work. All the figures in the composition represent one chronological sequence of movement – from diving, swimming, climbing into and coming to rest in the boat. When looked at as such, the canvas takes on a dynamism which the figures in *Football* (plate 36) seem to lack despite their apparent greater vitality. The relative success of the undertaking was heartening to Fry and it put the name of Duncan Grant in the forefront of the new movement. 'Mr Duncan Grant will one day be heard of beyond the walls of the Borough Polytechnic,' wrote Robert Ross in the *Morning Post*. The *Evening Standard* stuck out its neck and called the scheme 'the most important artistic event of 1911'. Several reviews mentioned the brightly painted corridor from which the dining-room opened – painted in sky blue, orange, white, and primrose. Much was made of the relatively low cost of the project – the materials and artists' payment came to a little under £100.[15]

Duncan learnt much from this experiment and he undertook several mural decorations in the following year. That autumn he had moved his studio again and joined forces with the Stephens at 39 Brunswick Square. A house in Bedford Square had been considered and another in Fitzroy Square. Vanessa rejected the Adam rooms of the latter: 'I believe elegance is becoming rather tiresome,' she told Clive. So Brunswick Square was settled on. Duncan and Maynard occupied the ground floor, Adrian the first, Virginia the second. The top floor was offered to Leonard Woolf, recently returned from Ceylon and in love with Virginia. Both the ground-floor and first-floor rooms soon contained large, startling wall paintings.

The room on the ground floor was curved at one end with windows at the other facing the square. In the middle on one side opposite the door was a fireplace. Although it was Maynard's room, Duncan made good use of it during the next three years. Over a sofa he threw a large multi-coloured rug; another chair was covered in a bright yellow and green material with a Greek-key pattern. On the mantelpiece stood a vase he had painted in a small pottery in Tunis, a black-outlined figure in a broken, distorted manner. And on one side of the fireplace Maynard hung a large picture by Etchells, *The Dead Mole*, which he had bought in 1912 and which was shown that year in the Second Post-Impressionist Exhibition. But the really notable feature of the room was a continuous mural from the fireplace round the curved end to the door, from ceiling to the dado (plate 38). It showed a London street scene with an accident between two horse-drawn cabs as the centre of interest. Women lean out of windows, children sit on the pavement, one driver cradles the head of his horse in his arms, men in flat caps look on and discuss the event. The scene was painted by Duncan and Etchells[16] in a loose, spotted style reminiscent of Signac. Many of the energetic figures are fantastically posed and distortion is used to witty effect in the figure of a very fat woman leaning on a window-sill.

In the first-floor drawing room used by Adrian, there was another wall painting of a game of tennis. The players are extremely simplified shapes and predominantly in reds and yellows. They bear some resemblance to the Polytechnic bathers but go beyond them in their reduction to essentials

37. *The Red Sea – Decoration*, 1911–12, by Duncan Grant. 48 × 59¼ in. City of Kingston upon Hull, Ferens Art Gallery. Possibly first intended to be shown at the Paris Salon but, after being exhibited once in London, it was disregarded. In the following year Grant painted a second version of *The Ass* on the reverse – hence the stretcher marks here visible

of line and are nearer the figures of Matisse's dancers in his Barnes Foundation mural or the cut-outs of his last years. They are quite featureless and without any suggestion of modelling. On this occasion Duncan was helped by Adrian who had, according to Duncan, a certain talent for painting; Adrian also decorated the four panels of a cupboard door with nude female figures.

Another wall painting undertaken somewhat earlier than these in Brunswick Square (which were destroyed through bombing in the Second World War) was in Maynard's rooms in Webb's Court at King's College, Cambridge. It was painted in late 1910 and early 1911 and bears distinct resemblances to *The Lemon Gatherers* and *Dancers* (both in the Tate Gallery) painted at that time. There are four panels with three figures in the first panel and two figures in each of the others; the scene represents grape-pickers and dancers. In the first, two women stand with baskets on their heads while a man on a ladder stretches his arm to the vine trellis above. In the next two panels, four dancers join hands in a circle moving to a stately rhythm, and in the last, two men hold baskets to their heads with their backs to each other. The rhythmic possibilities of a circle of dancers has been a feature all through

38. *Street Accident* (detail of mural), 1911–12, by Duncan Grant and Frederick Etchells. Destroyed by enemy action in 1940. Late in 1911 Duncan Grant became interested in pointillism and though he never embraced a severely systematic approach, many works in 1912 were carried out in what Vanessa Bell termed 'Duncan's leopard manner' – spots of close toned, clear colour graded towards a darker contour. Etchells used a similar manner and, judging from this unsatisfactory but unique contemporary photograph, worked harmoniously with Grant

Duncan's work – from this mural and *The Dancers* and an Omega decoration (plate 115) to the 1934 panel of dancers (Birmingham City Art Gallery). The painting is full, too full perhaps, of rhythmic complexities and there are recognizable affinities with his early love Piero della Francesca, though the colour is distinctly Post-Impressionist. Duncan apparently ran into difficulties towards the completion of the painting; he remembers throwing down his brushes and bursting into tears. In the event, the mural was not finished to his satisfaction. It remains on the wall, very well preserved behind a decoration on canvas panels which Maynard commissioned from Duncan and Vanessa some years later.

These murals give an indication of the invigorating effect of the Grafton Galleries exhibition. As Vanessa Bell later recalled, young artists in England needed to be rescued: '. . . here was a sudden pointing to a possible path, a sudden liberation and encouragement to feel for oneself which were absolutely overwhelming. Perhaps no one but a painter can understand it and perhaps no one but a painter of a certain age. But it was as if at last one might say things one had always felt instead of trying to say things that other people told one to feel.'[17]

By the end of 1912 Duncan's reputation in the 'forefront of the modern movement' was considerable. In the February exhibition of the Friday Club his large *The Red Sea – Decoration* (plate 37) had attracted favourable attention, the Contemporary Art Society had bought *The Queen of Sheba* and then showed his work in group exhibitions in Manchester, Paris, Cardiff, Leicester and Liverpool.[18] With the opening of the Omega Workshops in the following year examples of his painting could regularly be seen in London.

[1] The *Fortnightly Review*, January 1911.

[2] There was, for example, George Mallory, the young mountaineer, taking round a girl who had previously laughed at the pictures, and making her see the point of Cézanne and Gauguin. Cecil Taylor went round the exhibition with Saxon Sydney Turner and wrote afterwards: 'The galleries were full of sniggering society but there are so many of the pictures so clearly and immediately beautiful that I am surprised the ordinary person doesn't more often like them' (Cecil Taylor to J. T. Sheppard, 8 January 1911).

[3] His *The Post-Impressionists* was published in 1911, a brave but misguided account.

[4] 14 December 1910.

[5] 'How England Met Modern Art' in *Art News*, New York, October 1950.

[6] Louis Fergusson, *The Studio*, 1930, p. 111.

[7] The afternoons were not restricted to painters for Rutherston remembered appearances by Lady Ottoline Morrell, George Moore and Humbert Wolfe.

[8] Vanessa described him to Margery Snowdon as a 'somewhat uncouth north-country youth' (18 September 1912) and his sister as 'a nice character, also a painter and very silent'. Clive found them both 'dull and uncouth'.

[9] Bernard Adeney wrote (in a letter to a member of the Tate Gallery, 31 December 1953): 'We decided to employ the technique of graduating the colour tones to a dark contour to increase the rhythm of the design – as in Byzantine mosaics.' Some Byzantine influence also seems evident in the treatment of the background in both of Grant's panels and in the Etchells. Duncan explained what he had in mind to Etchells by painting a head similar in style to those found in their respective murals. He denies, however, any Byzantine influence.

[10] Gill was an architect and muralist, brother of Eric Gill.

[11] VB to RF, 5 June 1911.

[12] 'The Amusements of London' by J.B. in the *Spectator*, 11 November 1911.

[13] *The Times*, 19 September 1911.

[14] December 1911.

[15] The murals were removed owing to re-building in 1929 and were acquired two years later, somewhat damaged, by the Tate Gallery.

[16] A Miss Vera Waddington, who had been in Paris at the same time as Duncan was at La Palette, was also recruited but her contribution was white-washed out as not being in keeping; Duncan thought her work interesting but Maynard and the Bells found it deplorable.

[17] 'Roger Fry', memoir in manuscript by Vanessa Bell, 1934.

[18] These exhibitions included one at Leicester (January 1913), two at the Sandon Society, Liverpool (February–March 1913 and February 1914, where the Omega also exhibited its wares), a large show at Manchester (December 1911 to January 1912), the catalogue with prefaces by Fry and D. S. MacColl, and a Bristol exhibition, organized by Fry (Spring 1914).

Up to 1912 Duncan had only infrequently painted landscapes – on holiday with Maynard Keynes in the Orkneys, in Greece, and some studies on various English summer holidays. Landscape is even less frequent in Vanessa's work though visits to Studland Bay provided some opportunity. In February 1912, however, Virginia took a house in the Sussex downs and moved there from Little Talland House, the dreary villa she had rented two years before in nearby Firle village. The house played an important part over the next few years in the lives of most of Bloomsbury, not least Vanessa and Duncan was constantly painted there and in the country round about. Leonard Woolf has described its discovery in his autobiography.[1] Its name was Asham House, sometimes written Asheham or Ascham. A notable feature (besides the fact that it was reputedly haunted, indeed the ghost was seen gliding past the windows) was the neo-Gothic look of the three french windows that in summer were always open onto the terrace. The windows above were similar and the whole effect was 'curiously dreamlike'.

On 9 February 1912 there was a house-warming party and the people who came were to be among the most frequent visitors over the following years – Virginia and Leonard Woolf, Clive and Vanessa Bell, Adrian Stephen, Duncan and Roger. When Virginia married Leonard Woolf in August 1912 and went abroad on her honeymoon, Clive and Vanessa took Asheham until the end of September and for the next three years Asheham replaced Studland Bay as their summer retreat. They were also there in January and February in 1913 and 1914. Later on and during the War, the Woolfs were more often at Asheham for holidays and weekends. The house was finally given up in 1919.

Much of the talk at Asheham during August and September centred around the proposed Second Post-Impressionist Exhibition; Duncan and Vanessa were engaged in designing the poster for the show and Clive was writing his catalogue preface for the section of English pictures. Some of the exhibitors came down to visit. Henri Doucet arrived at the end of the month. Roger had met him the year before at the gallery of the poet and dealer Charles Vildrac in Paris and they had taken a great liking to each other. At that time Doucet, aged twenty-eight, was an exhibitor at the Salon des Indépendants and under contract to Vildrac (whose gallery for contemporary French painting Doucet had been instrumental in founding in 1909). In 1910 Doucet and a sculptor friend, Drouard, had taken over a

75

39. *Nursery Tea*, 1911, by
Vanessa Bell. 30 × 41½ in.
New Grafton Gallery,
London. Painted in June
1911 when she was recovering
from her illness in Turkey.
In a letter to Roger Fry
(5 June 1911) she wrote
'I am just in an exciting
stage as I flatter myself
that I am painting in an entirely
new way (for me). . . .'

40. *Studland Beach*, 1911, by
Vanessa Bell. 30 × 40 in.
Private Collection. A larger,
rigorously simplified version
of a sketch possibly painted
the previous year, this
picture, in its move towards
abstraction, counts as a
landmark in the painter's
development and was one of
the most radical works of the
time in England

dilapidated building in the rue du Delta in Paris which became a communal house for poor painters, one of whom, Modigliani, lived there for several months in 1910–11. He was finally thrown out, having destroyed in a drunken rage pictures and sculpture belonging to Doucet and the others. Roger invited Doucet to England and from then until his death in the War (1915) his visits were frequent. He was among the group of artists who painted Roger's daughter Pamela at Durbins, and he made portraits of Vanessa and her son Julian. While he was staying at Asheham, Vanessa painted him standing at an easel with Duncan sitting painting behind. On another occasion he sat to both Duncan and Vanessa, and the former's portrait of him, exhibited at the Second Post-Impressionist Exhibition, was bought by Charles Vildrac.

Frederick and Jessie Etchells arrived with their dog which caused trouble by attacking Vanessa's sheepdog and their visit was 'not altogether a success'. Clive in particular found them objectionable though he highly praised their painting. Vanessa painted them in characteristic attitudes at work in the sitting-room.[2] Like many of her portraits and figures in interiors at this time, the faces are featureless yet, as several witnesses maintain, absolutely recognizable (plate 42). Vanessa was adept at getting a likeness of the person she was painting, though she considered it the least important aspect, unless the portrait was a specific commission. Her sketchbooks over the years

41. *Asheham House*, 1912, by Vanessa Bell. 18½ × 21 in. Private Collection, London. On the reverse is a view of the front of Asheham House. With long, uninterrupted periods of painting at Asheham, Vanessa Bell rapidly developed those characteristics of her style first heralded with *Studland Beach*

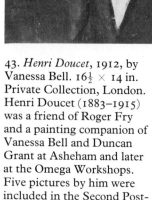

contain numerous drawings of people in trains, in cafés and in gardens, which
seem striking likenesses, sometimes to the point of caricature.[3]

The Second Post-Impressionist Exhibition, while always coupled with
the first, bears in retrospect a different complexion. Cézanne was now the
starting point as the old master of the movement, though not quite so well
represented as in 1910. Alongside work by the very latest French painters
(chosen by Roger) was shown a section by English artists (for which Clive
was responsible) and a consignment of Russian work chosen by Boris
Anrep. The passage of nearly two years had reduced the element of shock,
there were many more appreciative visitors and according to Clive the
pictures were 'selling like hot cakes' soon after the opening (5 October 1912).
Lectures and readings at the Grafton Galleries (where the secretary was
Leonard Woolf) by English and French writers helped people realize
that the modern movement was not simply confined to painting – something which the Russian Ballet season in July at Covent Garden had also
confirmed. Charles Vildrac came over and so did the revolutionary theatre
director Jacques Copeau, both of whom were entertained by the Bells at
Gordon Square.

Though Lewis Hind could write in the *News Chronicle*, 'Yes, Matisse has arrived', the critic in the *Morning Post* called it 'a deplorable and degrading show'. Matisse was the centre of furious abuse as the oldest and most degenerate of Cézanne's 'children'. He was represented by thirty-four paintings and drawings and seven bronzes; for those who liked the pictures, he was the star of the exhibition. The decadence of the English group provided another target for horror. Although it was admitted that they were not as uncompromisingly modern as the French, the tainted English works were singled out as being almost unpatriotic in their deference to the French movement. They look now of course a relatively restrained showing. Among the painters whose work Clive selected were Etchells (and a painting by his sister Jessie), Wyndham Lewis, Bernard Adeney, Henry Lamb, Spencer Gore and Stanley Spencer, Duncan, Vanessa and Roger. There were also seven sculptures by Eric Gill which were rather favourably received. Duncan was generally praised as the most talented of this group though his wavering between impressionism and downright modernism was considered shameful. Naturally impressionism was suggested as the path he should take, as illustrated by *Seated Woman* (plate 44) and *Pamela*. The latter is a portrait of Roger's daughter sitting by the garden pond at Durbins, painted in a low-keyed *intimiste* style of great delicacy of colour and drawing but already showing signs of a severer simplification of form, especially in the outlined treatment of the legs. He was saved, in the eyes of several critics, by the literary element detected in his *Dancers* and *The Queen of Sheba* though not unsurprisingly he came off very badly when his *Dancers* was compared to the huge *La Danse* of Matisse. The other two of Duncan's six exhibits included *The Byzantine Lady*, sometimes called *The Countess*, painted from a model accurately dressed in Byzantine clothes. (Vanessa had painted her at the same time (plate 45).) In its simplification, brilliant colour and exoticism, it was Duncan's most advanced picture there. The other work was the portrait of Henri Doucet already mentioned.

'I have four things at the Grafton which are quite ordinary and no one's ideas but my own, at least so I think!' Vanessa told Margery Snowdon.[4] Her *Spanish Model* was lent by the Contemporary Art Society which caused some derisory comment that an institution should patronize such shoddy work. Her tendency at this time to cube her shapes, to draw them towards an overall geometric conception, is well illustrated in *The Nosegay* and *Asheham House* (plates 48, 41). The sensuousness of flowers in the former is suggested entirely by the colour; in the landscape the structure is emphasized by the separate areas of colour, strongly outlined as in the landscapes of Spencer Gore (by whom there were two works *The Tree* and *Letchworth Station*).[5] While Duncan's work in the show varied widely in style from the Vuillardesque *Pamela* to the theatrical *Queen of Sheba* (plate 46), Vanessa's exhibits were very consistent with qualities of modest appraisal and a tough simplicity which are hallmarks of her work. Even her *Spanish Model* has no exotic references. Her gifts as a decorator and designer which were about to blossom are hardly in evidence; whereas Duncan's *Dancers* and *Queen of Sheba* are both strongly decorative. Vanessa's deep feeling for Matisse's

44. *Seated Woman*, 1912, by Duncan Grant. 36¾ × 20½ in. Courtauld Institute Galleries, Fry Collection. The model for this picture, shown at the Second Post-Impressionist Exhibition, was Katherine ('Ka') Cox (1887–1934). In 1912 and 1913 she frequently posed for Duncan Grant; there is a portrait of her in the National Gallery of Wales and two more in private collections

80

45. *Byzantine Lady*, 1912, by Vanessa Bell. 28½ × 20 in. Private Collection, London. Painted to be shown at a Hampstead charity fête. Duncan Grant's version of the same subject shows the model full face

work with its insistence on the painted surface and passion for clarity becomes more apparent in the necessarily flat organization of space in textile design. The release of pure colour which decorative work in the following year seemed to bring about, supported by a similar clarification of form, led her quite naturally to some of the earliest pure abstractions in modern British painting. But at first, the formal simplification was carried through without much alteration of colour and many of these paintings from 1912 are surprisingly muted – creams, pale blues, dark greens, greys and ochres. This can be seen in such works as *The Bedroom, Gordon Square* (plate 47), *Duncan Grant and Doucet at Asheham, The Cornstack*, and various Asheham landscapes of September 1912. When Vanessa and Duncan began to paint together frequently – at Asheham and in London – the question of mutual influence is often raised in Vanessa's letters to Roger and she is depressed on occasions when she sees what Duncan is making of the subject before them.

'As it has been so cold Duncan and I have been painting still lifes indoors – servants brought in flowers from the garden – I find that I am not now much impeded by working with Duncan although of course I always think why didn't I see it like that? But as I have come to the conclusion that I didn't see it like that I no longer try to think I did – I suppose one would get used to working with anyone in time.'[6] 'Duncan's is eatable and mine a stodgy affair,' she wrote a few days later of their still lifes.[7] In London later that

46. *The Queen of Sheba*, 1912, by Duncan Grant. 47½ × 47½ in. The Tate Gallery, London. Painted for a decorative scheme at Newnham College, Cambridge, where Grant's cousin Pernel Strachey had been a student. Lytton and Pernel were in the artist's mind at the picture's conception. The background camels were done from drawings and photographs taken in Tunis, 1911. The painting was widely exhibited 1912–14 through the Contemporary Art Society

47. *The Bedroom, Gordon Square*, 1912, by Vanessa Bell. $21\frac{1}{2} \times 17\frac{1}{2}$ in. Private Collection, London

48. *Nosegay*, 1912, by Vanessa Bell. Dimensions and present location unknown. This picture was reproduced in the catalogue to the Second Post-Impressionist Exhibition (no. 109)

autumn they did some designs together for fabrics and the depression returned. 'His are so gay and lovely – mine rather dull and stupid . . . and then Duncan's colour – Oh it's a long time since I've been so depressed by working with him.'[8]

While the difficulties of working together were solved in time, Vanessa was always conscious of being brought into comparison with Duncan. She was never envious or hurt by such comparisons when they were, as was often the case, to her disadvantage, convinced as she was of Duncan's greater gifts. But it always gave her pleasure when someone distinguished between their work, as did Segonzac for instance, thinking them 'fundamentally quite different' as she reported to Roger.[9]

Not only was Vanessa depressed at times about working alongside Duncan and the comparative feebleness, so she supposed, of her work but there were also moments when Duncan's own painting seemed equally depressing. Seeing a group of them which had been returned from an exhibition in Cardiff after being shown in Paris, she wrote:

It seemed to me suddenly that he had collapsed. I thought I could see that he had never since done anything nearly as good as the early one we have – that the *Queen of Sheba* was not only a failure because he had gone on and spoilt it, but that the whole conception was really sweet and

49. Vanessa Bell and Duncan
Grant at Asheham, 1912.
The vase of flowers bears
some resemblance to
Vanessa Bell's *Nosegay*

too pretty and small – that the *Whippet* which I had thought better was
not really very much and that the dancers on the hill was only better
because he hadn't carried it far. I thought that the usual English
sweetness was coming in and spoiling all.

But I also thought, perhaps I think this now because I have been
seeing all those French pictures since seeing the Cardiff ones before.
Perhaps they look so bad by comparison with Derain, Picasso, Matisse
etc. It's too awful if everyone turns out a failure and if even Duncan at
his age is already going for less fine things than he did.[10]

Vanessa here deplores in Duncan that sweetness which most people found
appealing at the Grafton show. The smallness of conception which she
mentions is alluded to in Rupert Brooke's review of the exhibition:[11]

50. Duncan Grant, Virginia
Woolf and Gurth, Firle
Park, Sussex, 1912

Mr Grant has painted better things, perhaps, than any he shows here.
But several of these are lovely. He is always a trifle disappointing. One
always feels there ought to be more body in his work, somehow. Even
his best pictures here are rather thin. But there is beauty in *The Seated
Woman*, and exquisite wit and invention in the delightful *Queen of
Sheba*, and a grave loveliness in *The Dancers*. His genius is an elusive
and faithless sprite. He may do anything or nothing. Also, he is roaming
at present between different styles and methods. What an eye for
beauty! Why aren't his pictures better? But it's absurd to suppose they
won't be when he has 'found himself'.

It is true that he was roaming but it was not so haphazard an exploration as
Rupert Brooke suggests. Influences come thick and fast in the years just

before the war but there is always some point to them, some definite ensuing richness in the delineation of his talent. The example of Picasso was particularly invigorating. They had first met in about 1909 or 1910 at one of Gertrude Stein's Saturday afternoon gatherings in her apartment in the rue de Fleurus, the walls crammed, in French style, with Matisses and Picassos and Miss Stein seated on a dais receiving, majestically and slowly, her guests.[12] In 1913 Picasso had moved to a flat overlooking the cemetery of Montparnasse in the rue Schoelcher where Duncan was very interested to see his collection of African masks and carvings. One Saturday at Gertrude Stein's, Duncan mentioned to Picasso that in his hotel room there were several rolls of unused, old-fashioned wallpapers. Picasso was intrigued; Duncan brought them along soon afterwards to the Steins' and Picasso went off with several of them, highly delighted, though not without some questioning, in a teasing way, of the honesty of such a 'theft'. According to Gertrude Stein it was 'at the rue Schoelcher that [Picasso] commenced . . . to use a kind of wallpaper as a background and a small picture [painted] in the middle, [and] he commenced to use pasted paper more and more in painting his pictures.'[13] Duncan himself had used cut-out paper in 1912 – mainly plain coloured sheets – and also dress materials and fabrics. Both are combined in the tall *Caryatid* (Manchester City Art Gallery), and a frequent use of materials – he included a string of beads, which were later removed, on the portrait of Lady Ottoline Morrell – continued until about 1916. A painting by Picasso which very much impressed Duncan at the Steins' was a 1907 study of a woman's head, one of a series which culminated in *The Nude With Drapery*.[14] Apparently an interpretation of the head of Giorgione's reclining Venus (Dresden), the study belongs to the 'tête nègre' period of Picasso's work and almost immediately follows his *Les Demoiselles d'Avignon*. Its vigorous cross-hatching and sharply differentiated planes had a decisive effect on Duncan's work for about a year – from the 1912 *The Tub* (plate 52) where the hatching is used sparingly though the woman's body is extremely simplified and angular, through the much closer woven texture of *The Ass* and *Tents* to the large *Adam and Eve* (late 1913, plate 79). Two dancing figures, elongated and entwined, of September 1914 (painted to hang outside the Omega Workshops) show the adaptation of Picasso's harsh and vibrant surfaces to painting of a more essentially lyrical kind, nearer to Duncan's temperament than the brave but somehow absurd distortions of *Adam and Eve*, a painting he later called 'a thankless offspring'.[15]

From 1910 until the War, Roger Fry produced some of his best pictures. In the work of Duncan and Vanessa, the transition from conservatism to progressive modernism is gradually detectable, picture by picture, month by month. With Fry, the change has something of suddenness about it. The timid though fresh poetry of his landscapes is brutally replaced by the angularities and tough composition of such pictures as *River with Poplars*, 1912, (plate 53) and *White Road with Farm* (c. 1912). The conventional Edwardianism and illustrative detail are brushed aside in a vigorous assault on the motif involved. Trees are ground down to the simplest geometrical shapes, clouds stalk the skies. Firm outlines and four-square areas of paint give to

51. *Man with Greyhound*, 1911, by Duncan Grant. $37\frac{1}{4}$ × $20\frac{1}{4}$ in. Pivate Collection, Ireland. The subject was suggested during a visit to London's East End

52. *The Tub*, 1912, by Duncan Grant. 30 × 22 in. The Tate Gallery, London. Bought from the artist in June 1912 by Vanessa Bell

these canvases a strong flavour of a convert's uncompromising spirit. 'I want clear cut shapes and clear colours,' he wrote, complaining of the gloomy, inky shadows of trees and overcast skies of an early summer's day.[16] His youthful love of picturesque scenery expressed in so many landscapes of the New English Art Club variety, has been abandoned for a more vigorous view-finding among the Tuscan hills and the rocks of Provence (plate 54), though not altogether to his satisfaction. 'I try to turn my back on the medieval castle and the distant towers of Avignon, but the beastly things will get into my composition somehow or another.'[17] He continued his interest in the capturing of light and mood of places, inspired in the past more by Claude Lorraine than contemporary Impressionism. It informs his best land-scapes and no matter how angular and severe his design, he extracts a lyricism that was developed in the French landscapes of his later years. 'Landscape was to remain the motif which best drew out his creative faculties.'[18]

Fry's portraits are a different matter and though among their enormous number there are works of distinction, many are blighted by extraordinary lapses of drawing. The dull hand of classicism shakes its grey dust over these compositions – casualties of petrified design and that roving intellect which 'manages to reduce it all', wrote Vanessa, 'to such a dead drab affair'.[19]

Vanessa was nearly always critical of Roger's painting and became more so when, after the First War, they worked together in the South of France. He was eager to have Vanessa's opinion on his work and she was naturally

53. *River with Poplars*, c. 1911, by Roger Fry. 22½ × 28 in. The Tate Gallery, London. Possibly painted in October 1911 when Fry was in France with Clive Bell and Duncan Grant. In 1910 and 1911 Fry's work showed in some respects a more advanced understanding than any of his English contemporaries (with the exception of Gore) of current French developments

reluctant to give vent to her true feelings but praised and gave suggestions where she honestly could. Of course, Roger gave 'criticisms at every point', which Duncan in particular found depressing. 'I begin to think that finally there'll be nothing for it but to tell him the truth – prevarication is becoming too painful and unsuccessful.'[20] Whatever Vanessa's feelings in 1912 and 1913 Roger appeared satisfied with her remarks and appraisals. Certainly he was ready to be influenced by Vanessa and Duncan. 'I did a sketch of Roger yesterday,' wrote Vanessa to Clive,[21] 'in Duncan's leopard manner with odd results but very like and today Roger is doing one of me. I've persuaded him to try the leopard technique too and he isn't at all happy in it but is spotting away industriously in the hopes of getting at something in the end.' But as a painting companion, Vanessa infinitely preferred Duncan's company and their association became closer in 1913 when Vanessa brought her affair with Roger to an end in favour of Duncan.

Vanessa had found Duncan sympathetic and amiable from the start and painting was an obvious bond. While she had periodic doubts about his work, she was in general overwhelmingly favourable and generous. About most of her contemporaries she was dismissive; little English work interested her. French painters are constantly held up for praise in her letters but English painters rarely figure. Of an old friend and ally, Henry Lamb, she wrote, 'I'm now quite clear what I think of him. It's simply too deadly – academic drawing niggled and polished up to the last point without life or interest, very

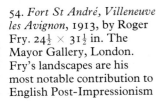

54. *Fort St André, Villeneuve les Avignon*, 1913, by Roger Fry. $24\frac{1}{2} \times 31\frac{1}{2}$ in. The Mayor Gallery, London. Fry's landscapes are his most notable contribution to English Post-Impressionism

55. Roger Fry at Brandon camp near Thetford, Norfolk, 1913

56. Vanessa Bell at a summer camp at Brandon, 1913. Maynard Keynes, Adrian Stephen, the Olivier sisters, Duncan Grant (who painted several pictures there including *Tents*) and Gerald Shove (1887–1947), one of the tenants at Brunswick Square, were also among the party

57. *Summer Camp*, 1913, by Vanessa Bell. Private Collection. Painted in August at Brandon, this sketch was used as the basis for Vanessa Bell's Omega Screen (plate III)

skilful, and utterly commonplace and second-hand in idea.' Steer is quite done for. Their Augustus John must be sold. Gertler soon begins to lose her attention. Sickert and Smith are the two most consistently admired. And of course Duncan. She had liked his painting before their close friendship and had bought *The Lemon Gatherers* from the 1910 Friday Club exhibition – 'in the principal place of honour is hung a sketch by Duncan which I thought far better than anything else – including the Puvis's. It is really very good indeed, very well drawn and a beautiful composition of women carrying loads on their heads. I was very much impressed by it and really think he may be going to be a great painter. . . . He is certainly much the most interesting of the younger painters.'[22]

While Roger shared Vanessa's admiration of Duncan's work and found him a delightful person, he saw with some alarm the growing intimacy between them. Vanessa playfully taunted Roger with descriptions of how Duncan had asked her to sit to him – 'Perhaps you could paint me at the same time which might console you'. On one occasion she told him that she had taken a bath in front of him to save time. She and Duncan not only worked together on the same subject or in the same room, but evolved plans and decorative techniques in friendly collaboration. This was what eventually so frustrated Roger – he loved collaboration (though by nature a leader) and being at the centre of any schemes that were afoot. He wrote of this to Clive: 'In painting Nessa and Duncan have taken to working so entirely together and not to want me, and altogether I find it difficult to take a place on the outside of the circle instead of being, as I once was, rather central. . . .'[23] He felt his passion for Vanessa gave him a right over her activities as a painter. He became philosophic over this but it rankled sometimes to hear 'what thrilling things you and Duncan do and say about art. . . . Of course you're doing splendid things, damn you. And mine will always be make-shift.'[24] He was taken by surprise that Vanessa, in the face of his passion and care, could be so completely under the spell of the elusive, seemingly indifferent, Duncan. How could Duncan look after Vanessa when she was unwell, find servants or deal with domestic crises in the way Roger could? He felt that 'the kind of intimacy and sympathy' he shared with Vanessa was inviolate so that when they separated he reproached himself for misunderstanding their relationship and doubted whether he had ever understood her. She had seemed so 'solid and real in a shifting world', had given him a feeling of security which 'made the break up so terrific when it came'.[25]

'Duncan Grant . . . was shy and vague and elusive, but always bewitching', commented Ottoline Morrell of the Duncan she knew before the First War – the young painter whom she took to meet the Russian dancers with Virginia Stephen; who was asked to meet Nijinsky and Bakst; who was seen flirting with Jelli d'Aranyi, the violinist, on the stairs at Bedford Square. He moved in and out of people's lives, silently, teasingly, soft-footed, hardly noticed by some, casting a spell on others that was to last a lifetime. His absolute dedication to his work always came first; his appearances at parties, at the

Russian Ballet, at reading parties in the country were from choice rather than habit. He was never a time-waster and everything was turned to use. His cultivation of independence was one of the strongest elements in his character and while it could lead to stubbornness it was tempered by a naturally mercurial manner. He was never aloof or overbearingly withdrawn. The expression of his feelings was reserved for a very few people and though his secrecy was maddening to some, it was never devious or scheming. He was incapable of that.

Unlike many of his friends, he was not a great talker. Like Vanessa he could remain quiet, amused and absorbed in the heady whirl of conversation that might be going on – Clive roaring and guffawing and slapping his knee in full flow, or Virginia erecting some fabulous theories on perverted love or family tragedy based on a five-minute talk with a complete stranger encountered in the Gray's Inn Road. Gossip of his friends was always welcome especially after silent hours spent painting in his studio. Virginia frequently supplied it with uninhibited relish. Living in the same house they were much in each other's company and while Duncan was aware of the dangers of taking her into his confidence they became increasingly fond of each other, encouraged of course by Duncan's intimacy with Vanessa. Virginia found Duncan extremely teasable with his highly personal and sometimes curious approach to doing things, his often surprising turn of language and the strange history of some members of his family,[26] though she was always aware that he could put up a very effective defence. And of course he was a painter, uninvolved in 'Grub Street' or quarrels about reviews, editorships, and the fluctuating reputations of this or that writer. There was none of the professional jealousy that was an element in her relationships with Lytton Strachey or Morgan Forster or Katherine Mansfield, for example. It is true she was sometimes vexed and irritated by discussions on painting: 'The furious excitement of these people all the winter over their pieces of canvas coloured green and blue, is odious.'[27] Her letters to him are full of affection, mainly concerned with the amusement afforded by their friends and with a continuing examination of Vanessa's character – not analytic or over-serious of course – but gently mocking:

> . . . old Nessa (who has become a Shakespeare character in my mind, so that I often put her into action for my amusement) – she, I suppose is long past reading letters by this time . . . and is it true, by the way, that she said the other day 'It's the last feather in the Camel's Cap,' meaning, it is thought (Heaven knows why) that she was unable to break the ice in her Po? And I suppose speech will be beyond her soon; Maynard seemed to think so, not that she ever had a complete vocabulary. . . .[28]

Vanessa's long silences, lapses into reverie were as much a subject for jokes with Virginia as was the state of Duncan's clothes with everyone else. They became a topic of conversation and hilarity. Duncan was poorer than most of his friends, receiving a small amount of money from his parents, occasional presents from Maynard, and sums from irregular and infrequent sales of his work. It was easy enough to eat since he could always be accommodated at the

58. Duncan Grant at
Asheham House, *c.* 1912

table in Gordon Square or Fitzroy Square if he happened to call in. But new clothes he considered a luxury and, being quite without personal vanity, he relied on cast-offs, more often than not, from Adrian. 'Duncan's clothes were grotesque. All belonged either to Adrian or his deceased uncle and were of course miles too large.'[29] Most memorable was his appearance at Virginia's marriage to Leonard Woolf on 10 August. 'A rumour has reached me that you might come up for the wedding. I should like it very much if you did – but this is only to say that we are going to be done on Saturday. . . .' wrote Virginia to him two days before. On the Saturday he arrived 'in a *very* shabby tail coat and silk hat all belonging to other people.'[30]

Duncan's involvement with the Post-Impressionist movement naturally brought new faces and new friends into his life. We find no more references to engagements with Holman-Hunts or Alma-Tademas or meetings with Steer and Tonks at the William Rothensteins. Of the older generation Walter Sickert was by far the most sympathetic, even if his views on the modern painters most admired by Duncan were exasperating. Vanessa was particularly fond of Sickert. 'I liked him better than I have ever done before,' she told Roger Fry after a meeting in July 1911, 'and was impressed by the ease with which I can get onto intimate terms with a man at once.' He had told her of his 'astonishing' love affairs and asked her to join his school, Rowlandson House. Mainly through Sickert, there were meetings with some of the Camden Town Group and, although less frequently, with younger painters such as the Spencer and the Nash brothers. Frederick Etchells was Duncan's closest painting companion apart from Vanessa and Roger. Wyndham Lewis appeared again in his life, to be met in Fitzroy Street or in conference with Roger about the workshop they proposed to start. In April 1913 there is a mention of a dinner with Edward Wadsworth followed by a meeting with Severini, the futurist, whose paintings were on show at the Marlborough Gallery. But none of these excursions into the London art world was productive of any intimate friendship; his strongest links were with Cambridge, and his visits to Maynard at King's continued to feature regularly in his life.

George Mallory was up at Magdalene College from 1905 to 1909 and was a year younger than Duncan whom he met in his last Cambridge year through James Strachey. Mallory's passion for mountaineering was already established but it was not his only preoccupation. He read a great deal of poetry and contemporary literature, admired Post-Impressionism, and published *Boswell the Biographer* in 1912. Duncan and Mallory rapidly became friends and Duncan visited him at Charterhouse where Mallory had become a schoolmaster. Duncan painted 'a large poster – a vivid green monk with uplifted glass' to advertise a new school magazine, *Green Chartreuse*.[31]

Mallory's splendid looks – Lytton Strachey said he had the 'body of an athlete by Praxiteles' – inevitably made him a subject for pencil and brush; he posed for Duncan on several occasions, mainly at Brunswick Square and most notably for a painting in Geoffrey Keynes's collection;[32] there were also numerous drawings. In March 1913 Duncan joined one of Mallory's Easter climbing expeditions at Pen-y-Pass, Snowdonia; he also visited him at his family home at Birkenhead.

59. *Virginia Woolf at Asheham*, 1912, by Vanessa Bell. 15½ × 13 in. Private Collection. Painted possibly in March, a few months before Virginia married Leonard Woolf

In 1914 Mallory married and Duncan attended the wedding at Godalming, just a few days before the declaration of War. During the next few years they continued to see each other and to correspond. At one point Duncan jokingly suggested that he should accompany an expedition to Mount Everest as the expedition's artist. It was on this proposed climb, in 1924, that Mallory and his fellow-climber Irvine disappeared in mysterious circumstances near the summit of Everest.

[1] *Beginning Again*, 1964, pp.55–6.

[2] *Frederick and Jessie Etchells in the Studio*, 1912, Tate Gallery.

[3] In 1933 she conceived a scheme of caricatures of Bloomsbury friends which were to be published as broadsheets with an accompanying page of text by Virginia Woolf. Drawings exist of Bertrand Russell and Roger Fry but the venture came to nothing. Other proposed subjects were Lydia Keynes and David Garnett.

[4] 15 October 1912.

[5] Vanessa's fourth exhibit was *The Mantelpiece*, untraced at the time of writing and not to be confused with *Still Life on Corner of a Mantelpiece*, 1914, Tate Gallery.

[6] VB to RF, Asheham, 11 September 1912.

[7] 16 September 1912.

[8] 2 November 1912.

[9] VB to RF, Paris, 2 March 1922.

60. *George Mallory*, 1913, by Duncan Grant. 21 × 25 in. Sotheby & Co., London

[10] VB to RF, August 1912.

[11] *Cambridge Magazine*, 23 November 1912.

[12] 'I love long poems,' she informed Duncan on one occasion, drawing out the 'long' in her deep voice. In early 1913, Gertrude Stein and Alice B. Toklas stayed with Roger Fry at his house Durbins.

[13] The chronology of the use of *papiers collés* in Picasso's and Braque's work is complicated and differs in so many accounts. Certainly pasted papers appear in 1912 and increasingly in 1913 and Gertrude Stein reproduces a Picasso still life *Au Bon Marché* dated Spring 1913 where considerable use is made of a striped nineteenth-century wallpaper. See *Picasso*, by Gertrude Stein, 1938.

[14] Museum of Modern Western Art, Moscow.

[15] Other paintings from 1912–13 which 'belong' to this group include *Slops* (Collection David Garnett), *Head of Eve* (Private Collection, London) and *Still Life* (Collection Mrs R. Peto).

[16] 31 May 1913, to Violet Dickinson.

[17] RF to DG, Villeneuve les Avignon, October 1913.

[18] Troutman, *Vision and Design*, Arts Council catalogue, 1966.

[19] VB to CB 21 November 1921.

[20] VB to CB, 21 November 1921. Before Roger Fry's Cooling Galleries Retrospective in February 1931, Vanessa wrote 'When I last went to his house I was horror struck to find an enormous portrait of myself looking like a handsome but shapeless cook in a red evening dress painted about 15 years ago. . . . The show will be very trying I expect. All sorts of things one hoped never to see again are being fished out . . .' (VB to CB, 23 January 1931).

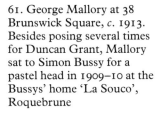

61. George Mallory at 38 Brunswick Square, *c.* 1913. Besides posing several times for Duncan Grant, Mallory sat to Simon Bussy for a pastel head in 1909–10 at the Bussys' home 'La Souco', Roquebrune

[21] Isle of Wight, January 1912.

[22] VB to CB, June 1910

[23] 9 May 1915.

[24] RF to VB, 23 August 1914.

[25] RF to VB, 16 September 1917.

[26] For the summit of Grant family eccentricities, Virginia Woolf cited a young man devoured by a Himalayan bear. No less remarkable and delightful was his aunt, Henrietta Grant, whose extraordinary behaviour was traced back to her having been dropped on her head from a carriage as an infant.

[27] VW to Violet Dickinson, 24 December 1912.

[28] VW to DG, *c.* 1917–18.

[29] VB to CB, 1910.

[30] VB to M. K. Snowdon, 20 August 1912.

[31] Robert Graves was one of the schoolboy editors. When Graves married Nancy Nicholson in 1918 Mallory was best-man and Duncan one of the guests.

[32] Sir Geoffrey Keynes (b. 1887), surgeon, bibliographer, collector, and younger brother of Maynard Keynes.

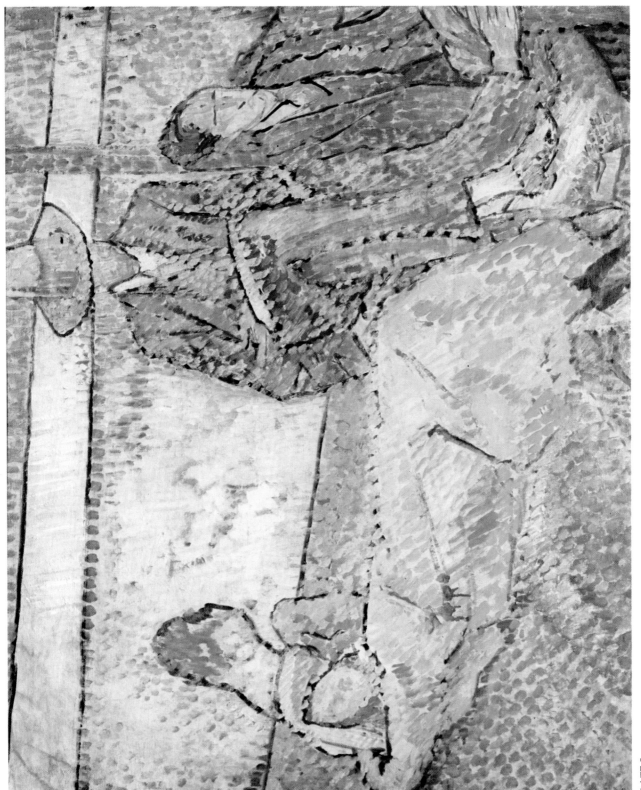

PLATE I

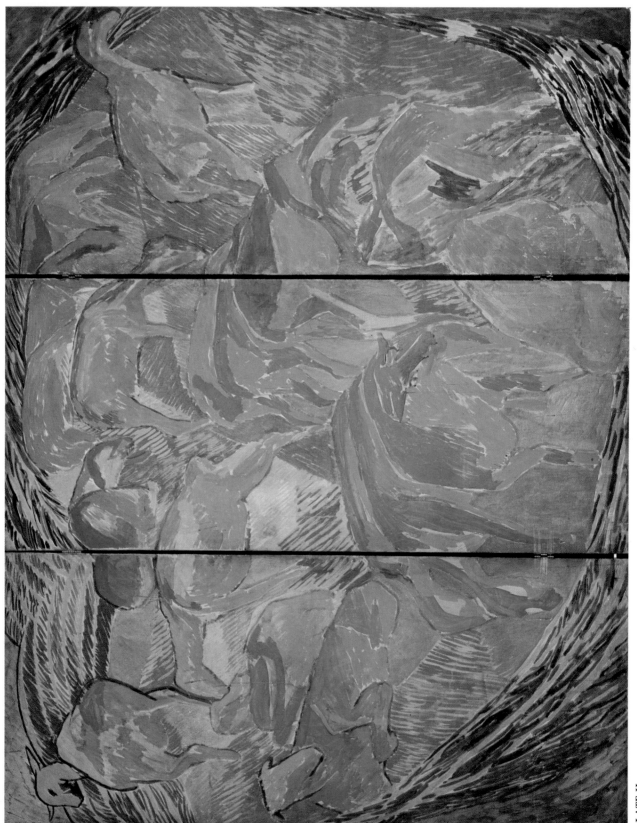

PLATE II

In his novel *The Pretty Lady* of 1918 Arnold Bennett describes a visit by his middle-aged, Albany-lodged hero G.J. to a room that is unmistakably Omega.

> The walls were irregularly covered with rhombuses, rhomboids, lozenges, diamonds, triangles, and parallelograms; the carpet was treated likewise, and also the upholstery and the cushions. The colourings of the scene in their excessive brightness, crudity and variety surpassed G.J.'s conception of the possible. . . . The place resembled a gigantic and glittering kaleidoscope deranged and arrested.
>
> G.J.'s glance ran round the room like a hunted animal seeking escape. . . . Regaining somewhat his nerve, he looked for pictures. There were no pictures. But every piece of furniture was painted with primitive sketches of human figures, or of flowers, or of vessels, or of animals. On the front of the mantelpiece were perversely but brilliantly depicted, with a high degree of finish, two nude, crouching women who gazed longingly at each other across the impassable semicircular abyss of the fireplace; and just above their heads, on a scroll, ran these words 'The Ways of God are strange'.

Even today, over fifty years later, when we look at the handful of photographs that were taken of Omega-decorated rooms, we can feel some of the astonishment that Bennett ascribes to G.J.[1]

Roger Fry was the originator and driving force behind the Omega Workshops. Its pervading aesthetic was quite new, established by the close, early cooperation of the artists Fry engaged. When Fry was in Paris in the spring of 1912 organizing the show of new English painting at the Galerie Barbazanges, it is more than likely that he saw the recently established workshop of Paul Poiret, the great designer. The Galerie Barbazanges rented rooms on the ground floor of Poiret's large fashion house in the faubourg St. Honoré and showed contemporary French painters such as Delaunay and Marie Laurencin. A little before the English painters exhibited there, Poiret had moved 'Martine', the name he gave to his group of interior decorators, a few doors away to their own premises, 87 faubourg St. Honoré. Most of the artists were untutored and there is a pleasant naïvety in the rugs and fabrics they designed and the murals they undertook. Pottery, painted furniture and whole interiors became part of their output, and Dufy, Segonzac and Matisse were among the artists who visited the workshop with Poiret. While

Roger Fry may well have found there some confirmation of his ideas for a scheme in London, the Martine products were more conventional, comfortable and 'pretty' than what was to come out of the Omega. Fauvism in its most mild aspect had some influence at Martine but its decorative possibilities were hardly explored in the way they were to be by Fry and his artists.

The Omega also had historical precedents, the most obvious being William Morris's workshop, Morris, Marshall, Faulkner & Company, which set up commercial production in competition with the soulless machining that so easily satisfied Victorian bourgeois taste. Morris's firm undertook mural decoration, carving and stained glass, furniture and embroidery. The venture was undermined however by an over-insistence on craft for craft's sake, the disparity between ornamentation and a real sense of design (with the exception of superb fabrics and wallpapers), and eventual deterioration into 'Ye Olde English' and farmhouse oak which still survive today under the name 'traditional English'. When the movement lost Morris's own personal impetus, it degenerated into archaism. The reason for this degeneration must be ascribed to the sorry state of painting in England at the time. The formless exactitude of Academic art was hardly conducive to a lively and original sense of design in the applied arts. And though it would be wrong to say that high achievements in the fine arts and in applied arts are mutually dependent, it certainly seems to be true of the revolution in both in the early decades of this century, above all in the influence of Fauvism and Cubism, which is most apparent in Omega fabrics and carpets.

One main difference between Morris's firm and the Omega Workshops was Fry's temperamental distrust of any politico-social motivation. He remained a sceptic in such matters though they deeply interested him. And with Duncan and Vanessa as his co-directors, it is unlikely that he would have found much support for any social motivation behind the establishment. It was not in any proselytizing spirit that he opened the Workshops. If a change did come about in the public's taste in furnishing and decoration then it would be a happy miracle on the side; his immediate aim was practical and altruistic in that he wished to help the many young artists whom he knew and whose work was in one way or another sympathetic. He was acutely conscious of the difficulty young painters had in selling their work or even showing it in a London still hostile to the Impressionists, let alone Picasso, Matisse and Braque. One of the first artists to get paid for work at the Omega, Nina Hamnett, testified to the financial help it was to her:

> One day somebody said, 'You might get a job to paint furniture and do decorative work at the Omega Workshops in Fitzroy Square.' The man who owned it was Roger Fry. I knew his name very well as he organized the first Post-Impressionist show in London in 1911 [sic].
>
> Feeling brave one morning I went to Fitzroy Square and asked to see Mr Fry. He was a charming man with grey hair, and said that I could come round the next day and start work. I went round and was shown how to do Batiks. I was paid by the hour. I made two or three pounds a week and felt like a millionaire.[2]

As a prelude to the Workshops, Fry organized the first Grafton Group Exhibition in March 1913, at the Alpine Club Gallery where, much to the public's frustration, works were shown anonymously. As early as February 1912 Fry had written to Lewis about a meeting 'to settle the nature of the group of artists which Duncan Grant, Frederick Etchells, and I propose to start.' The Friday Club was now too diffuse and miscellaneous to suit their aims. At the exhibition Lewis, Etchells, Duncan, Vanessa and Roger showed work alongside Max Weber from America and Kandinsky. Stanley Spencer was asked to show but apparently declined. Among applied art items there was a painted table by Etchells and a screen by Duncan which was decorated with brilliant blue sheep and created a stir, though *The Times* critic was quickly appreciative in spite of its colour. The paintings included a landscape by Spencer Gore, a large work by Duncan of the spirit of Sir Christopher Wren – a green giant towering above a model of St. Paul's – and a portrait of Molly MacCarthy by Roger. As for the pictures 'even outraged aesthetic virtue might admit that the general effect of the exhibition was gay, even though it be the gaiety of determined evil doing.' The new movement was still chastised on moral grounds – its distortions calculated to shock the public's natural decency. It was one of the achievements of the Omega over the next few years to mitigate such a line of condemnation. No matter how decorated, an object retained its function; it was still a cup, a bed, a parasol and thus half the battle was won. It must, however, be stressed that the Omega had only a small influence at the time and then mainly among the rich and cultivated patrons of a restricted circle. It had nothing like the widespread publicity of the Bauhaus. Advertising was on a tiny scale; it was the products and the wages that came first. Its initial notoriety was very good advertisement, for many people came to scoff but few left empty handed. Fry may have had no talent for commercial advertising but his charm, his enthusiasm and persuasive talk won over many customers. Here is Arnold Bennett in his journal for November 1916:

> Fry expounded his theories. He said there was no original industrial art in England till he started i.e., untraditional. He said lots of goodish things and was very persuasive and reasonable. Then he took me to the showrooms in Fitzroy Square. I gradually got to like a number of things, especially the stuffs. . . . I began to get more and more pleased with the stuff, and then I left with two parcels.

It is interesting that Fry here talked of industrial art and it must be emphasized that he did not conceive of the Omega as a 'Ye Olde Hand Made' crafts shop. If a machine could make an object better than a person or, in Fry's words, 'a purely servile and mechanical human being', then a machine was used. It has been said that Fry was against mechanical production and was all for the hand-made and the amateur craftsmen. What Fry was against was the utterly soulless production on a vast scale of badly designed objects that had arisen since the Industrial Revolution. Fry was no Morris-style Luddite. What he wanted and what the Omega tried to do was to bring the artist-designer into a much closer relationship with the craftsman or machinist so that the artist's ideas could be interpreted in a warmer and less formal manner. The spontaneity of immediate expression must be retained. This was certainly achieved in some of the early Omega furniture, in the desks of inlaid wood, the painted tables, and the chairs designed by Fry and Vanessa Bell. And it is seen to advantage in the carpets and textiles, especially those by Frederick Etchells and Edward Wadsworth (plates 73, 74).

During the later months of 1912 and in early 1913, work for the Omega (though it had not been designated as such) was rapidly going ahead. 'Can't we paint stuffs etc. which won't be gay and pretty?' Vanessa asked Roger. And so she and Duncan set to work. 'I have been doing designs with Duncan all day and his are much better than mine and I'm rather depressed,' she wrote to Roger in November 1912. Soon other artists were at work – Lewis,

62. Design for a Firescreen, 1912, by Duncan Grant. $32\frac{3}{4}$ × $29\frac{5}{8}$ in. Private Collection, London. Vanessa Bell mentions embroidering a screen from this design in August 1912 to relieve the boredom of a visit to her parents-in-law. Another version was in the Omega decorated room in Henry Harris's house, Bedford Square. A more elaborate and brilliantly coloured version was worked by Lady Ottoline Morrell

Etchells, Wadsworth, Cuthbert Hamilton, and John Turnbull, and by April Roger had finally leased 33 Fitzroy Square to house the venture. Vanessa was already planning a huge dinner party to be given in the Italian Restaurant in Great Portland Street to mark the opening: 'We should get all your disreputable and some of your aristocratic friends to come – and after dinner we should repair to Fitzroy Sq. where would be decorated furniture, painted walls etc. Then we should all get drunk and dance and kiss. Orders would flow in and the aristocrats would feel sure they were really in the thick of things.'

In April, Clive and Vanessa, Duncan and Roger set off for a month's holiday in Italy, spending most of the time at Viterbo, Ravenna and Venice. As always, Roger was the most restless and energetic member of the party hiring carriages everywhere, poring over railway timetables, painting and sightseeing and organizing his companions' day to an almost intolerable fullness. The other three were not so energetic. One day while at Viterbo, Roger had planned a whole day's extensive outing and was up very early, packed, the bill paid, and eager to go only to be enraged at finding Vanessa still asleep, Clive just beginning to dress and Duncan helplessly trying to boil a drop of water for shaving by a method known only to himself. On another day Roger went off on the steam-train to Toscanello to see the 'two great eighth-century churches outside the walls on the edge of a great ravine'[3] leaving the others behind. They invented a story of how Vanessa had been practically raped by a soldier in the streets of Viterbo to give themselves something to talk about on Roger's return, sufficient to withstand the certain blast of his adventures. But his solicitude for Vanessa was so great and touching that they guiltily had to confess to the fabrication. After a visit to Arezzo, Ravenna and Florence they took the train to Paris where they had dinner with Henri Doucet and were back in England by 20 May.

Memoirists and autobiographers of this time shower praise on the pre-War summer seasons of Diaghilev's Russian Ballet. Its influence was widespread in the theatre, in interior decoration and fashion, and painting. In England its appearance was very much bound up with the two Post-Impressionist shows. It was not simply the revelation of colour that astonished the painters but the dancers' command of space and the movement of bodies in a way never seen before. The Ballet's influence on 'pose' is difficult to pinpoint – photographs tell us only so much – but it seems that painters were made more conscious of the possibilities of pose in their figurative work from seeing Pavlova, Nijinski and Karsarvina. We see a new fluidity in figures, past and future movement implied through distortion. Bodies are posed as though in the act of dancing with exaggerated and often mysterious gestures of hands and feet, the turn of a neck or torso. This is well seen in Duncan Grant's *The Queen of Sheba* of 1912 with its brilliant Russian Ballet clothes, its wide proscenium arch, and the necks of the camels echoing the rhythms of the hands and arms of Solomon and Sheba. The 'wit and invention' in the painting, noted by Rupert Brooke, is particularly close to the spirit of such qualities in dancing, coming from the pose of the two figures rather than from any literary,

63. (*overleaf*) The upstairs showroom of the Omega Workshops from the *Daily News*, 7 August 1913. The screen on the right is by Wyndham Lewis and the one seen through Doucet's 'Adam and Eve' curtains is by Duncan Grant

extra-pictorial connotations. The influence of the Ballet on Duncan Grant's painting was deep and lasting, especially in figurative decoration over the next twenty or thirty years.

The impact of the Ballet at the Omega is most apparent in the clothes made there and in painting on panels, screens and walls, which were especially suited to large-scale figure decorations. Dancers and acrobats were a particular feature, as for example in Wyndham Lewis's screen shown at the opening of the Workshops, and such figures appear on pottery and furniture.

But influence flowed both ways and it is amusing to think that Duncan may have been the inspiration for one of the controversial ballets of the 1913 season. In the previous year, Nijinski and Bakst had visited Lady Ottoline Morrell's house in Bedford Square and seen Duncan, Adrian and others playing tennis in the Square gardens. The two Russians 'were so entranced by the tall trees against the houses and the figures flitting about playing tennis that they exclaimed with delight "*Quel décor!*" ' And in 1913 came *Jeux* with Nijinski's choreography, décor by Bakst, and Debussy's music; it was a short *poème dancé* between a man and two girls flirting together on a tennis court. Among other ballets given that July the most memorable was *Le Sacre du Printemps*, performed in London for the first time but without the riot which had greeted its reception in Paris, though there was some hissing and loud laughter – 'the applause was measured, but so were the cries of disapproval' commented *The Times* critic.

At about this time Duncan painted one of his best known portraits, that of Ottoline Morrell, at his studio in Brunswick Square. In her memoirs, Lady Ottoline wrote: 'I enjoyed these sittings immensely, for Duncan had more charm and humour, more childish enjoyment of life than anyone I knew, and we had endless jokes and fun together.' To emphasize the prominence of her chin Duncan added a piece of wood and also placed a string of real beads around her neck. Both these were later removed. But Ottoline declined to buy the portrait at the time – perhaps reluctant to acknowledge the truth of Duncan's fantastic image of her – a flaming, feathered, predatory bird of grandeur and absurdity. A few years later however she wrote to Duncan saying she had fallen in love with it but couldn't give the £40 asked for it. Although it is as much a caricature as Bussy's acid profile of her or John's hissing black-hatted Hapsburg, there is also something of the romantic melancholic noted by some observers and apparent from her memoirs.[4] Ottoline figured prominently in the summer entertainments and gathered people of many nationalities at her house. Boris Anrep came and talked about Russian legends to Nijinski; there were Simon Bussy, Békássy, Copeau and Doucet. Another hostess who was to be of great help to the Omega was Princess Lichnowsky, the wife of the German Ambassador who had arrived in England the year before. The gatherings were soon to be even more international – Austrians, Germans, Poles, Frenchmen and Russians all congregated in London the following year, a London becoming Europeanized, even, some thought, civilized.

Number 33 Fitzroy Square, which Roger took over for the Omega, is a large house at the end of the south side of the Square, on the corner of Conway Street. Like the east side, it was built between 1790 and 1795, to the design of Robert Adam. In the nineteenth century the residents of the Square were mainly professional, middle-class people. There were links with Bloomsbury ancestors: Lytton's grandfather, Edward Strachey, had lived at number 37 and a member of Leonard Woolf's mother's family, Nathan Jacob de Jongh, had lived at number 13. Ford Maddox Brown later occupied number 37 and at number 6 was Sir William Orchardson, one of the best of the Victorian 'subject' painters. Next door at number 7, lived Sir Charles Eastlake, P.R.A., and Landseer and Rosa Bonheur were entertained there. Other painters in the Square included William Dyce and Sir Frank Dicksee. Number 40 on the corner of Fitzroy Street had been taken by William de Morgan, the potter much associated with the firm of Morris, Marshall, Faulkner & Company, and figures as the haunted house in de Morgan's novel *Alice for Short*. [5]

The Square remained much the same up to the early years of this century. It was a little dingier perhaps, with a number of artisans coming to live in the tall well-proportioned houses with their railings and first-floor balconies, sculpted weather-worn friezes and Ionic columns. As one local historian noted, the Square never fell below 'a certain standard of respectability'. But when the Omega opened, it certainly did.

On 8 July the Omega received the press and held a private view attended by a large crowd. Roger showed at the same time a selection of his recent watercolours. 'We had a great success,' he wrote to his mother, 'the German Ambassadress was very keen and ordered a lot of our stuffs and gave names to the various designs. [6] And various other great ladies came and were very enthusiastic. I've been terribly hard at work to get this going, but it seems more worthwhile than I'd dared to hope.' He bubbled with enthusiasm as he showed round the first customers and reporters, explaining, persuading, inventing theories by the hour. The opening exhibition included tables and chairs, fabrics, bedspreads, clothes, large decorative curtains, screens, designs for murals, and a miscellany of pots, parasols and pencil boxes. Doucet had made long fern-leaves over the walls of the front showroom by spattering violet dye onto the cut-out shapes – an inverted stencil as it were. There were curtains at the window by Wadsworth. Screens were a feature with one by Wyndham Lewis called *Circus* – showing a slim little acrobat balancing on a strong man's shoulders next to a curly-haired woman with a whip and a clown beyond. ('But how much wit there is in those figures,' Roger told an interviewer. 'Art is significant deformity.') A screen by Duncan showed two long-waisted figures carrying a great blue pail across the four red panels as though part of some oriental procession; [7] another by Vanessa showed four women crouching against a tent and tree-like landscape rising to a point from a dark pool below.

Then there were the dress materials. Nina Hamnett had a loose top made from one designed by Roger – a strong black, orange and blue material which astonished her friends in Paris before the War. There is a photograph of her wearing it at a crowded studio party, with Modigliani and Frederick Etchells in the background.

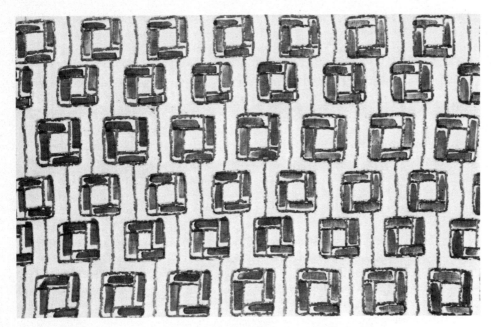

64. Two Omega fabrics, 'Mechtilde' designed in 1913 by Frederick Etchells and 'White', *c.* 1914, by Vanessa Bell. Victoria & Albert Museum, London. Vanessa Bell and Duncan Grant were making abstract textile designs a year before the Omega was officially opened. 'Mechtilde' was one of the simplest and most successful of all Omega fabrics

The critic in *The Times* saw that imitation was inevitable:

These artists have hit upon a method of design which needs ability and skill, but which is not hopelessly beyond their powers. It might be imitated by hack designers, and will no doubt be imitated if it becomes fashionable; but in that case the imitations will be just as absurd and ugly as the imitations of Morris's work. We confess that we do not care much for the tables already executed, which seem to us merely ordinary furniture decorated in an irrational manner, but there is great and novel beauty in the bedspreads, the parasols and stuffs. A design for a wall-paper, made of purely conventional forms, has more of the gaiety of flowers than any pattern imitating real flowers, and the design for a lady's dress is novel and at the same time has an air of fashion often painfully wanting in artistic designs. But what pleases us most about all the work of these artists is its gaiety. They seemed to have worked, not sadly or conscientiously upon some artistic principle, but because they enjoyed doing so. They are not pharisaically or aggressively artistic, but in doing what they like themselves they have managed to forget all the bad art they do not like. Anyone, we believe, can enjoy their work who will achieve the same forgetfulness; and we wish them all the success they deserve.

This review did much to induce customers to visit Fitzroy Square in those early months.

At the start of the Workshops, before the actual opening, Roger engaged a girl of twenty-two who since 1910 had been at Durbins as secretary to his sister Joan, attending the Slade School three days in the week. Winifred Gill was a godsend to Roger with her combination of talent and common sense,

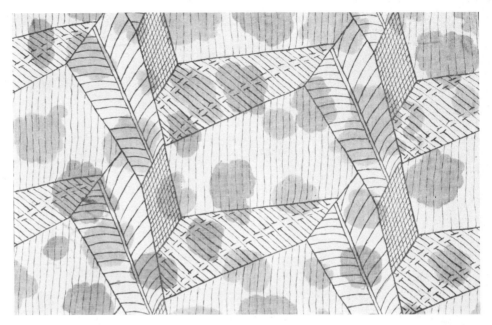

quick intelligence and energy, which she employed not only in decorative work but also as sales-girl and secretary. She had a particular aptitude for overcoming the many problems that initially confronted the venture and tackled them with high spirits and a sure sense of improvisation. She was with the Omega for much of its existence and it is owing to her splendid memory that we have so much information about production methods, the artists' day-to-day activities, and anecdotes of the Workshops which otherwise would be unrecorded.

Miss Gill would usually travel up with Roger on the train from Guildford and arrive soon after ten a.m. Mr Miles, the caretaker, opened the showrooms at nine by which time Mr Robinson the business manager would already be there. Size would be boiling on the gas ring, filling the studio with its smell and paints were soon set to warm. Anyone might come in to work, to leave drawings or designs, or discuss some new project with Roger. Gaudier-Brzeska might look in for a few minutes, or Duncan's towsled head appear round the door asking if Vanessa had been in; Lewis would be there in a black-and-white checked cap, and perhaps Jessie Etchells, working upstairs, dreamlike and beautiful.

There were two large working studios on the first floor and on the ground floor two showrooms divided by painted curtains representing Adam and Eve in a fauvist jungle. The studios were large enough to take several workers; there was always plenty to do and the whole place buzzed with activity.

At first, furniture was bought and then painted on the premises. Later, Roger and some others made designs which were carried out by Kallenborn, a Polish cabinet-maker who lived nearby off the Euston Road. The furniture was of unusual simplicity. A chair with a cane back and seat, in a deep red

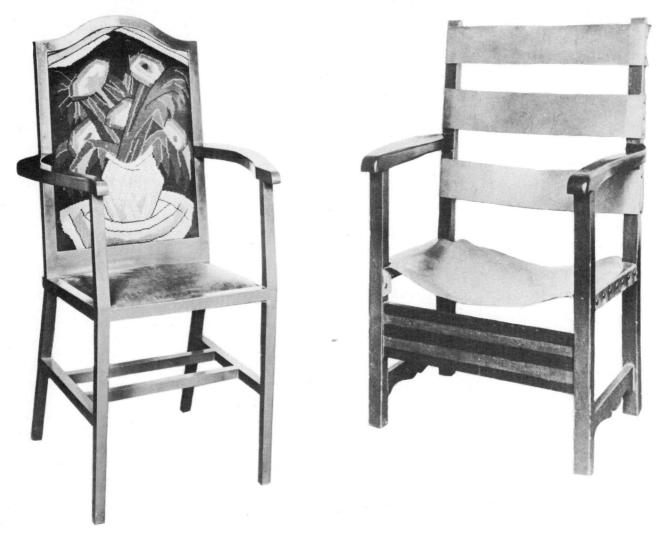

65. Two Omega chairs designed by Roger Fry, one with cross-stitch back. From contemporary photographs

varnish, was particularly popular and there were rorky chairs with soft leather strips at the back. In comparison the decorated ready-made chairs and tables seem tiresomely fussy.

The furniture was initially treated with size and then covered with gesso. This surface was then rubbed down and the colour applied (powder paint and size), and this in turn was coated with shellac varnish prepared laboriously in the studio; later, a cellulose varnish which gave a more matt finish was used. Of course there were mistakes to begin with – chairs collapsed, trays were not heat-resistant, paint rubbed off and varnish flaked away. But generally the standard was high and great importance was attached to the preparation and undercoating. For the chairs, an Indian red or dark blue were often preferred. Some were left unpainted. There is a set of the red cane chairs still in use at Duncan Grant's house, Charleston, sixty years or so after being made. Kallenborn was particularly good with inlaid wood, and tables; desks and trays in this method soon became a feature, including an elegant écritoire in white holly and ebony by John Turnbull, and a superb desk by Duncan. One of the most popular items, often repeated, was an inlaid tray by Duncan of a woman riding an elephant. The design was cut out of painted paper and copied in wood. Bernard Shaw on a visit chose to buy the tray and Miss Gill told him that Fry considered it the best article at the Omega. 'Would you very kindly tell him,' said Shaw, 'that I chose it myself without any prompting from you. He doesn't believe I've got any taste at all.' Shaw had been an initial subscriber to the Workshops when Roger was raising capital, but he was more interested in the social implications of the venture than in its aesthetic aims though he was highly pleased with his tray. A fine inlaid tray by Gaudier-Brzeska, 'The Wrestlers', was also on sale and a delicate, completely abstract one designed by Vanessa. These were among the more sober articles. In contrast, there were brightly painted chests. There was Duncan's still astonishing 'Lily Pond Screen' with its swirls of red, yellow and green paint on a black ground, based on a painting he had recently executed.[8] To many visitors, these brilliant colours were quite beyond the bounds of reason and decent taste.[9] On one occasion Winnie Gill went to Liberty's seeking a particular emerald green silk and was told by the indignant shop-assistant that 'Emerald, Madam, is a colour we never stock'. Such was the timidity of a shop which at the time was considered advanced. Hence the astonishment of many visitors to the Omega. Bright colours, spontaneity and freedom of treatment spelled decadence, dreadful taste and every kind of loose behaviour. Wyndham Lewis played up to these feelings with some candleshade-designs on the theme of prostitution ingeniously disguised. But what were people to make of Duncan Grant's to all appearances banal cross-stitch cover of a cat playing with a butterfly on a cabbage? of that bewildering circus scene? of severely geometric lampshades in chrome, deep blue and purple? of the enormous red stag for a nursery wall? of nudes on pencil boxes or an oyster-pink cloak of silk? The objects for sale not made by the Omega were equally strange – rough African jars decorated with dancing natives, Algerian water-coolers, muslin handkerchiefs from Broussa, bedspreads made up in India of fish among waves. Coloured beads were bought from a shop in Endell Street and Jessie Etchells made a bracelet from them which Maynard Keynes gave to Karsarvina when he brought her to the showrooms.

The Omega was hardly the place where casual shoppers dropped in to buy things. It did not possess the usual shop window nor was it on a normal shopping route. However, its proximity to Heal's in the Tottenham Court Road was to its advantage and those wanting the real article soon found their way to Fitzroy Square. On either side of the first-floor window hung two decorative panels of dancing figures, one by Lewis and one by Duncan Grant. In May 1915, Duncan painted a large free-swinging signboard. On one side was the Omega mark within a decorative framework and on the other, a simple still life of a lily and a yellow flower in a glass (plate 66).

Roger relied a great deal on private patronage, especially that of various rich and titled ladies caught up in the passion for the new interior decoration.

66. Omega Shop Sign, 1915, by Duncan Grant. 42 × 25 in. Victoria and Albert Museum, London. A free-swinging signboard which Grant painted in May 1915 to be hung outside 33 Fitzroy Square. On the reverse is the Omega letter Ω

67. Fan, *c.* 1913, by Duncan Grant. 9 × 17½ in. (open). Victoria & Albert Museum, London. Painted with dyes on silk. Hats, ties, cloaks and scarves were also on sale at the Omega

Before the Workshops opened Lady Cunard had commissioned a room – 'I'm cultivating her while the fit of art patronage lasts', Roger had told Duncan in the previous summer.[10] Sir Ian and Lady Hamilton subscribed £50 to the Omega and later gave a large commission for the decoration of three rooms in their house in Hyde Park Gardens for which Vanessa designed mosaic floors, and Turnbull a round stained-glass window. In 1916 Mme Vandervelde had her flat decorated by the Omega – though Roger was mainly responsible for the scheme.

Lady Ottoline made many appearances and in spite of a quarrel with Roger and their consequent estrangement she was a generous supporter who sent along many new customers.[11] There were the younger visitors – Diana Manners, Iris Tree and Nancy Cunard, a formidable trio of beauty and brains, and Naomi Mitchison ordering toys for her children. Roger's older friends came along: Wells and Shaw, Yeats and Bennett, Morgan Forster and Lowes Dickinson. Rupert Brooke made an appearance and Ezra Pound came in, keeping a sharp eye perhaps on what Wyndham Lewis was up to. Augustus John was another visitor. Nina Hamnett warned Miss Gill, such was John's reputation, that if she was alone when the painter arrived, she must ring at once for Mrs Upton, the caretaker's wife.

In the early autumn, Wyndham Lewis was up to a great deal. His machinations in the world of art politics led that October to his walking out of the Omega along with Hamilton, Etchells and Wadsworth. This event left a permanent scar on Lewis and made relations with Bloomsbury impossible from then on. He paranoically attributed to them his failure to win recognition as a painter after the War. He was being secretly followed, disparaged and hunted alive. From then on Bloomsbury was the 'enemy' – but then who was not? For the next thirty years or more, he attacked them in speech and in writing with compelling vindictiveness. His buccaneer secession from so many groups as soon as they became in any way established

was a prominent feature in his life but none was quite so complicated
or aggressive as his slamming the door of 33 Fitzroy Square. The reasons
are manifold and have been dealt with in detail by Quentin Bell and Stephen
Chaplin.[12]

  Lewis and the three others who left the Omega circulated an abusive letter
which accused Fry of double dealing and monstrous favouritism of his
Bloomsbury friends at the expense of Lewis and Co. A commission for a
Post-Impressionist room at the 1913 Ideal Home Exhibition had by 'a
shabby trick' been appropriated by Fry, whereas, according to Lewis, he and
an outside artist, Spencer Gore, had initially been asked to decorate such a
room where some Omega furniture would be displayed. Gore had been
approached by the sponsors, the *Daily Mail*, and, having left a note with
Duncan at the Omega for Lewis and Fry about the commission, he heard
nothing more. This episode occurred soon after the opening of the Workshops. Lewis and Gore had already made a mark with their famous
decorations for Madame Strindberg's 'Cave of the Golden Calf' night-club
in Heddon Street, Soho, the first of its kind, where there were also carved
figures by Jacob Epstein. Some time later, still according to Lewis, Fry
announced that the Omega had been asked to do a whole room at the Olympia

68. Some products of the
Omega Workshops. Inlaid
wood tray by Vanessa Bell,
table with inlaid wood
designed by Duncan Grant,
pottery and chairs by Fry,
carpet possibly by Edward
Wadsworth

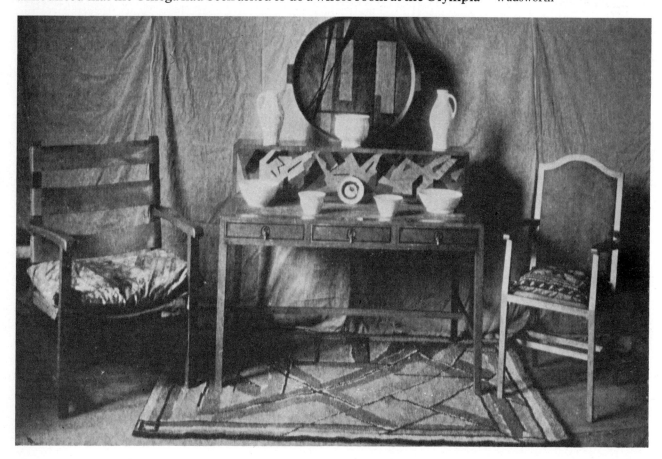

show, and asked Lewis to carve a mantelpiece as there were to be no wall decorations. According to Winifred Gill, Lewis disliked the task and angrily left with the three others. From her point of view it seemed indeed strange that the virtually unknown Lewis should have been asked to do a whole room at such an important show but that if in fact he had, then Roger's letter of acceptance to the *Daily Mail* would almost certainly have received the reply 'Well, we didn't ask you'.

Fry maintained that he had been directly approached by an official representative from Olympia to carry out the whole job and no mention had been made of any individual allocations. It was simply to be by the Omega Workshops. If there had been mention of names, Fry would have declined, upholding the rule of anonymity at the Omega. When the time came to designate work for the commission, Lewis, he maintained, suggested the carving and was eager to do the work. It was only when Fry was on holiday in Provence in October that the 'Round Robin', as the accusing letter was called, was circulated to friends and shareholders. Shortly afterwards, Vanessa wrote to Roger:

> We have had a day of it! This morning Molly [MacCarthy] telephoned to say that they had had the enclosed circular letter from Lewis, Etchells and Co. which you had better read at this point as it will explain matters. It is so absurd that perhaps you'll think it unnecessary to do anything but laugh at it. On the other hand Molly evidently thought you must somehow have given them cause to be very angry and Desmond [MacCarthy] thought that *your* enemies would be only too glad to get hold of any story against you and would be delighted at a split in the Omega and that you ought to defend yourself.

Bloomsbury rallied round, offering advice and sympathy. Clive favoured silence on Roger's part; then Vanessa decided Etchells should be seen. 'We [Duncan and Vanessa and Etchells] . . . talked for nearly two hours. He . . . could hardly be made to see our point at all. When he did see it he simply said that he didn't agree. . . . Evidently he had been storing up small things which had at last been brought to a point by this. It is all such a muddle that one couldn't convince him of anything. But I don't think that either he or the others will give in at all, or that there is any use in trying to get them to.'

Desmond then suggested that the *Daily Mail* representative should be asked for his evidence and Vanessa went along on 14 October. 'He said the names of Lewis and Gore hadn't been mentioned in his interview with you and that the commission had been given directly to the Omega. He was delighted to come forward and say this, so I gave him definite questions written out to be answered and he is going to send me a letter saying this.'[13] But there is evidence that Gore had been approached and one can only conclude that an administrative blunder had occurred, the left hand ignorant of the right. Gore did nothing and, as far as is known, made no effort to contact Lewis or Fry during the months before the exhibition.

Outlined in the 'Round Robin' is the signatories' second reason for complaint, that Fry had wilfully excluded Lewis and Etchells from a Post-

69. Teapot and cup and saucer made by Roger Fry, *c.* 1915. Victoria & Albert Museum, London. Pottery by Fry of this sober kind was, along with a few textiles, his most notable contribution to the Omega. His painted furniture is often lugubrious and fussy

Impressionist exhibition that Frank Rutter was organizing at the Doré Galleries for that autumn.[14] Evidence here is incomplete but almost certainly Fry was guiltless. A letter from Rutter to Lewis was found by Fry among his own correspondence at the Omega. He returned it to Lewis after the quarrel: 'I never saw it till now and can only suppose that you left it about and that it got put among my things. If this was due to my carelessness and want of method I am extremely sorry. I had read part of it before realizing it was addressed to you, and see that Mr Rutter has written to you before, so that I am glad to think that the accident of this letter getting mislaid here has not been, or need not have been, decisive in the matter of the exhibition.'

One might almost be forgiven in thinking that Lewis had planted the letter there himself, so devious had he been throughout the whole business, so oblivious of the need to substantiate his claims against Fry. By an odd coincidence Clive and Lewis met in Bond Street the day after the 'Round Robin' was made public and Vanessa reported their conversation: 'Lewis explained that he had had to use politics to defend himself, that he had his way to make etc. Clive pointed out that their letter had been a silly and "suburban" affair which would convince no one of anything but the folly of the writers. Lewis then tried to put the blame of the letter on the others and said it wasn't the sort of thing he liked doing.' Etchells later confirmed that Lewis alone was responsible for the letter. It is interesting to note that in the midst of this protracted quarrel, Vanessa was able to write appreciatively of Lewis's great lost painting *Kermesse* of 1912, then being shown at the Doré Galleries' 'Post-Impressionist and Futurist Exhibition': 'His picture (at the Doré)', she wrote to Roger on 16 October, 'seems to be the only English one at the show which seems at all interesting'; and a few days later (30 October) she referred to it as 'that large dance which he had at the Albert Hall [Allied Artists' Association Salon, 1912] but he's made it much better and I thought it good.'

It was soon understood that the defection of Lewis and his friends had more general causes. It was the rule of anonymity at the Omega which they disliked. Publicist that he was, Lewis was unlikely to be content to hide his brimming and pugnacious identity behind the incognito device adopted at the Workshops. Winifred Gill believed this to be the basis of the quarrel: anonymity was 'an intolerable burden to these young up and coming artists'. But of course the break was mainly brought about by aesthetic disagreement. 'As to its [i.e. the Omega's] tendencies in Art,' wrote Lewis in *Blast* (July 1914), 'they alone would be sufficient to make it very difficult for any vigorous art-instinct to long remain under that roof. The Idol is still Prettiness, with its mid-Victorian languish of the neck and its skin is "greenery-yallery", despite the Post-What-Not fashionableness of its draperies.'

In the second issue of *Blast* (Spring 1915) Lewis again attacked the Omega: 'The most abject, anaemic, and amateurish manifestations of this Matisse "decorativeness", or Picasso deadness and bland arrangement, could no doubt be found (if that were necessary or served any useful purpose) in Mr. Fry's curtain and pin-cushion factory in Fitzroy Square.'

What is so remarkable about these first few months of production at Fitzroy Square is the uniformity of design achieved, the definite *entente* between these variously gifted artists, the difficulty we have at identification. Lewis and his friends contributed vigorously to the Workshops with highly original designs. There are superb rugs by Etchells and fabrics by Hamilton and Wadsworth which in Pevsner's words are 'unique in European decoration of the period'.[15] The Omega was certainly the poorer after this break and 'Prettiness' ingratiated herself among the fabrics and some of the furniture. Decoration took the upper hand over design.

But the break was irreparable. Lewis soon set up his own business, 'The Rebel Art Centre', at 38 Great Ormond Street. The four ex-Omega painters were joined by William Roberts (after a brief 'apprenticeship' under Fry), and by Jessica Dismorr, Jacob Kramer and Helen Saunders, with Ezra Pound as frequent visitor and 'sparring-partner'. There were discussions and talks to 'familiarize those who are interested with the ideas of the great modern revolution'. Marinetti talked there in May 1914 and the following month there was a Rebel Art stand at the Allied Artists Exhibition at Holland Park which showed fans, boxes, scarves, and a table in the Omega manner. Saturday afternoons at the Centre were set aside for members of the public to come in and see what was happening, hear T. E. Hulme or Pound, or watch the incipient Vorticists at work.

From this new lair Lewis continued to abuse Fry whose silence Lewis found irritating and confusing. But Roger had already too much to do without adding a bitter argument with Lewis to his programme. Of course there were regrets, above all over the loss of Etchells. 'In a way I think it very bad luck on Etchells especially, who though he has behaved perfectly monstrously, has all along thought that he has been behaving from the purest motives. I mean I think it is bad luck because I think it quite likely that Lewis will quarrel with him quite soon,' wrote Duncan.[16] 'I quite agree with you about Etchells,' Roger replied, 'I always thought he would act on rather romantic impulses. The only thing is that I personally find it a little hard that he could turn so completely against me after having been so very friendly,

70. Design for an Omega
Workshops rug, *c.* 1913–14,
by Vanessa Bell. Private
Collection, London. In June
1914 this carpet was a
prominent feature of the
Omega Workshops display
at the Allied Artists'
Association Salon at Holland
Park Hall. It was praised by
Gaudier-Brzeska in a review
in *The Egoist* (15 June 1914)

and without ever listening to me. But I really want to help him and I quite expect that when he's seen the thing in a more reasonable way we shall be able to.' The mood is conciliatory, understanding, and shows a wish to help, but Etchells never returned. He became a Vorticist, did some of his best work and after the First War became an architect, translating Le Corbusier and becoming known for his knowledge of ecclesiastical architecture. He rarely saw any of his friends in Bloomsbury again though on one occasion he met Duncan Grant at a party and said that he thought Lewis was a madman and that he'd influenced his work deplorably.[17] He died in 1973. Cuthbert Hamilton (1884–1959) continued to paint and sculpt, founded a pottery, but drifted into obscurity and much of his work is untraced. Wadsworth moved away after his Vorticist venture and developed a distinctive style of his own between abstraction and figuration. Etchells' sister Jessie was not prevented by the quarrel from working at the Omega and was highly thought of by Duncan and Roger. She and Winnie Gill, another painter Gladys Hynes (1888–1958), and Nina Hamnett were an industrious and lively phallanx in the months that followed.

71. An Omega Lounge at the Salon of the Allied Artists' Association, Holland Park Hall, June-July 1914. From a contemporary postcard. The fabric hanging on the right was designed by Roger Fry

The Omega's sitting room at the October 1913 Ideal Home exhibition was a popular focal point for laughter and abuse (plate 71). The caretaker Mr Miles (whose devotion to the Workshops proved itself when he named his son Omega) would tell the artists the next day what an awful time he'd had the previous evening at Olympia. To one abusive visitor he replied, 'In saying that, you shows your taste and your breeding in one.' But of course it was all very good publicity and orders came in thick and fast. With four artists suddenly gone, there was an immense amount of work and Duncan and Vanessa 'really worked heroically to make up for the absence of the defectors.'[18] Paul Nash was briefly engaged to work; the aristocratic young Chilean painter Alvaro Guevara, still at the Slade, was also employed. Fry found him sympathetic and unusual and introduced him to other painters.

In December there was a show of recent work including a whole nursery and a model bedroom. The nursery, begun in August, had been temporarily abandoned when the Ideal Home room intervened. Vanessa had painted enormous simple animals on the walls among trees and pools of fish; Winnie Gill did the ceiling (plate 72). 'Upstairs there is a very gay nursery which children ought to like,' wrote *The Times* reviewer, 'even if it startles their parents; and it contains some toy animals which are life-like and seem full of energy. . . .' It was a 'great success' wrote Randall Davies in the *New Statesman* with particular praise for a doll's house that was 'perfection', complete with electric light and Omega furniture. The toys were large with plywood limbs that moved about on screws. Among the expected animals – camel and giraffe, rhinoceros and tiger – were effigies of the Kaiser and Crown Prince William.

This new display and the Ideal Home room were both opportunities to exhibit what is now recognized as perhaps the Omega's most original achievement in design along with its fabrics – namely the rugs and carpets (plates 70, 73, 74). Initially the English manufacturers would have nothing to do with the designs Roger showed them. They thought them so absurd that it would contaminate their machinery if they were to take them on. This consideration was not altered by the fact that they would be paid the same amount as they were for more conventional productions. So, like the linens, the first rugs were made in France. Soon afterwards the Royal Wilton Factory agreed to co-operate. The designs were transferred to squared paper to indicate every stitch. Designs by Duncan Grant and Etchells were first used for small rugs and a staircarpet 'Amenophis' was made from a linen design of the same name. Roger himself bought a large rug, made to Duncan's design, in viridian, chrome yellow and blue – his sister Margery had another in her house near Birmingham. It was of this work that *The Times* critic wrote:

72. Nursery at 33 Fitzroy Square, installed for exhibition in December 1913. Curtains and rug by Etchells, toy animals by Grant, murals and ceiling by Vanessa Bell and Winifred Gill, cane chairs by Fry

> There is . . . a carpet on the ground floor, designed on the principles of the earlier and grander Chinese art, and yet quite European and original, which seems to us the best modern carpet we have ever seen. Its very simple forms give it a force of colour never to be found in more complicated patterns and yet this colour is not in the least garish. And

the forms themselves, though they suggest nothing in reality, yet seem to have a life of their own and a logical relation to each other.[19]

Not until the carpets of McKnight Kauffer and Marion Dorn in the late twenties was there to be again such distinguished design in this particular field. It is work like this that saved the Omega from becoming that 'pin-cushion factory', commanding no more attention than 'a pleasant tea party' to quote Lewis again. As we have seen, there was a 'pretty' side to the Omega, a smart side of ladies' dresses, hats, parasols and beads. It was easy to cater for the taste of the premature Bright Young Things, the upper classes having fun, the theatricals and parties, those 'terrible gaieties' as Iris Tree called them afterwards. There was a bathing-dress for a Garsington weekend, a bracelet for Karsarvina, painted hats and clothes for fancy-dress. But of course, without such rich and influential patronage the Omega would have plunged into financial ruin. The man in the street hardly ventured into the Square. And Roger priced the goods very cheaply hoping this would induce the less well off to buy; instead, Omega designs were watered down by

73. Carpet for the Omega Workshops, 1913, by Edward Wadsworth. 94 × 74 in. On loan to the Victoria & Albert Museum, London, from Mrs Feo Stancioff. One of the Omega's most successful and striking products, this carpet was designed at about the same time as Vanessa Bell's (plate 70)

74. Carpet for the Omega Workshops, 1913, by Frederick Etchells. $57\frac{7}{8} \times 36$ in. Inner London Education Authority, Chelsea School of Art. The painterly abstraction of Wadsworth's and Vanessa Bell's carpets is eschewed by Etchells in this magnificent and compact geometrical design

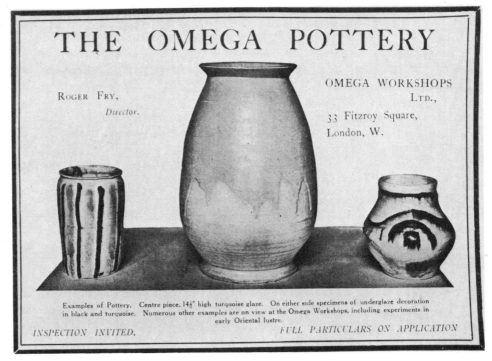

commercial manufacturers[20] and sold at double or treble the Omega price. This was especially true of the fabrics and the pottery.[21]

At the July opening there was pottery for sale but it was overglazed painted ware from ready-made factory products. Eager to produce pottery more in keeping with the other Omega work and unsatisfied with conventional shapes, Roger decided he must find someone to carry out his own designs. He contacted a potter at Mitcham, Surrey, and tried to get him to throw the simple shapes he wanted. The potter was unable to alter his long-practised throwing and Roger realized he would have to learn to do it himself. He started with great gusto and was soon producing some really distinctive work. He wrote enthusiastically to Duncan of his experience:

> Vanessa and I have been potting all day. . . . We went when the potter wasn't there and got the man to turn the wheel. It was fearfully exciting at first: the clay was too stiff and V. very nearly bust with the effort to control its wobbliness – and in vain; then we got some softer clay and both of us turned out some quite nice things – little ones mostly, but they'll make quite nice little bowls and pots. It's fearfully exciting when you do get it centred and the stuff begins to come up between your fingers. V. never would make her penises long enough, which I thought very odd. Don't you?[22]

The pots were unadorned, the surfaces rough and the bottoms of bowls and vases thick and heavy where the surplus clay had been retained – the result was enormous flat plates, solid vases, bulging tureens. The Mitcham potter gave some of them a turquoise glaze and they were offered for sale in early 1914.

When War broke out and the Mitcham man was called up, Winifred Gill suggested another potter, Roger Carter of Poole, who came to see Fry at the Omega. During the War years, Roger Fry made several visits to Poole. He made a prototype dinner service which was then reproduced in quantity by the Poole workers, retaining the personal irregularities of surface and thickness. There were three glazes – black, dark blue, and a particularly beautiful white tin glaze with its film of blue-grey. These were often repeated and in 1916 Roger threw more and was generally pleased with his progress: 'The pottery is very swell, though I say it as shouldn't – some of the little bowls are as good as I can ever hope for I think. The black's lovely and one dull yellow green is charming. The purple ain't a success.'[23]

The best decorated Omega pots are, however, by Duncan and Vanessa – especially vases and shallow dishes. Roger knew he was better at making rather than painting them. Of course people were continually attributing his style to this or that tradition – Italian, early Mahometan, Sung – so it gave him particular pleasure to have his work praised by a porcelain expert at the British Museum, R. L. Hobson, who 'was most enthusiastic and thinks we have done better than any modern pottery he has seen. He thinks the turquoise quite remarkable, though the peculiar beauty of the colour is, I think, more due to some mistake in the firing than to calculation.'[24]

[1]   'I must say I'm not surprised people were shocked by the Omega products', Duncan Grant commented recently when shown a photograph.

[2]   *Laughing Torso*, 1934, pp.42–3.

[3]   RF to G. L. Dickinson, 31 May 1913.

[4]   The portrait, owned by The Viscount Moore, is reproduced in *Duncan Grant and His World*, Wildenstein catalogue, 1964.

[5]   Duncan Grant had met de Morgan and his wife in Florence in 1905.

[6]   Princess Lichnowsky named one after herself, Mechtilde, another after Roger's sister Margery, and a third Maud after Lady Cunard.

[7]   Collection the artist.

[8]   The screen is in the Victoria and Albert Museum and the painting in the collection of Mrs P. Diamand.

[9]   One newspaper called the furniture immoral and Winnie Gill had to deal with two inquisitive women eager to see these immoral objects: they apparently had in mind, as the very depth of degradation, an armchair combined with a commode. Shown everything there was to the last cupboard, they had to go away unsatisfied.

[10] Other early patrons included Lady Ottoline Morrell, Lady Tree, the Princess Lichnowsky, Lady Desborough, Madame Vandervelde, the wife of the Belgian Minister, and the young Countess of Drogheda.

[11] One story related by Winifred Gill illustrates that indomitable Portland side to her character. When she took her daughter Julian to buy some material for a dress and the choice was finally whittled down to two, Ottoline asked the young girl which she preferred, the blue or the green. The child wanted the green. 'Then we'll take the blue' Ottoline stated. Her curiosity was boundless. On another occasion she arrived when Nina Hamnett was working upstairs. As Miss Gill mounted the stairs behind Lady Ottoline she

raised her voice on the words 'Lady Ottoline' to warn Nina of the arrival. 'Oh God, not that old bitch,' cried Nina, diving behind a curtain. After looking at the various things in the room, Ottoline inevitably pointed to the curtain. 'And what's behind there, Miss Gill?' And Nina was discovered smoking a cigarette. 'Ah, Miss Hamnett' was the surprised, still inquisitive and drawled response.

(12) 'The Ideal Home Rumpus', by Stephen Chaplin and Quentin Bell in *Apollo*, October 1964.

(13) VB to RF, 13 October 1913.

(14) The exhibition included works by Lewis and Etchells as well as by Bonnard, Vuillard, Van Gogh, Delaunay, whose *Cardiff Football Team* was conspicuous, Epstein, Herbin, Severini and Nevinson.

(15) 'Omega' by N. Pevsner in *Architectural Review*, August 1941.

(16) DG to RF, 20 October 1913.

(17) Years later Vanessa Bell met Etchells by chance in London: 'He is now a flourishing architect', she wrote to Roger Fry, 'and has a house in Davies St. where he lives and has offices and employs several young men and a youngish woman who also lives there. He owned a car and also a house and a wife near Uckfield! Altogether I have never seen anyone so changed except that he is still a bore' (Spring 1931).

(18) RF to Rose Vildrac, 4 November 1913.

(19) 10 December 1913. The carpet can be seen in the Courtauld Insitute Galleries, Fry Collection.

(20) An example of this can be seen in a handout published by Heals's in May 1914, 'The Modern Note in Fabrics,' though admittedly many of the Post-Impressionist fabrics came from France and Australia. Among designers of French fabrics, Constance Lloyd is mentioned as working almost entirely for French printers. It will be remembered that she was an old friend of Duncan's from his student days.

(21) Omega block printed linens 31″ wide were priced between 2s. 9d. and 4s. a yard.

(22) RF to DG, January 1914.

(23) RF to Pamela Fry, *c.* mid 1916.

(24) RF to Lady Fry, 5 December 1914.

8

While the activities at the Omega naturally occupied a great deal of time, other projects were afoot among the painters. One of the most exciting was Duncan's commission to design costumes and screens for a French production of *Twelfth Night*. The producer was Jacques Copeau who, with Charles Vildrac, had been invited to lecture on French literature on the occasion of the Second Post-Impressionist Exhibition at the Grafton Galleries. He met Roger, the Bells, and Duncan at this time and found them congenial and sympathetic friends. The following year, 1913, he started his 'Théâtre du Vieux Colombier' in Paris with its plain white walls and ceiling and small auditorium. His love of Elizabethan and Jacobean drama shared by Gide (and by his friends in London) prompted his first production, Heywood's *A Woman Killed with Kindness*. The theatre also became a meeting place for young French writers and there were lectures and discussions. Gide, for example, talked there on Verlaine and Mallarmé. In the summer of 1913, before the opening of the theatre, Copeau wrote to Duncan asking him to undertake the costumes and what little scenery he intended to have for a production of *Twelfth Night* to be given in May 1914.[1] By

76. Copeau's production of *Twelfth Night* with costumes by Duncan Grant (1920 revival). The actress to the left is wearing a dress made from an Omega fabric. Among the cast for the original production were Valentine Tessier and Louis Jouvet

September, Duncan had done drawings for the costumes (some of which were to be made from Omega fabrics) and later he went to Paris and attended rehearsals. He was enchanted with the theatre and the actors and immensely enjoyed working with Copeau. He got to know Copeau and his family well and saw something of Gide and the Vildracs; Vanessa also came over for a few days to help with the final fittings. Copeau found in Duncan *'un homme véritablement épris de son travail'*.

The premier in May was a great success with packed houses and laudatory reviews – in Copeau's words *'Toute la presse a été unanime dans l'admiration; ce qui vaut mieux encore le public vient chaque soir en grand nombre et nous fait fête.'* [2] Duncan's costumes, eschewing historical truth and combining several styles with *'une adorable fantaisie'* of Edwardian hats, brilliant full-skirted Omega dresses, fantastic shawls and fans, Cromwellian coats and high Renaissance breeches, were particularly praised. After the War the production went to New York with painted screens by Duncan added to the décor.

In late 1913 and the first half of 1914 several exhibitions, ballets, and operas contributed to the increasing excitement and novelty of a London becoming caught up in the general artistic ferment in Europe. We have already noticed the summer impact of the Russian Ballet, the opening of one of the city's first cabaret night-clubs, the visits of the Futurists, culminating in Marinetti's talk at the Rebel Art Centre. In June there were large, very mixed Bloomsbury parties, notably one given by Adrian where Duncan appeared as a heavily pregnant whore and Marjorie Strachey wore nothing but a miniature of Prince Albert. Karin Costelloe gave a party the following week where a farce by Lytton was performed, *The Unfortunate Lovers or Truth Will Out*, in which a great deal of transvestisism helped to explain in very theatrical terms certain current liaisons within Bloomsbury. Later that week Karsavina could be seen at Drury Lane in *Salomé* and Dame Nellie Melba in *Faust* or *Aida* at Covent Garden. On the following day, 1 July, *Khovanshchina* was given and on the 2nd a full ballet programme of *Schéhérazade, Jeux, Thamar* and *L'Après-Midi d'un Faune*. *Boris Godunov* the next night was followed by more ballets on the 4th including the popular *Carnival* and *Narcisse*. On the same day you could buy Dostoevsky's *The Idiot*, just published, and hear Yvette Guilbert at the Bechstein Hall in the afternoon. The weekend newspapers were blazing with the 'Scott Will Case', a typical Edwardian scandal of the Ouida variety involving Lady Sackville and her supposed influence over a will of a million pounds. Her daughter, Victoria Sackville-West, was soon to be engaged to Harold Nicolson. There was the Balkan War and the war of the Suffragettes who hit the headlines on the 8th – Sylvia Pankhurst was arrested at Bromley Public Hall and a group of women set fire to Southport Pier for reasons that puzzled the press. On the 8th, the private view day at the Omega, you could have gone in the evening to *Ivan the Terrible* at Drury Lane or, if suffering from Russian indigestion, Irving Berlin was appearing in the review *Hello Ragtime* which was enjoying a long run at the London Hippodrome. There was an exhibition of Pre-Raphaelites at the Tate Gallery which wasn't much visited and the enormous Allied Artists Exhibition at the Albert Hall where you could brandish your umbrella – for it was a rainy mid-summer – at the awful Cubists or, of course, buy them, depending on your tastes.

In August and September, there were the usual long excursions to the country. Clive went fishing up in Scotland – 'I find a purely animal existence very soothing', he wrote to Molly MacCarthy who at that time was writing her novel *A Pier and a Band*. He joined Vanessa and the children in September at Asheham which once again was inundated with visitors, including several Stracheys, Gerald Shove and Hilton Young for one weekend, Roger and Goldie Dickinson on another. Duncan was there a good deal. He and Vanessa had earlier been camping at Brandon near Thetford, Suffolk, with the Olivier sisters, Roger and Maynard (plates 55, 56). Vanessa has left a vivid picture of Duncan at this time – waiting for her at Liverpool Street Station – 'I found Duncan in his usual paint-covered clothes but with a spotless new white hat. With about 20 packages – easel all coming to pieces – camp-stool etc. and a bottle of champagne!'[3] Duncan also spent a fortnight painting alone at the Hutchinsons' house, Eleanor, and a week-end at Wissett Lodge, Suffolk, with his family – a house which he was to live in three years later under very different circumstances.

Amidst the hurly-burly at Asheham, Clive tried to write to Molly MacCarthy. 'It's all up with this letter now. They have come in and settled round the fire and begun to discuss how you ought to translate into French 'The Roaring Girl' which Copeau proposes to play at his new theatre of the Vieux Colombier. My suggestion '*La Cabotine*' is preferred to Marjorie's '*La Fille qui Hurle*'. Now they've got on to Vanessa's feet which she hasn't washed after playing Badminton barefoot; and that is leading on to the question of dirt in general which, I foresee, will soon lead on to the questions of morals. So there we are.' The following day he continued with 'Just as I feared'.

With his immensely sociable and affectionate nature, his love of talk and jokes, Clive found happiness and well-being among his friends. 'It seems very absurd,' he wrote again to Molly, 'that people who are fond of each other shouldn't all live together always. What's this modern notion of pairing off instead of living in rookeries? Vanessa and I are happy enough alone, painting and writing and reading and mooning and pottering about, but we should be happier in the thick of our friends.' Of course it all depended on *how* fond you were of your friends and what degree of fondness it was. The friendly commune Clive envisaged could so easily become fraught with emotional and sexual undertones.

During Lytton's stay at Asheham time was set aside from gossip, Badminton, and discussions on morality, to paint his portrait. He sat in a straw hat in a rorky chair reading, and the painters gathered in front in a confusion of easels, stools and children – Pamela and Julian Fry were encamped with their father in a nearby field. Roger's portrait was not a success. Duncan's included the whole figure. Vanessa went closer, bang in front and produced a brilliantly fauve portrait in a very high key of colour with red beard, and pure violets, yellows and rose pink (plate 77). This spontaneous and unqualified

77. *Portrait of Lytton Strachey*, 1913, by Vanessa Bell. 36 × 24 in. Collection Richard Carline

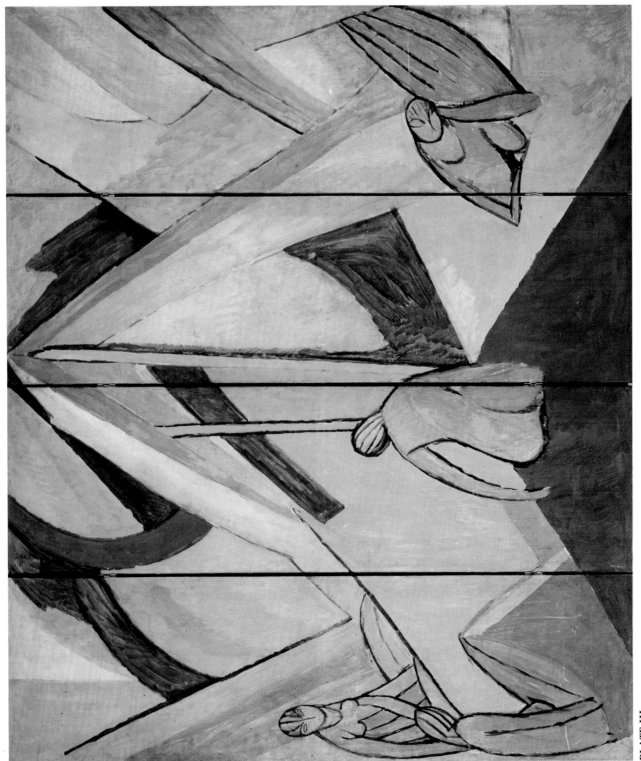

PLATE III

PLATE IV

78. *Oranges and Lemons*,
1914, by Vanessa Bell. 29¼
× 20½ in. Private Collection,
London. The fruit was sent
to Vanessa Bell from North
Africa by Duncan Grant in
February 1914 and was
painted simultaneously by
Roger Fry. The background
curtain is an Omega fabric
'Maud' probably designed
by Vanessa Bell in 1913

release of decorative colour, the simplified form and seemingly effortless
control and aptness of placing, mark Vanessa's maturity at this period of her
work, especially in portraiture. The various influences of the previous two
years have been assimilated; she is absolutely in command. As Sickert wrote
of her a decade later, 'The medium bends beneath her like a horse that knows
its rider.'

'I have been busy lately with a large picture which I brought to birth with
great labour and pain and I see is likely to be a thankless offspring.' So
Duncan wrote to Lytton on 6 January 1914 about his *Adam and Eve* which by
then was already hanging in the Alpine Club Gallery as part of the Second
Grafton Group Exhibition. With the defection of Etchells and Lewis, the
Group's nature became more defined – impoverished according to some.
Only the names of Fry, Grant and Bell appeared on the catalogue. *Adam and
Eve* (plate 79) was one of Duncan's most ambitious paintings to date and with
its jocularity and distortion put much of the surrounding work in the shade.
It attracted a great deal of attention, especially as it was a commission,
through Clive Bell, from the Contemporary Art Society. The picture roused
Randall Davies of the *New Statesman* to some facetious comment:

> Mr Duncan Grant has hit upon a most ingenious device for baffling the
> malignant stupidity of 'hanging committees', who have been known to
> disguise their spite against a picture that strikes them as eccentric under
> a veil of seeming innocence, and to hang it upside down. Mr Duncan
> Grant has taken a leaf out of the book, or shall we say a card out of the

79. *Adam and Eve*, 1913, by
Duncan Grant. Approx. 7 ×
11 ft. Severely damaged by
floods at the Tate Gallery in
1928. Present location
unknown. Both Picasso and
Matisse had a direct
influence on the work and
the decorative treatment of
the trees relates it closely to
the Omega style. Grant's
characteristic fantasy is
revealed in the figure of
Adam

pack, of common sense, and improved on the customary method of representing the King and Queen of Hearts, by painting Adam and Eve, side by side, on the same canvas, in such a manner that it is of no consequence which way up the picture is hung. In a word, Adam is standing on his head.

It is to some extent mournful to see our cherished ideas toppled over, and in this instance we take leave of tradition with a more than usually bitter pang, as we wave our moist handkerchief in a sad but forever farewell to Dürer and Titian. However far back the modern painters have to go for their inspiration we did feel, somehow, that Adam and Eve were safe. Though it is consoling to think that perhaps as Titian's picture at the Prado is catalogued as 'El pecado original', so Mr Duncan Grant's may be called 'The Fall of Man' and be regarded as the impression of an incident rather than as ancestral portraiture. . . .

In the painting of *The Ass* the same artist seems to have been more at home with himself. A really congenial subject often brings out an artist's best qualities.

The painting *The Ass*, which was bought by Roger, was loosely based on a Persian miniature where the ass is treated not as some particular creature with individual characteristics but as an image of vitality and a source of wonder. Both *Adam and Eve* and *The Ass* belong to a series of paintings where borrowings and influences – from the Byzantine, from Picasso, from Persian miniatures, from newspaper photographs and 'contemporary' life (*Man with Greyhound*, plate 51), from Matisse, the Bible and the early Italians – are used in an intoxicating shuffle and reshuffle, all equally suitable and suggestive as catalysts to work. It was not a question of the old formula of going back to go forward. Going back did not exist. Everything and anything could be used – much as in collage – for immediate and pressing expression. In that sense the paintings are anti-historical.

As for the rest, there were 'positively archaic' landscapes by Roger, and a large *Nativity* by Vanessa ('a protest against the popular *Firstborn* at last year's Academy. Here the baby is black; a charming touch of local colour . . .'). Apparently Roger also contributed to the sculpture section with 'a little block of wood painted maroon', vaguely suggestive of something human; there was some 'pedantic cubism' from William Roberts, and a marble cat and some drawings by Gaudier-Brzeska who thought that Duncan with his *Adam and Eve* was 'the Phoenix of English painting'. Among the forty or so canvases were a number from Charles Vildrac's gallery in Paris, including works by Marchand, Lhote, Friesz and Doucet, Picasso's *Tête d'Homme*, then owned by Roger Fry, and some photographs of 'certain "sculpture" devised by M. Picasso by means of egg-boxes and other débris . . . [which] could not be trusted to cross the Channel without falling to pieces . . .'.[4]

Roger was exhausted with all the bother of the hanging and left London for a few days rest. On 7 January Duncan went to the South of France, accompanied as far as Paris by James and Marjorie Strachey, and did not return until March. Reports from London reached him of the Grafton show including the following account from Lytton: 'I could not look much at the pictures as I found myself alone with Hamnett [then secretary to the exhibition], and became a prey to the desire to pass my hand lightly over her mane of black hair. I knew that if I did she'd strike me in the face – but that, on reflection, only sharpened my desire, and eventually I was just on the point of taking the plunge when Fanny Stanley came in and put an end to the tête-à-tête.'[5]

In February 1914, the Friday Club had its annual exhibition. It was generally thought extremely tame with the exception of two pictures by David Bomberg. His large composition *Ezekiel* with its cubed marionette-like figures arranged round a platform seen from above was, as Lewis pointed out, an academic subject but treated with real originality. For the next few months, Bomberg was the most talked about young painter of the avant-garde, receiving much intelligent and favourable criticism. Among the newer exhibitors at the Friday Club were the Nash brothers, Nevinson, Allan Gwynne-Jones and the landscapist Darsie Japp. Although the Friday Club continued for some years, its membership was considerably decreased by a new, more catholic society which with a sweep of the board gathered together in the ensuing years most of the prominent small groups among the younger generation – Grafton, Camden Town, Fitzroy Street, Cumberland Market. All spiced the cauldron of what was simply known as 'The London Group'. There had been a meeting on 15 November at number 19 Fitzroy Street mainly composed of Lewis and his group and the Camden Towners. Duncan was asked to attend. 'They proposed both you and me as members,' Vanessa wrote to Roger, 'but I gather that we may be blackballed! Lewis is a member and so is Duncan as I think all Camden Towners are. Etchells, Hamilton and Wadsworth also seem to have been proposed.'

In fact, the Grafton Group were excluded. Roger only became a member in 1917 along with Nina Hamnett. Duncan and Vanessa were elected in 1919 – long after such contemporaries as Paul Nash, Gertler and Ethelbert White. The father figure, Sickert, refused to join at the last moment with characteristic unexpectedness, but returned to the fold in 1916. The Group was not associated with any particular aesthetic doctrine and the hanging committee was broadly representative of the various trends in painting at the time, with J. B. Manson as secretary representing the more cautious English impressionist school, and Lewis and Wadsworth the most advanced movement. Their first show was at the Goupil Gallery in Regent Street in March 1914. It turned out however to be predominantly Vorticist with Lewis, Nevinson, Etchells and Wadsworth showing important work. Bomberg at this time was unwilling to be associated with the Lewis group though the reviewers naturally lumped his magnificent *In the Hold* along with the others. *The Times* dismissed it as merely kaleidoscopic glitter, no better than the noisy 'pattern-making' of Wadsworth's *Scherzo* or the Cubist-contaminated works of Etchells. The latter's *Head of a Man* was, wrote *The Times* critic, 'like a thousand boring diagrams in three dimensions that are to be seen every year in Paris'. This was one way of turning the tables on such experimental work – to accuse it of both plagiarism and academicism. As usual, all the blame was laid at the feet of Monsieur Picasso for the ruination of the talents of these fine young English painters. Cubism was sullying the flag. Infinitely preferable it seemed was the impressionist *Interior* of Miss Ethel Sands, a fine flower of the Sickert group, and *The Green Bed* of Miss Sylvia Gosse. Bernard Adeney was simply 'clumsy Cézanne' but there was praise for John Nash and Spencer Gore. Roger wrote favourably of Bomberg's *In the Hold*; it seems to have confirmed his ideas about the real possibility of abstract painting which he had tentatively advanced when writing about Kandinsky's work the year before. All the pro-modern critics like Hulme and Frank Rutter gave it serious and approving attention. The reviewer in the *Athenaeum*, however, after describing it as the 'most entirely successful painting in the exhibition . . . a complete success' then suggested that it should really be carried out as a textile. Fry found Bomberg highly interesting and sympathetic and for a short time Bomberg worked at the Omega and his drawings were for sale in the portfolio there but found no buyers. With the departure in the following year of Lewis and his confederates, the London Group took on a more recognizable character which it steadily developed without much fervour or ado for the next twenty years. Fry, Grant, Bell, Gertler, Smith and Dobson, Adeney, Baynes, Meninsky and Porter – these were the names most commonly associated with its pleasant and restrained annual shows in the 1920s and '30s, and there was often a high standard of painting, if little to rival the brilliant daring of *In the Hold*.

The Exhibition attracted a lot of attention and numerous visitors; Ezra Pound, aping *The Times*, called the private view 'a very brilliant occasion'. It was one of the many such occasions that lent vivacity and glamour to the last few months of peace.

Another feature of these months was Bloomsbury's excursions into Society – mainly encountered in Lady Ottoline Morrell's drawing room. With the recent blurring of the until then rigid class structure, Edwardian society was becoming less exclusive, more flexible. Various hostesses became prominent, generally combining two particular kinds of interest, the political and, for want of a better word, the artistic, the emphasis fluctuating from party to party. Chief among them was the Prime Minister's wife, Margot Asquith, who entertained at Downing Street[6] 'then a centre of such an abundance and intensity of life as it had not seen for a hundred years and is never likely to see again'.[7] Especially notable were the supper parties held after the opera or the Russian Ballet performances. Maynard became a frequent guest and a particular favourite of Violet Asquith. Indeed his intimacy with the Asquiths and their circle was later to be the source of some criticism of Maynard by his old friends.

Generally, Bloomsbury abhorred smart society but they responded to hostesses like Lady Cunard and Lady Ottoline where the gatherings were predominantly artistic and intellectual. Lady Cunard, who took over 20 Cavendish Square when the Asquiths moved to Downing Street, became more important in their lives after the First War though she was always a welcome patron of the Omega Workshops. Her daughter Nancy was a more

80. *Still Life on Corner of a Mantelpiece*, 1914, by Vanessa Bell. 22 × 18 in. The Tate Gallery, London

congenial spirit at this time. Nancy, Iris Tree and Diana Manners were the centre of another group 'The Coterie', a group whose rebellion was primarily a social one and directed at the very society that had armed them with the weapons of their rebellion – confidence, money, and a spirited articulateness. They were of a younger and, in superficial ways, a freer generation than Bloomsbury. Bloomsbury were their spiritual parents. '. . . [We] were bandits, escaping environment by tunnelling deceptions to emerge in forbidden artifice, chalk-white face powder, scarlet lip rouge, cigarette smoke, among roisterers of our own choosing. . . .'[8] 'Our pride,' wrote Lady Diana Cooper, 'was to be unafraid of words, unshocked by drink and

unashamed of "decadence" and gambling – Unlike-Other-People, I'm
afraid. Our peak of unpopularity was certainly 1913 and 1914.' It was at this
time that Diana Manners and Iris Tree briefly attended the Slade School and
had a room near Fitzroy Square which was rumoured to be hung with whips.
When War came their patriotism was unquestioning and many of the
'beautiful, intemperate young men' of the group were killed. But they were
among the few who viewed with respect, albeit critical, the pacifist stand of
those such as Bloomsbury.

The gatherings at the Morrells' house in Bedford Square certainly contained an element of politics though almost as a concession on Ottoline's part
to Philip Morrell's political career. Ottoline much preferred reserving her

81. *The Mantelpiece*, 1914,
by Duncan Grant. 18 ×
15½ in. The Tate Gallery,
London. Both pictures,
plates 80, 81, were executed
at 46 Gordon Square.
Among the objects
represented are an Omega
painted box (on the right of
Grant's picture) and some
paper flowers which were
made and sold at the Omega.
Vanessa Bell's approach is
grave and restrained, more
architectural in concept than
Grant's restless treatment
where collage is used for
'immediate expression'. The
cut-out papers were applied
in front of the subject

vitality and daunting ability to get people together for the artists and writers
she knew. With Bloomsbury she had been on intimate terms for some years,
but it was in 1914 that she came to know the two Spencer brothers and Mark
Gertler. The latter was to play an important part in her life for several years to
come. As a buyer for the Contemporary Art Society she bought Gilbert
Spencer's *Seven Ages of Man* and Gertler's *Fruit Sorters*, and also acquired
work from them for her own collection. Her Thursday afternoons took on a
more varied flavour: guests ranged from young Slade students to Bertrand
Russell, Desmond MacCarthy, Boris Anrep, the painters Doucet and Bussy,
and the writers Vildrac and Békássy.

The painters and critics of Bloomsbury were also becoming familiar
figures in Paris, welcomed there by Vildrac and Copeau. In January 1914 the
Bells, Roger and Molly MacCarthy were there. Gertrude Stein took them
along to meet Picasso – Vanessa's first meeting with the painter. She wrote
afterwards to Duncan that 'he is probably one of the greatest geniuses who
has ever lived. His gifts seemed to me simply amazing' (29 January). They
also visited Matisse and saw the great collection at Michael and Sarah Stein's
in the rue Madame. The Bells added to their own small collection of modern
paintings by buying from Kahnweiler Vlaminck's *Village in Provence*. Their
collection already included Vlaminck's 1909 *Poissy-le-Pont, Les Oeufs*, 1912,
by Gris and a still life by Picasso. This last appeared as an illustration in Clive
Bell's *Art*.

In his essay 'Before the War', written in 1917, Clive Bell offers a picture
of that time, the memory of which coloured the subsequent gloom and
restrictions of four years of War. 'In the Spring of 1914 Society offered the
new-comer precisely what the new-comer wanted, not cut-and-dried ideas,
still less a perfect civilization, but an intellectual flutter, faint and feverish no
doubt, a certain receptivity to new ways of thinking and feeling, a mind at
least ajar, and the luxurious tolerance of inherited wealth. Not, I suppose,
since 1789 have days seemed more full of promise than those spring days of
1914. They seem fabulous now. . . .'[9]

This atmosphere of international cultural exchange and the exciting
feeling of being '*au mouvement*', was inseparable from the freedom accorded to
an English citizen. 'He could live where he liked and as he liked. He had no
official number or identity card. He could travel abroad or leave his country
for ever without a passport or any sort of official permission. . . . Unlike the
countries of the European continent, the state did not require its citizens to
perform military service.'[10]

It was the reversal of this last that brought those in Bloomsbury directly or
indirectly into confrontation with 'the state' when, two years later, conscription was introduced. Their objection was to the curtailment of liberty in
circumstances not of their choice. 'How damnable it is,' wrote Vanessa, 'that
people with ideas utterly different from one's own should have so much
power over one's life.'[11] Their despair in August when War was declared
was a reflection of the personal upheaval such an event implied and of their
shocked sense of the world rolling over into the mud. Of course such despair
could be mitigated. There was always work, and more work, and the stability

82. *Still Life with Beer Bottle*, 1913, by Vanessa Bell. 19 × 13 in. Private Collection. The subject of a still life in front of a window runs through Vanessa Bell's work, a revealing *leitmotif* – compare plates 27 and 132

of like-minded friends. For a time even some organized official resistance seemed a straw to clutch at. Then that hope dwindled as the War machine bulldozed into their lives and the old existence became more and more untenable. 'Why shouldn't we spend May here?' wrote Vanessa from the country.[12] 'How idiotic to go home and listen to talk about the War and Rupert.' Such an exclamation seems at first escapist, and no doubt partly was so but it expresses too the realization of the impossibility of participation. The vividness of that pre-War clarity of behaviour was to contrast strongly with the confusion and tragedy of the subsequent years.

Before 1914, as Leonard Woolf wrote later, 'There was no shadow of past defeat; the omens were all favourable. . . . We were not part of a negative movement of destruction against the past. We were out to construct something new: we were in the van of the builders of a new society which should be free, rational, civilized, pursuing truth and beauty. It was all tremendously exhilarating.'[13] It seemed then, as it increasingly did up to 1939, that the best defence against the onslaught on their private life was a passionate absorption in work. And as far as possible during the War this was the self-protective line they took with an almost ferocious concentration. And so the paintings and the Omega Workshops continued, the Hogarth Press came into existence, *Eminent Victorians* and *Night and Day* were written, and there was an enormous amount of journalism, pamphlets and criticism.

On 4 August most of Bloomsbury were out of London. The Woolfs were at Asheham with Vanessa and Duncan. Maynard was in Cambridge, and Lytton was cocooned with 'Cardinal Manning' at his cottage near Marlborough. In London, Clive was discussing what steps should be taken with like-minded pacifists who, in the first week of War, gathered at the Morrells' house in Bedford Square. Philip Morrell had bravely spoken against the declaration of War but was booed in the House of Commons into silence. It effectively ended his political career. Among others, Ramsay MacDonald had blotted his political copybook with objections to the Government's foreign policy and an advocacy of neutrality. He was a founder member of the Union of Democratic Control, formed to prevent the diplomatic 'crimes' which were seen then as an immediate cause of the War. Ottoline Morrell's hospitality and sympathy did much to encourage the formation of this group, whose other supporters included E. D. Morel and Bertrand Russell, both of whom were subsequently imprisoned on charges of anti-War activities.[14] On 6 and 7 August we find among the names of visitors at Bedford Square those of Maynard Keynes, Duncan Grant and Adrian Stephen. But it was only with the introduction of conscription that Bloomsbury worked actively against the War. The rest of 1914 was spent in uncertainty as it rapidly became clear that the War would last longer than the few months that Maynard had predicted to his friends. On 20 August we find Adrian Stephen thinking of volunteering; he later became the secretary of the No Conscription Fellowship. Clive was enquiring of James Strachey how best he could join the Army Service Corps; in 1916 his pamphlet 'Peace at Once' was burnt by order of the Lord Mayor of London. Duncan entertained the idea of a commission in the Artists Rifles: he was to be condemned to two years agricultural labour. Continually the news came of friends who had enlisted, were preparing to go or had gone. Maynard's brother Geoffrey joined the

RAMC and stayed at Brunswick Square before leaving for France in October. Rupert Brooke took the step that made the myth. Artists from the Omega – Turnbull and Gaudier-Brzeska – were soon missing. And many of Maynard's most promising undergraduates volunteered at once.

Some extracts from Vanessa's letters to Roger give a picture of her life during those months.

> Duncan and I do nothing here [Asheham] but paint. He has started on a long painting which is meant to be rolled up after the manner of those Chinese paintings and seen by degrees. It is purely abstract. We have also both started on a still life and on different landscapes. I don't think you need be afraid that any works of genius have been perpetrated yet but of course I have moments of despair when I see Duncan really does seem to be producing anything of the sort.[15]

> Duncan has begun to paint a picture of me in my red evening dress but it hasn't got very far yet as I don't sit very often.[16]

> It's finer today and we have nailed up your canvas outside the house in front and have started on it. Duncan and I are each doing one. Do you mind? Perhaps I oughtn't to be – but it's such fun and if you don't like mine I will get more canvas for another. As a matter of fact I think unless I do one Duncan will never do his. We are doing two modern dress dancing figures in each – red, black, white, cadmium yellow and a little green – trying to keep them rather bright and full of accent as I think with London greyness all around that's necessary.[17]

In September, Adrian Stephen became engaged to Karin Costelloe; their marriage in October put an end to life at Brunswick Square. Maynard moved to rooms at 10 Great Ormond Street and Duncan had a room in 46 Gordon Square (and a studio at 22 Fitzroy Street) though he spent much of the time painting at Asheham. Leonard and Virginia moved to a house on the Green at Richmond. Roger spent most of his time in his new studio at 21 Fitzroy Street with only occaional weekends at Durbins since a family of refugees were living there and had 'nearly wrecked the household'. Virginia Woolf has described Fry's Fitzroy Street studio: 'It was an untidy room. He cooked there, slept there, painted there and wrote there. There was always a picture on the easel, and on the table an arrangement of flowers or of fruit, of eggs or of onions – some still life that the charwoman was admonished on a placard "Do not touch".'[18]

After an initial setback the Omega soon picked up and orders and commissions began to come in again in the winter months. 'Had there been no war we should have been doing a very good trade by now judging from the greater appreciation and liking we get from our work,' wrote Roger in January 1915. During the War the Omega increasingly became a sympathetic centre for meetings, exhibitions and experimental theatre, and a place where magazines and photographs from abroad, virtually unobtainable elsewhere, could be seen, but of the original artists only a handful remained. Henri Doucet was killed on 5 March, his first day in the trenches, near Ypres. Roger referred in

83. *Portrait of a Lady*, 1913,
by Vanessa Bell. 27 × 22 in.
Collection Duncan Grant.
A certain unemphatic air of
mystery emanates from this
painting, as in several of
Vanessa Bell's pictures at
this time such as *The
Bedroom, Gordon Square*
(plate 47) and *Portrait of
Mary Hutchinson* (plate 107)

later years to his unclouded friendship with the little bearded painter whom,
he felt, had contributed not a little to his own practice of painting. In July
1915 the Hungarian poet and ex-King's student, Ferenc Békássy, was killed.
Some years later a volume of poems by Békássy was published, on Maynard's
suggestion, by the Hogarth Press.

In the spring, Clive and Vanessa rented St. John and Mary Hutchinsons'
house Eleanor near West Wittering in Sussex. It was here that Duncan and
David Garnett (known as Bunny) began their close friendship which determined in some ways the course of their lives together until after the end of

the War. David Garnett has acknowledged the striking influence of Duncan on his own thinking about art and an artist's approach to his work, a debt recorded in the dedication in Garnett's first novel *Lady into Fox*. Garnett was to pose many times over the next few years for paintings and studies, and he introduced various new elements into Duncan's life as well as new friends (plates 96, 97). At first Vanessa was somewhat resentful of their friendship, finding it intrusive in the quiet life she and Duncan led together. But her resentment was short-lived. She liked David; she praised his generosity and strong affections; and he in turn was dazzled by her beauty and talent and capacity for a logical appraisal of a situation. He soon became part of all their lives though remaining sceptical of much that was taken for granted in the thought of 'old Bloomsbury'.

Eleanor was a small house and various arrangements had to be made to accommodate everyone – at one point Clive had to take a room in the village, and Maynard slept in a caravan for a night or two. Duncan meanwhile was sleeping and working in a studio boat belonging to Professor Tonks of the Slade. It was a perfect spring, the prelude to a baking summer. Vanessa and Duncan painted panels on the dining-room doors. Duncan did mosaics and completed a signboard for the Omega Workshops. He also painted a portrait of Vanessa (plate IV) seated in an armchair, her head back, eyes gazing at the ceiling, arms loosely crossed. It was a characteristic attitude, dreamy and meditative with a certain melancholy in the languor of her face and curve of her neck, that neck which Roger described as 'swelling like a great wave' when she threw back her head. At this time Vanessa was reading her sister's first novel published in March, *The Voyage Out*. She recognized parts of herself in the character of Helen Ambrose who often sits, composed, listening, embroidery on her lap, a pool of apparent calm.[19] 'It seems to me extraordinarily brilliant,' Vanessa wrote to Roger,

almost too much so at times. It makes it too restless I think. However it is of course very good in its descriptions of people and conversations and all the detail. The obvious criticism I suppose is that it isn't a whole but I haven't quite finished it yet so I oughtn't to make a final criticism. Lytton is very enthusiastic and was raving about the writing and the wit and observation and sympathy with all sorts of characters. Novel writing does seem a queer business – at least this kind. If it's art, it seems to me art of quite a different sort from making a picture but I don't think all novel writing is. The quotation from Jane Austen even though it's only a sentence seemed to me at once to put one into a different world, one that's the same really that one is in when one looks at a Cézanne. Did you feel it? I suppose it's because one knows the rest of the book and one couldn't feel it from only one sentence. Reading V.'s book is much more like being with an extraordinarily witty and acute person in life and watching all these things and people with her. But that may only be because I have actually done so. I wish I could really get outside it all. As it is I know all the people nearly and how she has come at so much of it which makes it very difficult to be fair.

Breaking into the genial life at Eleanor, came two events which, while treated as farce, left a disturbing undertone. Duncan was rumoured by the locals to be a spy because of his darkish appearance and Scottish accent, particularly when pronouncing 'Rothiemurchus'. On telling the police that his father was a Major, he was exonerated at once. Clive was the next victim of the locals' suspicions but at the mention that his father was a County High Sheriff he too was spared from further questionings. They were the sort of rumours that at that time turned swiftly into nasty hysteria. D. H. Lawrence in Cornwall was the object of such hysteria, naturally enflamed by the presence of his German wife.

On 23 April Rupert Brooke died and the news travelled swiftly to Eleanor. Vanessa took up an uncompromising line among the rather sentimental reactions of her friends and the myth-making of the press, and wrote:

I am sorry for her [Ka Cox] and James [Strachey] who did care about him but otherwise I think it's queer how all these people who couldn't stand him alive are driven to talking about the waste and meaninglessness of life by Rupert's death. After all it's not the first time a young person has died. He would have been a great popular success and enjoyed himself very much but I can't say I see a great deal beyond his looks to regret and it seems to me not to be compared to the death of someone like Doucet who would have been able to be happy in a way that did matter. However I suppose it's natural to be insincere about death . . . I think you're one of the few people who isn't.[20]

June was spent in London where Vanessa was having a small show of costumes she had designed from Omega fabrics. Simultaneously at Fitzroy Square was an exhibition of woodcuts by Roald Kristian, Nina Hamnett's Norwegian husband who had come to London after the outbreak of War and had changed his name to de Bergen. They were living in the Camden Road and both worked at the Omega. De Bergen was responsible for a marionette show at the Omega where his rather African looking dolls danced on strings to Debussy's *Boîte à Joujoux*.[21]

Duncan, surprisingly enough, was exhibiting with the Vorticists at their only exhibition. They had approached him some months before, as Vanessa informed Roger: '[He] was doubtful about it but they said all kind of other outsiders were sending and that it meant nothing personal – so in the end he has sent two abstract pictures and a still life. He was afraid you mightn't like him to send but I said I thought you wouldn't have any feelings about it – and he wants to sell if possible as he's rather hard up.'[22] This caution on Duncan's part was induced not only by the break with Omega by Lewis and his friends but also by their continued hostilities, the most recent being in the second issue of *Blast* that spring. However, the three pictures were hung, the two abstracts made up of pieces of wood stuck to board, paper collage and paint. He went to see the exhibition, which was held at the Doré Galleries, and admired a work by Etchells and the Bomberg drawings but found little else to interest him. His own works were badly hung and a piece of wood came unstuck from one and had to be nailed on again.

84. *The White Jug*, 1914, by Duncan Grant. 41 × 16½ in. Private Collection, London. The lemon, jug and écriture were added in *c*. 1918 to the original geometrical abstract painting

85. *Abstract, c.* 1915, by
Vanessa Bell. $17\frac{1}{4} \times 15\frac{1}{4}$ in.
The Tate Gallery, London.
One of Vanessa Bell's few
extant abstract paintings (a
large one, now lost, was in
Roger Fry's collection). It
relates to the 1913–14 rug
designs made for the Omega
now in the Courtauld
Institute Galleries. Sensuous
colour is tied to a
characteristic formal
economy

Among other abstracts by Duncan of this time there is a small vertically
composed picture *In Memoriam Rupert Brooke* (plate 89), of sober colour and
simple geometric forms. There was also the long roll which he had completed
the previous autumn (plate 88). It was nearly fifteen feet in length, eleven
inches high and composed of seventeen sections of pasted paper shapes
with paint sometimes overlapping the papers, sometimes simply surrounding
them. It was intended to be seen through the aperture of a box as the roll
passed through slots at the back at a pace dictated by a slow movement from a
work by Bach. There was also to be lighting inside the box. It was essentially musical in conception, partly inspired by an announcement Duncan had
read in a newspaper of a concert of Scriabin's music which was to be accompan-

86. *Abstract, c.* 1914, by Roger Fry. Dimensions and present location unknown. Exhibited as *Essay in Abstract Design*, with two others, in Fry's Exhibition at the Alpine Club Gallery, November 1915. Fry's abstract paintings were few and tentative though he was, with T. E. Hulme, one of the first critics in England to appreciate the possibility of non-figurative painting

ied by changing coloured lights. The Russian composer's work had been well publicized before the War when he had visited London and aroused interest.[23] The roll in fact was never completely performed and the box existed in idea only. Roger was discouraging about the experiment. So too, in a different manner, was D. H. Lawrence when it was shown to him. Lawrence had become warm friends with David Garnett through the latter's father Edward, and David introduced the writer to Duncan. The Lawrences, E. M. Forster, Garnett and Duncan met at the latter's studio. But the episode was painful. Duncan developed toothache. Lawrence became more aggressive with each new picture, especially one representing a large naked male – the spirit of Christopher Wren – holding in one hand a model of St.

Paul's. Frieda Lawrence tried to save the situation; Morgan Forster, almost secretly, left to catch a train, and Duncan sat gloomily, head in hands, as Lawrence proceeded with his tirade. It was then that the roll was produced with David Garnett holding one end while Duncan gradually unfurled it. The meeting was over. Lawrence later wrote to Ottoline Morrell that he and Frieda both liked Duncan very much but the letter condemned his work, and called the roll 'a silly experiment in the Futurist line. Other Johnnies can do that!' While there was little further personal contact between Lawrence and Bloomsbury, they supported him against the suppression of *The Rainbow*. Lawrence did not forget Duncan and in *Lady Chatterley's Lover* he appears as the painter Duncan Forbes – 'that dark skinned taciturn Hamlet of a fellow with straight black hair and a weird Celtic conceit of himself.'

87. *Interior at Gordon Square, c.* 1915, by Duncan Grant. 15¾ × 12⅝ in. The Tate Gallery, London. A schematic interpretation of a view from one room through to another at Gordon Square. A larger version in collage is in a private collection

From April to July, Roger was in France helping the Quakers on their relief mission – a visit prompted by his sisters Ruth and Margery who were over there and by the inevitable curiosity for a new experience. He saw something of the organizational side of the War and something of its bureaucracy when he was mistaken for a spy. He went down to paint at the Bussy's house at Roquebrune and returned via Paris where he saw various painters, gave news of his English friends, and visited Rose Vildrac.

With a reference from Roger, and help from Ruth Fry, David Garnett joined the Friends of War Victims Relief Mission and in July went to France for six months, to help rebuild devastated villages in the Sommeilles district. He was accompanied by Francis Birrell who was soon to become an intimate of Bloomsbury and a critic and occasional writer of distinction.

At this time the National Registration Bill was introduced, known as the Derby Scheme, whereby 'men of military age "attested" their willingness to serve when called upon'.[24] Conscription became increasingly an issue and unmarried men who had not attested – who did not wear the prescribed armband – were open to public rebuke and the gift of a white feather. Duncan considered doing some work such as labouring or working in an armaments factory – he felt he could not stand an office job. Clive was thinking along similar lines. But again decision was delayed and a summer excursion to Bosham was arranged, just a short distance from Eleanor. A large painting by Duncan of the village church is untraced – 'an odd, rather old-fashioned picture, a strong effect of sunlight with a great deal of very sharp detail'. This description by Vanessa adds to our knowledge of the multiplicity of styles Duncan was using to explore and structure the variety of his responses. The stimulus of decorative work for the Omega introduced into his painting a more emphatic, more purely calligraphic distribution of overall rhythm. The rather literary lyricism of paintings such as *The Queen of Sheba, The Dancers* or *Idyll* has been subdued in favour of a way of handling paint that is expressive of a more abstracted visual lyricism. There are, from this period, few works of a literary or mythological inspiration, the *In Memoriam Rupert Brooke* being an exception. It was a matter of reduction and simplification to gain the sort of reality he wished for. So in the space of a few months there is

89. *(far right) In Memoriam Rupert Brooke*, 1915, by Duncan Grant. 21¾ × 12 in. Collection the artist. The square of silver paper from a cigarette packet was added some years later

88. *Abstract Kinetic Collage Painting with Sound* (detail), 1914, by Duncan Grant. 11 × 168 in. The Tate Gallery, London. Duncan Grant's most radical contribution to the new movement in England and indeed a pioneering work in European abstraction in its combination of sound, light and movement

the gradually unfolding theme and variation of the roll collage; the small compact and geometric *Interior at Gordon Square* (plate 87), a radical re-interpretation of an actual place; the uncomplicated decorativeness of the Omega signboard; and there are the portraits – the lapidary image of Vanessa at Asheham[25] and the languorous one at Eleanor and the two large portraits in interiors – *Iris Tree* and *David Garnett*[26] – both painted at 46 Gordon Square. Iris Tree posed for Duncan, Vanessa and Roger simultaneously in 1915 when she was eighteen, already writing the poems that were to be published in the Sitwells' *Wheels* the following year. These twin brilliant portraits (plates v, 92) – Vanessa's and Duncan's – seem particularly evocative of that 'pre-War' nursery before the painful growing up amid the sound

90. *Abstract with Collage, c. 1914*, by Vanessa Bell. 22 × 17 in. Collection David Garnett. The most vigorous of Vanessa Bell's surviving abstract works. A large abstract painting in Roger Fry's studio in 1919, was subsequently destroyed by fire (along with Grant's 1916 *The Tub*)

of explosions, the casualty lists, 'all the metal and struggle, trains, ships, mourning. . . .'[(27)]

In early November it was brought home to Duncan, through an unnerving experience, what he must expect if he remained out of the armed services or unengaged in warwork of a recognized kind. David Garnett had returned to England in October on a short leave from Sommeilles and it was arranged that Duncan should accompany him back to visit Jacques Copeau in Paris. There was to be a revival of *Twelfth Night* at the 'Vieux Colombier' and Copeau wished to discuss with Duncan a new production of Maeterlinck's *Pelléas et Mélisande* for which he wanted Duncan as designer.

The two men arrived at Folkestone where 'Duncan was abused and insulted by an English officer for not being in the army – the officer apparently having no power to prevent him leaving England and no duties to perform.'[(28)] Duncan chanced his luck and went on board but at Dieppe a French officer detained him while letting David Garnett continue to Paris. Duncan, deported as a 'pacifist anarchist', had to take a boat back the following day and arrived frustrated and miserable at Gordon Square. The incident was taken up in various quarters, mainly by St. John Hutchinson with the Foreign Office and by Maynard with influential friends. Duncan's aunt, Daisy MacNeil, appealed to the British Consulate in Paris but was told that her nephew acted in such a strangely eccentric manner that the officer at Dieppe felt he could do nothing else but ask him to leave the country, in spite of an official letter from Copeau which Duncan produced. Soon after this event, Maynard wrote to Bunny to persuade him to return home where there

91. *Abstract*, c. 1913–14, by Vanessa Bell. 19¼ × 24 in. Private Collection. Vanessa Bell first used collage in May 1912 and continued to do so intermittently until 1915

was a possibility of a job at the War Office. Sommeilles was becoming intolerable and soon after Christmas Bunny returned.

In November, Roger held a large show of his work at the Alpine Club Gallery. There were over fifty paintings as well as carpets, furniture and pottery from the Omega. It was widely reviewed and well attended ('30 or 40 people come daily. But of course I don't sell . . .'). Three 'Essays in Abstract Design' were denounced in derisive terms, especially one containing two London bus tickets (now in the Tate Gallery). Many of the paintings were of the South of France – of Cassis, St. Raphael, St. Tropez, Roquebrune and

92. *Portrait of Iris Tree*, 1915, by Duncan Grant. 29½ × 24½ in. Reading Museum and Art Gallery. Painted at the same time as Vanessa Bell's portrait (plate v)

93. *Portrait of Iris Tree*, 1915, by Roger Fry. Private Collection, London. Iris Tree (1897–1968), daughter of Sir Beerbohm Tree. Her early poems were published in Edith Sitwell's anthology *Wheels*. She also posed for Epstein and Alvaro Guevara

Monte Carlo – all of them places in which, after the War, Duncan and Vanessa were to stay and paint. There was a collage of 'Queen Victoria'[29] and a portrait of Iris Tree, painted at a separate sitting from the portraits earlier mentioned (plate 93). It is among the more vital of Roger's many wartime portraits, which included Iris's sister Viola Tree, Mme Vandervelde and Edith Sitwell.

[1] In 1912 H. Granville-Barker had asked Duncan to design a production of *MacBeth*, but though many drawings were made for costumes, the idea never materialized.

[2] Copeau to DG, 27 May 1914.

[3] VB to RF, August 1913.

[4] *Athenaeum*, 10 January 1914.

[5] Fanny Stanley was one of several spinster members of the Grant family.

[6] The hall of 10 Downing Street was the scene of an unfortunate encounter. Rupert Brooke's break with his oldest friend James Strachey was inexplicably extended to James's friends. He had never been on intimate terms with Duncan Grant but they liked each other and had often met since their schooldays. But Brooke had paranoically turned against these friends having come to the illogical conclusion that they were in league to thwart his love for Ka Cox. On seeing Duncan at the Asquiths he contemptuously passed by with 'What! You here Duncan.'

[7] Osbert Sitwell, *Great Morning*, 1948, p.208.

[8] Iris Tree, 'Nancy Cunard', in the *London Magazine*, August 1966.

[9] *Pot-Boilers*, 1918, p.247.

[10] A. J. P. Taylor, *English History 1914–45*, p.25.

[11] VB to RF, Spring 1915.

[12] VB to CB, April 1915.

[13] *Sowing*, 1961, p.161.

[14] Other supporters included Arthur Ponsonby, Liberal MP, and Sir Charles Trevelyan.

[15] VB to RF, 25 August 1914.

[16] VB to RF, 10 September 1914. The portrait which includes fabric and paper collage is in the collection of Mr and Mrs Quentin Bell.

[17] VB to RF, 17 September 1914. Duncan Grant's panel hung outside the first-floor window at 33 Fitzroy Square. A sketch is in the Victoria and Albert Museum, London.

[18] *Roger Fry*, 1969, p.201.

[19] The portrait also bears similarity to Julia Stephen, and the Ambroses are an early study for the Ramsays in *To the Lighthouse*.

[20] VB to CB, April 1915.

[21] De Bergen was also a painter and sculptor.

[22] June 1915. Fry was also asked to send but declined.

[23] Saxon Sydney Turner, the most musically educated in Bloomsbury, talked admiringly of *Prometheus*, Scriabin's 1910 'Poem of Fire' in which he used a colour organ.

[24] A. J. P. Taylor, *English History, 1914–45*, op. cit.

[25] A full-length portrait *The Red Hat, c.* 1917, is in the author's collection.

[26] The Museum and Art Gallery, Reading, and the artist's collection respectively.

[27] Iris Tree, 'Nancy Cunard', op. cit.

[28] D. Garnett to J. M. Keynes, December 1915.

[29] Collection Raymond Mortimer.

After the indecision of 1915 and the deaths of friends, Bloomsbury were no longer able nor, it seems, willing to remain uncommitted in their attitude to the War. The events of January forced them to define more rigorously their conduct during the rest of the War and to formulate their opinion about conscription. The Military Service Act was introduced on 5 January 1916 and became law three weeks later, imposing compulsory military service for the first time in Britain. Conversation down at Asheham, where a New Year's party was gathered, inevitably revolved round the personal consequences of the Act and its national reverberations. The party found themselves completely united in their opposition to conscription, though the reasons of course were various. 'Duncan and Bunny and Lytton', Vanessa wrote to Roger on New Year's Day, 'are all agreed that they would rather go to prison than be forced to become soldiers and horrible though that would be it would be better than the other.' The outlook was bleak but there was the conscience clause in the Conscription Act which exempted, among others (for example, the unfit or the sole supporters of dependants), those able to demonstrate a conscientious objection.

In January and February Bloomsbury's practical action against conscription took the form of office work at the Fleet Street headquarters of the National Council for Civil Liberties. This and the No Conscription Fellowship were the two organizations that not only led the attack against compulsory service but looked after the individual interests of conscientious objectors, distributed propaganda (the most dangerous of their activities), and kept the authorities on their toes with respect to administrative aspects of the Act.[1] On the committee of the No Conscription Fellowship was Bertrand Russell, a ceaseless agitator against compulsory service. His influence can be seen in Clive's pamphlet 'Peace at Once'. Russell's unflinching iconoclasm and the lucidity of his ideas – especially in his lectures at the Caxton Hall in early 1916 – were, in Lytton's words, 'a wonderful solace and refreshment . . . I don't believe there's anyone quite so formidable to be found just now upon this earth.' For Russell, as for Bloomsbury, pacifism was an indestructible expression of a personal faith that permeated daily conduct.

In one way or another most of Bloomsbury at this time were involved in pacifist and anti-conscription activities. Leonard Woolf, deeply pacifist, was not however a conscientious objector. He would certainly have joined up (like his four brothers) but for the continuing ill-health and instability of

Virginia whom he continued to nurse towards recovery. He was called up at the end of May and after a medical examination where a diagnosis of his constantly trembling hands was incorrectly given as a form of St. Vitus Dance, he was given complete exemption from all forms of service for the duration of the War. Meanwhile he was engaged on the research and writing of a book under the auspices of the Fabian Society which later in the year was published as *International Government*. It drew upon much of the findings of his 1915 report, another Fabian commission, on the causes of the present conflict and the possible chances of success of 'an international authority to prevent war'. Maynard, as a Treasury official, was issued with an exemption certificate by the Permanent Secretary to the Treasury on the grounds of doing work in the national interest. But he also made a carefully considered plea for exemption as a conscientious objector, making it clear that, in Clive's words, 'He was not a pacifist, he did not object to fighting in any circumstances: he objected to being made to fight.' The application was rejected because of the Treasury's previous exemption; but Maynard felt that his convictions should somewhere be recorded. A week earlier he had sent £50 to the National Council for Civil Liberties where Lytton and James, Duncan, Vanessa, Adrian, Bunny and Bob Trevelyan worked intermittently, helping to distribute leaflets and undertaking clerical work. Adrian later became the Council's Treasurer, before taking up farm-work. Lytton wrote a leaflet accusing the Government of introducing conscription as an anti-Labour move to tie the hands of possible strikers. The leaflet was considered seditious and though many copies had gone out the rest of the printing was destroyed.

When the Military Service Act came into direct effect on 2 March, the rumbling machinery of the Local Tribunals was set going throughout the country for dealing with questions relating to exemption. Applicants could receive absolute, temporary, or conditional exemption. Conscientious ob-jectors did not expect their cases to be sympathetically reviewed amidst the patriotic frenzies of 1916 – this was the time of the Germans' attack at Verdun when quarter of a million men were killed or wounded with no appreciable difference to the outcome of the War. Some Tribunals were notoriously harsh. For the most part, they consisted of local worthies, borough councillors, schoolteachers, parsons, retired military men, and representatives of the various interests of the neighbourhood. Cases were tried in a way that in peacetime would have been considered scandalous. The resulting injustices – the solitary confinement, the foul conditions of work camps, the beatings, humiliations, and deaths – naturally enough excited little public sympathy when compared with the sufferings at the Front.

Early in March, Duncan went to Suffolk to look at a neglected farmhouse called Wissett Lodge near Halesworth that had become vacant on the death of its owner Mrs Florence Ewebank, a relation of Duncan's mother. It was left to Major Grant to dispose of and it was soon settled that Duncan should rent it for himself and Bunny to set themselves up as fruit-farmers and to undertake agricultural work of a domestic nature. It was felt that by so doing they would, when their turn came, be viewed more leniently by the Tribunal

94. *Huntley and Palmer's*, 1915, by Vanessa Bell. 22 × 22 in. The Mayor Gallery, London. Painted at Bosham, Sussex. The name 'Huntley and Palmer's' appears on the biscuit tin behind the goblet

than if they had continued living ordinary lives in London. Duncan's father, though disapproving of his son's position, tried to understand his convictions, and gave advice and practical support. He came up from Kent on more than one occasion to look into the question of the orchards, asparagus beds, and the planting of potatoes.[2]

Wissett was a small early Victorian farmhouse set slightly apart from the village, surrounded by trees which darkened the already dim, small-windowed rooms. A huge wistaria, rambler roses and creepers smothered the walls, overshadowed by a large ilex tree. There were flower-gardens, a pond, a pergola and vegetable beds. The house was comfortable but fussily furnished and when Vanessa and her children arrived, she gradually banished the bric-à-brac, made new curtains and chair-covers from Omega stuffs, and with Barbara Hiles, who had been summoned to help, marbled and stippled the walls. Later, Vanessa and Duncan copied Fra Angelicos from postcard reproductions in watercolour on her bedroom walls.

Although life at Wissett during the next six months was dominated by the worry of preparing defences and answering questionnaires for the Tribunals, by often uncongenial farm-work, and shortage of supplies, it was not an entirely unhappy period. Vanessa's presence was infinitely reassuring. Deep in the country with her children and Duncan, and with uninterrupted hours for painting, she found periods of calm and relative happiness. She never wanted to give up this 'countrified existence' where 'becoming a savage' seemed an entirely satisfactory way of life. Her occasional visits to London distracted and exhausted her. Friends who arrived with fresh and absorbing news of the outside world hardly compensated for the invasion of her solitude. They interfered with the slowly evolving pattern of her feelings for

95. *Flowers in a Vase, c.* 1915, by Duncan Grant. 30 × 25 in. Private Collection, London

those near her and the rhythm of their existence together. Duncan and Bunny worked hard – mainly to counteract the strain and depression of waiting for the inevitable summons. Imprisonment was never far from their minds. In London, Clive was facing the same possibility: 'I daresay I shall be in jail before Duncan and Bunny,' he wrote to Vanessa. Lytton, reluctantly moving on from the Morrells at Garsington, joined Charles Sanger and Leonard and Virginia for Easter at Asheham; Maynard went to Wissett bringing with him the luxury of a bottle of whisky; Roger bicycled about Oxfordshire with Pamela, Omega problems for a while forgotten. A week later he spent a weekend at Garsington with Clive, Mary Hutchinson and Molly MacCarthy. Talk of the War and approaching Tribunals was not allowed to dominate the proceedings: there were other preoccupations. 'Ott's was amusing,' Roger wrote to Vanessa, ' – she and I very affable – no "*explications*" even when I sat with her in her boudoir. No, there was no chance for me to do any love-making so I had to listen to the doors opening and shutting all night long in the big passage, though in common decency I suppose I ought to have gone out to the W.C. once or twice to keep up appearances.'[3]

Duncan and Bunny soon received notice that their cases were to be heard on 4 May by the Blything Tribunal sitting at nearby Bulcamp. As early as March, Vanessa had written about her fears of the Tribunal which 'consists of country gentlemen I believe, who I'm afraid are likely to be very bad about conscientious objectors.' On the evening of 3 May, a barrister, a member of Parliament and a Treasury official arrived at Wissett Lodge – Adrian Stephen, Philip Morrell and Maynard Keynes. At a quarter to ten the next morning two dog-carts took the company off through little villages and hedgerows brilliant with blossom. Of the hundreds of cases already heard by the Tribunal, this was the first to be attended by an advocate and character witnesses. The presence too of a member of Parliament caused a good deal of surprise. Adrian and then Philip Morrell spoke on Duncan's behalf for, went a local report, the

> appellant was not accustomed to attend a law court or a tribunal, therefore it was difficult for him to express his views. Mr Morrell could assure the tribunal that his friend would scorn to take advantage of an Act of Parliament in order to escape military service unless he had a real conscientious objection. At the beginning of the War he could have had a commission and he (Mr Morrell) urged him to accept it, but he said his conscientious feelings forbade him to do so. If he was offered alternative service to meet his case, he would be pleased to do that for the good of his country – in fact he was most anxious to do something for his country compatible with his feelings.

Bunny added a characteristically passionate note to the defence of his views when he described what he had seen when working for the Quakers in the Marne. Maynard added that the applicant's mother had visited Tolstoy. What difference could it make to the case *where* Mrs Garnett had been on her foreign travels was the response. In such circumstances, explanation seemed

96. *Portrait of David Garnett*, 1915, by Duncan Grant. 24 × 21 in. Agnew & Sons, London. After the First War David Garnett began a successful career as a novelist with *Lady Into Fox* (1923). His first wife was Ray Marshall (d. 1940) and his second Angelica Bell

futile. 'It was rather horrible (yesterday)', Vanessa told Roger. 'Both applications were refused – not even non-combatant given. The whole thing was a complete farce. I think the tribunal had made up its mind from the first to refuse Duncan. . . . Maynard was the only person who made any impression on them and he couldn't say much as they simply wanted to get through to the next case. The Chairman admitted he believed Duncan's convictions to be sincere, yet refused him. Bunny spoke for himself. . . . They are appealing of course – but I haven't much hope. It seems unlikely that an Appeal Tribunal at Ipswich will be any better than this. My only real hope is that it may be possible to get them out of prison before very long.' And Duncan himself commented that 'The whole business was a Provincial

97. *Portrait of David Garnett*, 1915, by Vanessa Bell. 30 × 20½ in. Private Collection, London. Painted at the same time as plate 96, possibly at Eleanor House, West Wittering, Sussex

Farce but when a thing is funny with disastrous possibilities for oneself it is difficult not to be bored. And though the whole event seemed infinitely petty and unreal at the time it left me completely shattered in the nerves. It is odd that an unreal experience should exhaust one more than a real one.'

Their Appeal came before the Ipswich Tribunal on 16 May. Both were awarded non-combatant service with leave to appeal to the Central Tribunal. The result was better than expected, imprisonment had been averted, they were recognized as conscientious objectors and there was a strong possibility that the Central Tribunal would refer them to the Pelham Committee. There was general relief all round. Ottoline assured them both that the Appeal would be a great success.

Ottoline Morrell's hatred of the War was intense and unflinching and Garsington rapidly became a centre for conscientious objectors. Philip Morrell supervised a farm for many of them to work on and a nearby cottage, Home Close, was furnished for their use. Clive volunteered to work there on and off until the end of the War. Though Lady Ottoline disliked him and found his relish for gossip intimidating, he was immensely popular on the farm. He managed visits to Wissett however, with Mary Hutchinson, and found time for occasional weekends in London where he could escape the clutches of Garsington's more persistent visitors. A friend who joined him at Home Close was Gerald Shove, now married to Fredegond Maitland[4] who was, wrote Clive, '. . . the queerest mixture of intelligence and silliness and inexperience and wide acquaintances, [she] talks to me a good deal about the nature of love and I broaden her mind with smutty and scandalous stories.' Another visitor was Violet Bonham-Carter, and Ottoline entreated Maynard to come – 'you must bring bath salts and brilliant talk' – for Violet Bonham-Carter was known for her intolerant attitude towards conscientious objection. Maynard was tactful but Lytton, also a guest, quarrelled violently with her and the weekend was not an easy one. Her father, the Prime Minister Asquith, and various members of his family, including Elizabeth, later the Princess Antoine Bibesco, also visited Garsington. Asquith had all along been against conscription, believing that it would not measurably increase the size of the forces. When it was introduced, he was partly responsible for the clauses concerning exemption for conscientious objectors. His appearance in this hive of 'conchies' was not thought unduly compromising. At tea-time, the climax of a Garsington weekend, he was more interested in talk of poetry and painting than the War.

It is astonishing how Ottoline managed to provide for so many guests – liberal politicians, badly-behaved intellectuals, painters, writers, and Oxford undergraduates. The weekends merged into one another. On cushions, in deckchairs, lounging in hammocks, sprawled on rugs, the company would assemble for tea like some travelling circus. Ottoline presided, whipping up the conversation, putting people through their hoops and paces, attentive, intimate, murmuring to her neighbour, or addressing the pugs and peacocks, pacifists and poets. By some of her visitors she was treated abominably, and it needed all her courage to continue to make Garsington 'a harbour, a refuge in the storm'. Lawrence's portrait of her as Hermione Roddice in *Women in Love* was a bitter blow and she regarded it as a cruel caricature. A tremendous quarrel ensued. 'Ottoline dimly perceives,' wrote Clive to Vanessa, 'that Lawrence's portrait may represent the general opinion; she is positively subdued.'[5]

In spite of this setback, she was indomitable; life continued to the full. Bertrand Russell informed everyone, with a queer satisfaction, of the latest humiliations undergone by the 'conchies'. Siegfried Sassoon, 'very handsome, very agreeable' turned up and Ottoline was particularly attentive; the twenty-year-old Aldous Huxley, already a brilliant conversationalist, came over from Balliol 'folding his long, grasshopper legs into a deckchair'; Katherine Mansfield was another visitor; and Gertler, telling Ottoline all the evil he had ever heard of her. 'I think' wrote Clive to Vanessa, 'they are all rather sorry they took such a fancy to Gertler at first. They have been clever enough to discover that he has only one topic of conversation – himself.' Middleton Murray came, 'shifty, backboneless, fearful, ill, but rather nice and pathetic' as Gertler wrote to Carrington;[6] the d'Aranyi sisters, Jelli and Adila, appeared for a concert, after which Carrington wrote in her peculiar vein: 'Never have I seen the garden look so wonderful. A moon shining on the pond, covered with warm slime, bubbling and fermenting underneath and great black shadows cast from the trees over it all. And inside, music and these strange villagers with their babies, and young men in hard white collars and thick serge suits. Clive sitting lost in thought on the steps. Maria[7] in her yellow trousers, lying, covered in a black cloak in the passage, distractedly in love with Ottoline. We acted a play. Katherine sang songs and danced ragtimes.' And over all Philip Morrell 'monumental, like one of the togaed statues outside the old House of Commons, remained immersed in his own nobility of mien and character.'[8]

At the Omega Roger was worried by the shortage of artists and, with a temporary revival in sales, much of the extra work fell on his shoulders and those of the tireless Winnie Gill. Nina Hamnett and her husband had been sporadically working there for a few months.[9] Soon afterwards, de Bergen was imprisoned for three months as an unregistered alien and then deported to France. Nina and he never saw each other again, much, it seems, to her

98. Invitation Card for the Omega Workshops designed by Roger Fry. His interest in calligraphy resulted in a pamphlet 'English Handwriting' written with Robert Bridges, 1926

relief. She continued working at Fitzroy Square and painted a good many portraits (including ones of Osbert and Edith Sitwell, Sickert and W. H. Davies). Roger found her a delightful companion; she became his mistress and helped to alleviate his domestic loneliness through this busy but benumbing period. He began the first of several portraits of her painted over the next twelve months.

At the end of June, Roger went to Paris with Madame Vandervelde, the beautiful wife of the Belgian statesman and an energetic friend to many Belgian refugees and English writers and painters in the War. In between visits to Matisse and Picasso ('Picasso a little *dérouté* for the moment but doing some splendid things all the same') there was time to talk to friends, show photographs of his work, and discuss 'the man we'd overlooked', Seurat, whose work was still virtually unknown in England. For Vanessa, his correspondent, this was all most tantalising news, it being impossible to see much new painting at the time. Had he photographs? what was Matisse doing? what had he seen in the studios of Montparnasse? But Roger was still reluctant to visit Wissett for it was 'too painful' not to be able to see Vanessa alone. He still could not come to terms with the idea of simply being a friend of Vanessa's and the more he realized that he must do so for the good of them both, the lonelier he felt. At the end of July he went with his children to Bosham, Sussex, and remained there through August.

On 20 June Lytton arrived at Wissett for a week's stay, with Harry Norton as fellow-guest. In spite of some minor friction between Vanessa and himself, he thoroughly enjoyed his visit and was reluctant to leave. He read and wrote, flirted with Bunny, walked in the fields and laid an extravagant but futile plan to capture the heart, ostensibly, of the local postboy. In the evenings there were long discussions in true 'Thursday' style. Vanessa wrote to Roger:

> Lytton admitted in the end that he had very little sense of anything but the human interest in painting. He is very suspicious of our attitude about art and thinks we don't understand our own feelings and are trying to prove a theory. I on the other hand think him almost entirely dramatic in his appreciations. I mean I believe he only feels character and relationships of character and has no conception of the form it's all being made into. Then we have had long discussions about Ottoline. Norton and Duncan and I took the line that she was a terrifically energetic and vigorous character with a definite, rather bad taste which she put into practice but it was different from having any creative power – but Lytton thinks Garsington a creation.[10]

Vanessa's feelings for Ottoline, nearly always critical, were confirmed in August when Ottoline arrived for the weekend. Vanessa, it seems was not only anxious on her own behalf for as she told Roger in August, 'Quentin I find has a strong taste for a bawdy joke. Julian is rather shy about them but I think will be educated. I only hope Quentin will have enough sense as to who he makes them to – Ottoline comes for two days next week and I don't know what will happen if he pinches her bottom as he did Duncan's the other day with winks and giggling. But it might be a great success.'

99. *Portrait of Nina Hamnett,*
1917, by Roger Fry.
32 × 24 in. Courtauld
Institute Galleries, Fry
Collection. The most
successful of Fry's several
portraits of Nina Hamnett
(1890–1956) painted in 1917
and 1918 at 21 Fitzroy Street

On 27 August, the weekend over, she wrote to Roger, 'We're recovering
from Ott whose visit nearly destroyed us . . . I've decided that woman isn't
for me. I can't stand it and hope I shall never spend more than a few hours in
her presence again – or at most one week-end a year. This is final.'[11] During
the day, Duncan and Bunny were away from the house and contributed little

100. *Charleston, c.* 1950, by Vanessa Bell. 23 × 19 in. Collection Quentin Bell. The house changed little between 1916 and the time this was painted though an ugly Victorian porch was removed. Vanessa Bell had a particular liking for water in her landscapes and the pond was a constant subject

to her Ladyship's entertainment. Harry Norton, again a visitor, went to the other extreme. 'Norton gave her boxes of Bengal Lights to light her cigarettes with and she was always taken in and lit up with a flash! and was furious. Hers was not a happy life'.[12] Ottoline's own retrospection recollective of the visit, however, was of a time of gaiety and enjoyment.

On 28 June Philip Morrell telegrammed – 'Appeals just decided. Both successful'. Duncan and Bunny were exempted from non-combatant service providing they took up some work approved by the Pelham Committee. It soon became apparent, however, that Wissett would have to be given up. The local people were now most suspicious and disapproving of this odd house of 'pasty faces' as COs were popularly called. Moreover, it seems they had influenced the War Agricultural Committee to report unfavourably on Wissett. A second enquiry was held but again the Committee came out against, without actually visiting the place, and the two men were asked to find more appropriate work elsewhere. Sussex seemed a possible choice as they had heard that a farmer called Gunn at Glynde was well disposed towards conscientious objectors, though he himself had no more room for them. They would be near to Leonard and Virginia at Asheham, and nearer to London. On one of her walks near Firle village, Virginia had noticed and taken a fancy to a farmhouse just below Firle Beacon, one of the high South Downs, called Charleston and thought it a possible place to rent. It was agreed that Vanessa, leaving Duncan and Bunny to the harvest, would travel down to Sussex, look into possibilities of employment for them (for self-employment was now out of the question) and see if Charleston was available. She did so and after some rapid transactions on market-day in Lewes, the nearby county town, a young farmer agreed to employ the two men and they were to rent Charleston on Lord Gage's Firle estate.

Bunny went ahead to the Ram Inn in Firle getting to know his employer Mr Hecks of New House Farm, 'a very quick-witted young man'. While he set about pulling and topping mangolds, the upheaval from Wissett fell mainly to Duncan and Barbara, for Vanessa was unwell and Quentin added to the chaos by breaking a leg. Hens, ducks and rabbits had to be crated and sent ahead by rail, apples gathered in the orchards, canvases tied up and easels packed and, together with fishing rods, two bicycles and the dog Henry, all had to be transported to Sussex.

After a short stay in London, seeing friends, visiting the Omega and going to the theatre, the new occupants arrived and Charleston became their temporary wartime home, ramshackle, unfurnished, an outside pump for water, without gas or electricity, a remote and primitive refuge for two conscientious objectors, Sir Leslie Stephen's daughter, and her two rather wild and inseparable children.

Late in October, Vanessa described the house in which she was to live for forty-four years:

> It really is so lovely that I must show it to you soon. It's absolutely perfect I think . . . as one comes to it from the front one sees the less good side of it. It has been refaced with some kind of quite harmless stucco of plaster and has a creeper growing over it. The other sides are wonderful. I suppose it's 17th or early 18th century (but my word doesn't go for much), anyhow it's most lovely, very solid and simple with flat walls in that lovely mixture of brick and flint that they use about here and perfectly flat windows in the walls and wonderful tiled roofs. The pond is most beautiful with a willow at one side and a stone or flint wall edging it all round the garden part and a little lawn sloping down to it with formal bushes on it. Then there's a small orchard and the walled

garden like the Asheham one and another lawn or bit of field railed in, beyond there a wall of trees – one single line of elms all round two sides which shelters us from West winds. . . . Inside the house, the rooms are very large and a great many – 10 bedrooms I think – some enormous [in reality seven at the most]. One I shall make into a studio. It is very light and large with an east window. But the sun doesn't come in much after quite early morning and it has a small room out of it with another window so one might get interesting interiors I think.[13]

It was the setting of the house and the surrounding landscape that particularly pleased its new inhabitants[14] – the magnificent slow curve of Firle Beacon to the west, gently sloping down to fields at the back of an enormous barn and outhouses. From the main Lewes to Eastbourne road an unmade track cut through meadows and pasture to the house, quite hidden among the elms except for its two broad and comfortable chimneys. Remote it certainly was for there was no public transport on the road and visitors either bicycled or walked from Glynde or Berwick stations. Molly MacCarthy, struck by its seclusion as she walked to it for the first time across the fields in pouring rain, thought it the nearest thing to Wuthering Heights she had ever seen and burst into tears.

[1] Closely involved in both organizations was Clifford Allen (later Lord Allen of Hurtwood) who, between increasingly debilitating bouts of imprisonment, helped maintain peace between these pacifist groups with compassionate diplomacy.

[2] Barbara Bagenal (*née* Hiles) reports that some of Duncan's ideas on agriculture created great amusement and sometimes dismay in the village – chicken eggs were put to hatch in the oven with grotesque results, and six pedigree Leghorns had their tails dyed blue to distinguish them from the other poultry.

[3] RF to VB, May 1916.

[4] Fredegond Maitland (1889–1949) was a poet, a second cousin of Virginia and Vanessa and daughter of F. W. Maitland, historian and biographer of Sir Leslie Stephen.

[5] 2 February 1917.

[6] 12 October 1917.

[7] Maria Nys, later Mrs Aldous Huxley.

[8] O. Sitwell, *Triple Fugue*, Grant Richards, 1924.

[9] This ill-assorted couple appear in Sickert's painting *The Little Tea-Party* (Tate Gallery) painted at The Whistler, Sickert's studio at 8 Fitzroy Street.

[10] *c.* 25 June 1916.

[11] 27 August 1916.

[12] VB to J. M. Keynes, 29 August 1916.

[13] VB to RF, October 1916.

[14] 'We were all delighted when we saw it. It was exactly what we might have imagined. I first saw it on a bicycle as well, which was the only way of getting about in those days. There were no buses on the main road. Vanessa said that there was this great lake in front. We were rather surprised when it wasn't a very big one. Her sense of proportion was rather odd.' (Duncan Grant in an interview with James Fox, *Vogue*, 15 March 1972.)

At Charleston, Vanessa at last found a house she could furnish and decorate in a manner completely original, putting into practice ideas she had had for some years, her scope widening as the house became a more permanent home. Naturally the practical experience gained from the Omega was much to the fore and Omega objects were soon in evidence – textiles, lampshades, pots – 'the Omega dinner service looks most lovely on the dresser' Vanessa wrote soon after their arrival. Dining-room chairs came – cane-seated, straight-backed, with red-stained wood – which Roger had designed before the War. Duncan and Vanessa transformed rough-and-ready furniture, bargains from Lewes, painted door-panels and cupboards, improvised decorations on bedheads and logboxes. Spontaneity was the keynote. An enormous dog appears below a window, an improbable bird above, daisies stand upright in pale blue goblets, a crouching angel of impish pink plays a lute on a logbox, a swimmer glides across a chest in kaleidoscopic water, women carry baskets through the panels of a door. Witty and fantastic postures were devised to suit whatever object or surface came to hand. These athletic and graceful figures were nearly all Duncan's work. They are part of a whole series beginning with the tennis players on the wall at Brunswick Square and the swimmers and footballers of the Borough Polytechnic.

101. One side of a logbox, decorated c. 1916 by Duncan Grant at Charleston. There are alternate dancers and musicians on the four sides

Vanessa inclined to a passive and generally less figurative mode: bowls of fruit and jugs of flowers, instruments without their players, laden baskets set down, their carriers vanished, a woman having taken her bath, standing pensively by a window. 'I have started a large picture meant as a decoration for one of the walls in the garden sitting-room. There's very little in the picture and it's mostly one colour – or two, yellow ochre and a greenish grey. The subject is principally floor with a bath and a semi-nude female rather too like Mary and the pond through the window. As it's 6 feet by 5 feet 6 inches it will I'm afraid tend to be monotonous' (plate 109).[1] Some time later she again wrote to Roger: 'I've been painting that odd still life of apples in the dish every day lately and also painting two doors in Duncan's bedroom. They come on either side of the mantelpiece you know which makes it a rather amusing whole but I'm not doing anything very startling – only pots of flowers and marbled circles.'[2] The fireplace was of course brought into the scheme with repeated circles and bands of terracotta and pale green (plate 102). The sometimes garrulous patterning characteristic of the early Omega designs has developed into a calm disposition of circles, squares, and broad striping which are a more personal reflection of Vanessa's natural

language. The gentle marbling in the circles seems, beside the stately alloca-
tion on the fireplace, almost animated. And cool colours hold the flowers
in check.

The garden was not neglected. The views of it from the house are inseparable from the interiors. Duncan planned and dug paths, flowers were planted, Bunny saw to the orchard. A terrace was made in the walled garden.
'We're busy . . . making a small cemented place to sit out on and we're going
to make a small inlaid piece of mosaic of odd bits of china, glass etc. in the
centre and also a narrow border round the edge.'[3]

Roger became an eager accomplice in all these projects – giving advice and
making suggestions. He was rarely more happy than in these intimate,
creative discussions with Vanessa. But in the main he was an epistolary
accomplice, for visits to Charleston were difficult to arrange – emotionally as
well as practically. There was always an overwhelming amount of work in
London at the Omega, for the *Burlington Magazine*, organizing exhibitions,
and of course his own painting.

Exhibitions by young painters unconnected with the original nucleus of
Omega artists were a feature of these wartime activities. They show Roger
Fry's willingness to welcome new talent and go some way to correcting the
allegation that he was interested only in the promotion of his immediate
circle. In August 1916, Alvaro Guevara, aged twenty-two, exhibited twenty-
eight paintings at Fitzroy Square. Guevara, known universally as 'Chile',

102. Decorated doors and
fireplace, 1918, by Vanessa
Bell in a bedroom at
Charleston. The carpet was
worked from a design by
Douglas Davidson

was one of the most florid figures of the period, a South American aristocrat, a boxer as well as a painter and a poet, a gifted student at the Slade, prospective husband of Nancy Cunard and an early victim of Nina Hamnett. His old world Latin morality and fastidious manners made him slightly disapproving of Bloomsbury and his sometimes tiresome monologues irritated them. Nor was he a success at Garsington. But Roger, Sickert and John all agreed he was gifted and Sickert generously praised Guevara's exhibition in the *Burlington Magazine*, though, characteristically, the article is more interesting on Manet than on Guevara. His paintings of figures in cafés – he was a master of café portraiture, to further, perhaps, his acquaintance with an attractive boy – dancers practising, and bathers at the Chelsea and Hackney Baths had a freshness and originality and a compositional daring which in his later and more famous series of figures in interiors, of which *Miss Edith Sitwell* is the best known, became theatrical. From time to time Guevara worked on decorative schemes at the Omega when commissions arrived – which to Roger's surprise, they continued to do.

In 1916 there had been a room to decorate for Arthur Ruck in Berkeley Street which took the London Underground as its theme (plate 103). Roger made a large circular carpet and designed marquetrie tables; Vanessa was asked to design a stained glass window; and the murals, carried out by Roger, Dolores Courtney, Nina Hamnett and de Bergen, depict crowds emerging from the tube station into the streets and parks of London. Sir Ian and Lady

103. Mural in a room at 4 Berkeley Street, London, decorated by the Omega Workshops, 1916, for Arthur Ruck who dealt in Old Masters and objets d'art. An article illustrating the murals appeared in *Colour* magazine, June 1916, and Fry contributed an article on 'The Artist as Decorator' to the same journal in May 1917

Hamilton had commissioned a large number of candleshades to be painted from Roger's design. This work was responsible for the introduction of a new painter at the Omega who rapidly became friendly with its artists: Edward Wolfe.

Wolfe was twenty at the time (1917) and had arrived the previous year from his native Johannesburg, equally prepared for a career in the theatre or as a painter. Painting won and he began to attend the Slade School and became a friend of 'Chile' Guevara and Geoffrey Nelson, both ex-Slade students. Nelson and Augustus John gave a large studio party, nominally in honour of a Chelsea barmaid, which Wolfe attended. He was treated to some advice from John as they wandered down the embankment after breakfast – 'Don't go to Sickert – he'll only teach you how to paint pisspots.' So, at Nina Hamnett's suggestion, he went to the Omega as assistant candleshade painter. His variations on the theme pleased Roger. 'Ah, yes Wolfe,' he would say, 'a perfect genius for candle-shades.' For this high-spirited South African, Fry and his friends became a sympathetic circle, prepared to discuss, unlike Tonks at the Slade, the new painting which interested him. When drawing from the nude, Wolfe invariably managed to make his figures too large for the paper. This magnification occurred once too often and, such was Fry's reputation, Tonks thought it was a deliberate plot contrived by Fry to annoy him. Soon afterwards, Wolfe left the Slade for more congenial full time work at Fitzroy Square.[4] As well as being a fellow painter, Teddy Wolfe was a lively and intelligent companion. Naturally he was asked to Lady Ottoline's. He had first met her at the Omega when having tea with Nina and the others. When news reached them of Ottoline's arrival, Wolfe was hotly persuaded to go down to meet her. He started down the stairs, framed by the open doorway of the lavatory across the short landing. Ottoline advanced, 'bashed-in' pearls around her neck, 'waterfalls of feathers from her hat, and trailing trains behind her. . . . "Ah", she gurgled and moaned, "so you are the new artist" – looking over his head into the lavatory – "Maynard has told me all about you".'

In February and March 1917 an unusual exhibition of drawings by children opened at Fitzroy Square. A young art teacher from Dudley High School, Birmingham, a friend of Marjorie Strachey's, asked Fry's advice about a teaching post in London and showed him work by her pupils. Her method was for the pupils to hear a poem ('The Forsaken Merman' for instance), draw their impression with their eyes shut, and then make a second drawing, eyes open. Fry was extremely enthusiastic, wrote an article for the *Burlington* and opened a show of the drawings on 19 February. It was well-received and much visited. On 7 March he wrote to his daughter, 'I'm trying to get the Minister of Education to see them and see if we can't do something to stop the teaching of art'; and in another letter '. . . here's an inexhaustible supply of real primitive art and real vision which the government suppresses at a cost of hundreds of thousands of pounds. If the world weren't the most crazily topsy-turvy place one would never believe it possible.'

About this time another development of Omega life emerged – an evening club, the Art Circle, where members paid a small sum to attend talks and

concerts and put on theatrical performances. One of the reasons behind this
venture was the influx into the neighbourhood of many Belgian refugee
artists and musicians. Nina Hamnett wrote: 'After the arrival of the Belgians,
Charlotte Street became very gay. There were Bal Musettes all up the street.
A big Belgian played an accordion and everyone danced and a hat was taken
round after for halfpennies, as they do in France and Belgium in work-
people's dances.' A puppet performance in aid of the Belgians was given –
the Prologue to Lowes Dickinson's morality play *War and Peace* – showing
a scene outside the Gate of Heaven with the arrival by aeroplane of Violence,
Futurist, Reason, and Cynic. Another play had puppets designed by Duncan. The d'Aranyi sisters often played at parties and at the Omega, and the
celebrated Madame Suggia gave a 'cello recital.

Arnold Bennett was often among the guests at these evenings. He was a
generally valuable supporter of the business – even after a table he had
ordered was mistakenly sent to his wife instead of his mistress. Edward Wolfe
was given his first commission through the Omega when Bennett asked to be
painted. It was Bennett's favourite picture of himself. Yeats also came to the
evenings and sometimes looked into the showroom on his way from visiting
Eva Gore-Booth who lived above and was awaiting the release of her sister,
the 'rebel' Countess Markevitch, from prison. He bought fabrics and one of
the large green Algerian water-coolers for his cottage in Ireland.

But despite the Art Circle evenings contact between friends was erratic.
'It's this wretched separation of everybody that makes one uncomfortable.
But my hope is that if the house at Tidmarsh comes into being, it may be
possible by the summer to have some pleasant reunions in the old style
whether the war's going on or not,' wrote Lytton to Clive.[5] Completing the
general exodus from London, Lytton left Belsize Park Gardens and set up
home in December with Carrington at the Mill House in Tidmarsh, a small
Berkshire village. It was rented by Oliver Strachey, Harry Norton, Saxon
Sydney Turner, Maynard and Lytton himself, who was to live there more or
less permanently. Carrington supervised the decoration and furnishing,
helped by Barbara Hiles, and managed the domestic side of life as well as
setting up her studio there. Her dogged devotion to Lytton's comforts and
her imaginative plunge into housekeeping prevented her from painting in
any regular way, though she did accomplish a surprising amount of work at
Tidmarsh over the next six years, including her best known painting of the
back of the Mill House with its Spencerian foliage and black fantastic swans.

Before his move to Tidmarsh, Lytton corrected the manuscript of *Eminent
Victorians* and in December, at Clive's suggestion, sent it to Chatto and
Windus. This firm was emerging as one of the go-ahead and popular pub-
lishers of the time under Geoffrey Whitworth and Charles Prentice. Clive's
Art had been published by them and in the following years Fry, Aldous
Huxley, Aldington, David Garnett, Wilfred Owen and Charles Scott-
Moncrieff were among their authors. Lytton joined them when *Eminent
Victorians* was accepted for publication.

Chatto and Windus was a very different concern from the firm which in
1917 began its life on the dining-table of Hogarth House, Richmond. 'The

Hogarth Press', as it came to be known, was started by the Woolfs mainly as a therapeutic and welcome practical alternative to writing for Virginia.

A month after purchasing a printing press, the Woolfs felt sufficiently capable of beginning their first publication which they proposed selling by subscription, circularizing their friends and likely purchasers. Carrington was commissioned to make four woodcuts, and in July *Two Stories*, by Virginia Woolf and L. S. Woolf, was issued, Virginia's being 'The Mark on the Wall' and Leonard's the 'Three Jews'. It was a success and the Woolfs were soon looking for something to do for their second publication. On 3 August Vanessa wrote to Roger who was staying at Eleanor with the Hutchinsons: 'Virginia has asked me to get together enough woodcuts to produce one of their numbers – of woodcuts only which might be rather fun. I have always wanted to try to do some again. Will you contribute?' Roger started work and Vanessa and Duncan did some; at the Omega de Bergen and Edward Wolfe were also asked to contribute. By September the project was called off, Vanessa unable to have the last word aesthetically over the production and unwilling to trust Leonard's taste. The book was later published under the Omega Workshops imprint.

Initially, the Hogarth Press was regarded in Bloomsbury as a joke and was laughed about in private but defended with passion in public. By 1921 publications included stories by Leonard and Virginia, by Katherine Mansfield and Morgan Forster, a critical essay by Middleton Murry, *Poems* by T. S. Eliot (among them 'Sweeney among the Nightingales'), *Paris*, a long poem by Hope Mirrlees, Pearsall Smith's *Stories from the Old Testament* and Gorki's *Reminiscences of Tolstoy*, translated by Leonard Woolf and S. S. Koteliansky. The Press's reputation as publishers of Russian literature was launched by this last book. Works by Chekhov, Dostoevsky, Bunin, Tolstoy, Goldenveiser and Andreev followed – mainly hitherto untranslated short works, often biographical. In the years that followed other European authors were published at the Hogarth Press, notably Italo Svevo, Rilke and, of course, Freud. Hogarth books soon became distinctive in appearance, many of the jackets being in the Post-Impressionist style.[6] The Woolfs found unusual binding papers from as far afield as Yugoslavia and Roger Fry's daughter Pamela, studying in Paris, sent over hand-made 'marbled' papers.

A similar marbling process, this time on fabrics, was used in another venture that helped alleviate the depression of a never-ending War. In August 1917, Duncan received a letter from Jacques Copeau about the Vieux Colombier's 1918 season in New York. Duncan was again asked to paint some panels for the revised production of *Twelfth Night*, which had been frustrated in 1915, and to design costumes for Maeterlinck's *Pelléas et Mélisande*. It was arranged that the costumes should be cut out and painted at Charleston and that Maynard would take them and the additional *Twelfth Night* screens to New York where he was going in September on a financial mission. Roger sent a copy of the play and work was soon underway. Barbara, who was camping near Charleston for the summer, helped in the making and dyeing of the costumes, 'marbled' in the Omega tradition:

104. Group at Charleston, August 1917. Standing l. to r. Duncan Grant, David Garnett and Saxon Sydney Turner, seated Barbara Hiles

We mixed the dyes, splashing them onto the large wooden kitchen table, two of us held the material in both hands, laid it on the table, then lifting it up continued until it was marbled for certain dresses. Each dress was of a different coloured marbling.

We also sewed patchwork onto cotton for the King's robe. For the King's serenading scene, Duncan Grant painted the bodice and wings on the cotton material, I made a wig with skeins of yellow wool. Vanessa and I cut out the dresses and roughly tacked them together so that photographs could be taken. Our dyeing process was very unprofessional, we became splashed with dye and marbled all over, hair and skin.[7]

Before the costumes went to New York, Vanessa, Duncan and Barbara tried them on and photographs were taken by the pond at Charleston and at the kitchen window. *Twelfth Night* was given in New York in January 1918 and in Paris in 1920: and *Pelléas* had two, perhaps three, performances later in the year before Copeau, ordered to produce a new play a week, tired of New York and returned to France.

Early in 1917 Roger conceived the idea of an exhibition of 'copies' at the Omega, and various friends were asked to contribute. Duncan and Vanessa frequently made copies, mainly from the early Italian Renaissance masters. Among other things, Duncan sent his copy of Piero della Francesca's hatchet-nosed *Federigo da Montefeltro* which he had painted in the Uffizi in 1905. 'I hope it won't arrive in pieces and that the frame will fit. What a time you'll have had with all our badly put together objects.' Roger tackled a version of Cimabue's *St. Francis* (from the Assisi Church) which pre-cipitated a revision of his estimate of that painter, and at Charleston Vanessa struggled with a Sassoferrato which, she wrote to Roger, 'may be as beastly as the original'. During the show Gertler offered a 'Yiddish Cézanne'. But the critics were either hostile or silent, the public didn't come. It was a con-spiracy, according to Roger, of 'art-politics' origin. It seems more likely, however, that these often 'free translations' seemed to the critics a pointless exercise, at worst, another joke of Fry's perpetration – his name still aroused the gravest suspicions among most of the critics. Roger pronounced the show 'a fiasco', though a few sales were cheering. Maynard bought two of Duncan's copies for £10 each – Pollaiuolo's *Apollo and Daphne* and a detail of a Piero. Vanessa gave Sickert a Bronzino detail which he had admired. Nina, usually critical of Vanessa's work, thought her exhibits the best in the show. Gertler was appreciative and over the next few months saw a good deal of Fry. He wrote to Carrington: 'I was so encouraged today by Roger Fry's appreciation and understanding of my work and especially my statue, which so few people can make anything of.'[8]

In July, Clive launched into print again. He took Ottoline at her word – that he 'should be a traitor to civilization' if he did not spend the mornings writing and 'mustn't dream of farm work'. In a *Burlington* article he lambasted contemporary English painting as provincial, inveterately sub-urban, and completely adrift from European currents. Inevitably, he draws on the old English/French comparison, urging the English painter to look to Paris both for painting and for an example of civilization. Surprisingly, he has praise for other than French painters – Larionov, Goncharova, the Italian Futurists, Kandinsky, and the Munich school. There was nothing comparable in England – even Sickert was ignored, though possibly because he belonged to an earlier generation. Of the Camden Town Group he writes: 'Theirs is no vulgar provincialism; but in its lack of receptivity, its too wily aloofness from foreign influences, its tendency to concentrate on a mediocre and rather middle-class ideal of honesty it is, I suspect, typically British.' Vorticism is swept under the carpet as 'a little backwater . . . as insipid as any other puddle of provincialism' and Eric Gill is pursued by 'those twin hags insularity and wilful influence'.

Not only is the essay sharply dismissive but, less usual, a streak of bitterness drives through the prose. The pent-up frustration of life at

Garsington and the interminable weariness of the War seem to be vented on the unfortunate English painter. As was to be expected Bell exempted Fry and the Omega circle from his attack.

The appearance of this vitriolic essay coincided with an exhibition of work by Fry and his circle and some contemporary French painters entitled 'The New Movement in Art'. Fry had been invited by the Royal Birmingham Society of Artists to make a selection of work by young painters representative of the 'New Movement'. It opened in Birmingham in mid-July and two months later came to London, with some additions, to be shown at the Mansard Gallery in Heal's Furniture Shop at 195 Tottenham Court Road. In Birmingham the show had, in Fry's words 'created some indignation and interest', but writing to Vanessa he added that 'except for Gertler we are fearfully tasteful'. Many of the pictures came from his own collection, among them three Marchands, a Gris, a Derain, a Friesz, two Vlamincks, a Lhote, and a bronze head by Brancusi. Of the English painters, Nina Hamnett had the largest showing with eleven paintings, there were seven by Fry, eight by Vanessa, and nine by Duncan. The 'tasteless' Gertler showed four works, among them two recent ones, *The Mill* and *The Pond*. Of that 'backwater' Vorticism, there was no sign. In London a group of thirty watercolours by the American E. McKnight Kauffer was simultaneously shown at Heal's. It was about this time that Fry wanted Kauffer to relieve him of the editorship of the *Burlington Magazine*, a post he also offered to Aldous Huxley. In December 1918 some of the American's work was on sale at the Omega.

Vanessa's *Portrait of Mary Hutchinson* (plate 107), first shown the year before and highly praised by Sickert in the *Burlington*, again created a strong impression. Duncan sent mainly older work such as *The Ass, Pamela, The Lemon Gatherers* and the Asheham *Lytton Strachey* of 1913, the last two lent by Clive, as were Vlaminck's *Poissy-le-Pont* and a Friesz landscape. The exhibition sold well and Michael Sadler bought eight pictures including Vanessa's *Bottles*, now known as *Triple Alliance* (plate 105), one of her most successful and uninhibited collages. The sales were particularly heartening in this bleak period. Nina Hamnett was able on her proceeds to move from her squalid Camden Town lodging to begin a lifelong affair with Fitzroy Street, where she took a studio.

At Charleston, the world of exhibitions, of publishing and art politics seemed very distant. The grind of farmwork continued (worsened by appalling weather in the winter). Vanessa's two boys rampaged in healthy high spirits and Bunny taught Julian some basic science. Vanessa continued furnishing the house while Duncan planned the garden and painted on his free Sundays. As the year went on his health deteriorated and in November his working hours were reduced to afternoons only. There were many visitors. Molly MacCarthy, peregrinating to avoid the bombs in Chelsea, came with her children Rachel, Dermott and Michael. Rachel made a splendid Ottoline in a play devised for the adults by Julian, and Michael was in disgrace for using, for want of anything else, a fine edition of a French novel as lavatory paper. In late August, Lytton arrived and in the evenings read 'Cardinal Manning' and 'Florence Nightingale' – Vanessa criticized the

105. *Triple Alliance*, 1915, by Vanessa Bell. 33 × 25 in. Weetwood Hall, Leeds. Vanessa Bell used collage much less than Duncan Grant in her work. This painting, bought by Sir Michael Sadler in 1917, uses newspaper, bottle labels, maps and a used cheque

style, Duncan slept, weary from farmwork, and Bunny soaked it all up, grasping its implications as the first explosive 'post-War' book. This was the first of Lytton's almost annual summer visits to Charleston until his death.

In the first week of September Clive stayed at Charleston with Mary Hutchinson. The house was rather primitive for Clive's taste – 'very pleasant, dirty and uncomfortable' – after Garsington's well-manured beds of roses. His son Quentin writes: 'his children greeted him with excited joy. They were moved, not only by affection, but by a feeling that, in coming to Charleston, he brought something of the great world. He would come in a taxi from the station, at this time any kind of motor vehicle at Charleston was an event; then he was likely to bring chocolate which, in the third year of the war, was the gastronomic equivalent of a taxi; then too he would bring a lovely companion who, from her hand-bag or band-box, might produce anything from a storybook to a toy-theatre.'[9]

Domestic drawbacks mattered nothing to Roger – squalor was his element and he rejoiced in tackling practical problems. But he was a rather difficult and, through his own choosing, an infrequent guest. He was charming of

106. *Portrait of Mary Hutchinson*, 1915, by Duncan Grant. $24\frac{1}{2} \times 17\frac{1}{4}$ in. Private Collection.

107. *Portrait of Mary Hutchinson*, 1915, by Vanessa Bell. 30×23 in. Collection Mrs Pamela Diamand. Vanessa Bell wrote to Roger Fry (February 1915): 'On Friday we painted Mary. Duncan got very desperate and began his again which I think I ought to have done too but I didn't. It is a frightfully difficult arrangement for I'm bang in front of her and everything is very straight and simple and very delicate in colour.' Vanessa Bell did begin another version which is in the Tate Gallery, London

course, brimming with ideas and theories and well-considered gossip – the news from Fitzroy Street, who was with whom and why, Nina's latest adventure, Sickert's madcap disguises, the latest of studio love-life. But it was mainly for Vanessa's benefit; it was Vanessa he had come to see. With Duncan, though on the friendliest of terms when they met, he was still apprehensive; Duncan was the barrier between Roger and Vanessa and their former intimate understanding which he vainly tried to recapture. Bunny he regarded as some silent, unproductive barnacle on the bows of the splendid galleon that was Vanessa as she sailed serenely through all the driftwood around her.

Generally, Roger was kept busy in London by the Omega. He wrote to Vanessa in June 1917 saying, 'I should like to kill it personally, but I don't think it would be right to do so and if it should survive after the war, there will be giant hopes.'[(10)] And so it went on, at times exciting, at others a tiresome interference with his writing and above all his painting. During the autumn and winter he was engrossed in several portraits – of Lalla Vandervelde, of Iris Tree's actress sister Viola, and of Nina Hamnett (plate 99). For several months Roger and Nina had been having an easy, friendly affair. She was high-spirited and generous, a francophile, and very companionable. She enjoyed his perfect manners, his eagerness to explore life, and the often interesting company that assembled at his studio or, during weekends, at Durbins. She also sat a great deal for drawings and paintings – as she did a little later to Duncan. One drawing of Duncan's in particular vividly catches her lightness as she leans against a fireplace, laughing and waving a cigarette in the air.

Following the success of the 'New Movement' exhibition at Heal's, a small show was held at the Omega in November and attracted good notices and several sales, which in turn helped business in the Workshops. *The Times* reviewer was particularly complimentary to Duncan, noticing especially his growing individual fluency in the handling of paint. Virginia Woolf was a visitor and wrote to Duncan about his pictures there: 'I liked the one over the fireplace immensely: the green and blue one, I mean, which seemed to me divinely romantic and imaginative. Lord! how tired I got of those sturdy pots and pans with red billiard balls attached to them! I daresay I am saying all the wrong things – I was taken round by Roger, and felt innumerable eggs crack beneath me. I was very much struck by his sensibility: he showed me minute patches of black, and scrapings of a sort of graining upon which the whole composition depended. And I believe it did too. Certainly, it is a most remarkable art.'[(11)] In the next month Roger showed twenty flower pieces at the Carfax Gallery in Bury Street and sold most of them. 'I don't think there's any compromise in them,' he wrote to Pamela, 'it's just that the subject is so pleasant.' The best of the flower pieces were those in which Fry succumbed most readily to the charm of the subject – such as *The Lily*, bought by the Contemporary Art Society. The more formalized and 'abstracted' ones appeared dehydrated. Academic was the word for them, quickly pounced on by those who still saw Fry as an anarchist in the English art scene.

108. Mary Hutchinson at Charleston, 1917, in front of *The Tub* (plate 109) by Vanessa Bell. Mary Hutchinson (*née* Barnes), a cousin of Duncan Grant, married St. John Hutchinson in 1910. She was a valuable patron of the Omega Workshops and commissioned decorative work from Grant and Vanessa Bell for her house at Hammersmith and later at Regent's Park

109. *The Tub*, 1917, by Vanessa Bell. 71 × 66 in. The Tate Gallery, London. The picture can be seen at an earlier stage in plate 108. The round tub itself seems a distillation of the silent, reflective mood of the figure – a psychological territory explored in many of Vanessa Bell's domestic subjects

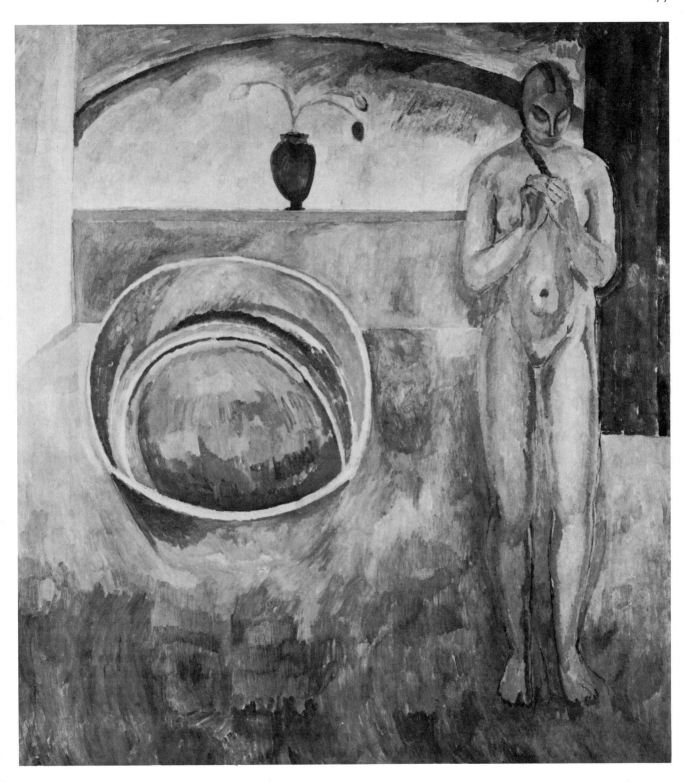

While the show was on, Duncan and Bunny came up to London for a week's holiday and Clive arrived from Garsington. Roger wrote to Vanessa, 'Clive suggested a great historical portrait group of Bloomsbury. I think I shall have a shot at it, it would be rather fun. Lytton, Maynard, Clive, Duncan, me, you, Virginia, Mary, Molly, Desmond. Is there anyone else that ought to be in? P'raps Walter Sickert coming in at the door and looking at us all with a kind of benevolent cynicism.'[12] Already it seems Roger thinks of Bloomsbury as in the past – 'historical' – looking back to the few intense years before the War when everyone constantly saw each other and stayed together for weeks on end, and when there was leisure and freedom.[13]

[1] VB to RF, September 1917. The decoration was purchased by the Tate Gallery in 1975.

[2] VB to RF, 22 February 1918.

[3] VB to RF, 3 August 1917.

[4] Fry bought several of Wolfe's drawings and one was published in the *Burlington Magazine* with others by Grant, Sickert, Gaudier-Brzeska and Nina Hamnett, all illustrations to Fry's article 'Line as a Means of Expression', December 1918.

[5] 6 November 1917.

[6] Vanessa Bell designed the jackets for all her sister's books published by the Hogarth Press and illustrated *Flush*, 1933. She also designed the jacket for Henry Green's *Back*, 1946. Duncan Grant did the cover for *Olivia* by Olivia, 1949. Other artists who worked for the Hogarth Press include John Banting and Graham Sutherland.

[7] Barbara Bagenal quoted in 'Jacques Copeau and Duncan Grant', by D. Sutton in *Apollo*, August 1967.

[8] 15 May 1917. He is referring to *Acrobats*, now in the Tate Gallery.

[9] 'Clive Bell at Charleston', catalogue introduction by Q. Bell to an exhibition at the Gallery Edward Harvane, 1972.

[10] 11 June 1917.

[11] VW to DG, 17 December 1917.

[12] 12 December 1917.

[13] It is interesting to note the omission of Leonard Woolf's name. A decade earlier this would not have been surprising, for he was then in Ceylon. Already his political activities were drawing him into a world with which Bloomsbury was unfamiliar and of which they inclined to be dismissive. How could Leonard sit on these earnest committees? The fluctuating nature of the group is illustrated also by the inclusion of Mary Hutchinson, an inclusion that would have appeared, I think, highly suspect to Vanessa for one and certainly to Mrs Hutchinson herself. She knew well all the people mentioned by Roger (and was related to Duncan and Lytton), but knew them more as individuals among a varied circle of friends. She told Vanessa that she was 'outside and not of Bloomsbury' and that 'she disagreed fundamentally from [them] all in many ways. . . .' Her shy and perhaps proud temperament was often mistaken for a standoffish arrogance, an easy target for malicious badinage. It was her poise, her way of confronting life at exactly the pitch which circumstances demanded that caused disagreements in Bloomsbury.

During the winter of 1917–18 Roger received a new kind of commission for the Omega. Helped by Edward Wolfe, he did the sets and costumes for Act I of a play by Israel Zangwill, *Too Much Money*, starring Lillah MacCarthy, which opened in Glasgow and later ran at the Ambassadors Theatre in London. Fry was also working on the decoration of some virginals made by Arnold Dolmetsch. The outside of the case was treated in an abstract, marbled manner, mellow in colour, and on the inside of the lid was a rather cramped nude female in a tight, dry style. 'Your design for the virginal does look very antique but I don't see that matters as it will depend on how it's done,' wrote Vanessa disingenuously. She was painting the doors in Duncan's Charleston bedroom and on 19 February Duncan had begun 'an enormous painting about six feet by five – an interior of the dining room here with me painting and Bunny writing, taking in three walls and a great deal of floor and ceiling. It's lovely colour of course and I think should be very interesting space. He's doing it entirely from sketches and drawings.'[1] This is one of the largest and structurally most complex of Duncan's long series of Charleston interiors (plate 111) and bears comparison with the *Man at a Table* (*c.* 1925) and *Girl at the Piano* (1940). The design is governed by the central axis of the bowl of fruit on a stand, vertically continued above in the tall chair back and strip of illuminated wall, and below in its reflection on the table top running through the books at David Garnett's elbow and the table leg and chair spindle in the foreground. Around this axis a variety of orthogonals and curves emphasizes a space that is very confined and intimate. The strong vertical lines of the curtains and fireplace converge on the curve established in the central cross-section – through Vanessa's back, her head and the nearby sharply lit jug, the window-sill, the bowl on the table to the right, through the arms of the chair and the hunched figure of David Garnett at the edge. The heavy curve of his arm begins a shallower concave through the books, the top of the chair, the bottom of the picture on the easel, and up to Vanessa's painting arm and head. This multiplicity of line juxtaposed with the echoing of shapes – the canvas and the small window, the bowl of fruit and the vase of flowers on the mantelpiece – contributes to a highly wrought design of great gravity, the paint applied with more deliberation and solidity than is usual (compare for instance the *Vanessa Bell at Charleston* of the previous year – plate VII. It foreshadows the new post-War direction that Duncan's painting was to take.

On a brief visit to London in March, Duncan picked up a catalogue in Roger's studio of the forthcoming sale of Degas's picture collection at the

110. Omega Screen 'Provençal Valley', 1913, by Roger Fry. Private Collection. In October 1913 Fry was with Henri Doucet in Provence and discovered a valley at Aramon near Avignon which is the subject of this screen. Exhibited in January 1914, second Grafton Group Exhibition

Galerie Georges Petit in Paris. He was greatly excited by the illustrations and tackled Maynard on the possibility of his persuading the Treasury to draft money for the National Gallery to buy from the auction. Maynard liked the idea. A few days later, at Charleston, he went through the catalogue with Duncan and Vanessa and became very enthusiastic, especially over the Cézannes. On 21 March Duncan was gloomily working on the farm when he was handed a telegram from Maynard: 'Money secured for pictures.' Two days later Maynard wrote to Vanessa that he was leaving for Paris the following morning as the sale coincided with a financial conference which he had to attend.

My picture coup was a whirlwind affair – carried through in a day and a half before anyone had time to reflect what they were doing. I have secured 550,000 francs to play with; Holmes[2] is travelling out with us and I hope we shall be able to attend the sale together. The prime object

111. *Interior*, 1918, by
Duncan Grant. The Ulster
Museum, Belfast. Vanessa
Bell painting and David
Garnett writing in the
dining room, Charleston

is to buy Ingres; his portrait of himself being first choice; after that the Perroneau. I think Holmes also has his eye on a Greco but admits there would be another chance for this. I am fairly sure I can persuade him to go for the Delacroix Schwiter; I shall try very hard on the journey out to persuade him to buy a Cézanne as a personal reward to me for having got him the money, but I think his present intention is not to buy a Cézanne; I have not yet discussed the question of Corot with him.

Duncan and Vanessa's original plan was to get Roger to see Charles Holmes and advise him over the purchases. But Roger was at Poole throwing pots for the Omega. So their hopes were placed – a little uneasily – on Maynard's powers of persuasion. The sale took place on 26 and 27 March while Paris was being shelled, the Germans having broken through the Allied lines. Consequently, bidding was slow though excitement mounted when the National Gallery secured Delacroix's *Baron de Schwiter* against keen competition from the Louvre. Maynard bought for himself an Ingres drawing *Femme Nue* for 1,900 francs, a small painting by Delacroix, *Cheval au Pâturage*, a study by Delacroix for the Palais Bourbon decorations and a still life *Pommes* by Cézanne for 9,000 francs. On the following day, Duncan, Vanessa, Clive and Bunny were finishing dinner at Charleston when a tired and hungry Maynard arrived. Vanessa takes up the story in a letter to Roger:

> Maynard came back suddenly and unexpectedly late at night having been dropped at the bottom of the lane by Austen Chamberlain in a Government motor and said he had left a Cézanne by the roadside! Duncan rushed off to get it and you can imagine how exciting it all was. . . . Holmes' purchases are idiotic considering his chances. He wouldn't hear of Cézanne and in the end didn't spend all the money but came back with £5,000 unspent and no El Greco which he might easily have had. He did get the Delacroix *Baron de Norvins* [Vanessa has confused the *Baron de Schwiter* with another purchase, Ingres's *Baron de Norvins*], *Angelica and Roger* by Ingres and I think some drawings, a Corot landscape (not one illustrated), Manet's *Lady with a Cat*, a Gauguin still life. I can't remember the rest. Maynard got for himself the Cézanne *Apples*, a wonderful Ingres drawing, a small picture by Delacroix and a drawing by Delacroix which he's given to Duncan. The Cézanne is really amazing and it's most exciting to have in the house.

A Cézanne in a private collection was rare indeed; there was none in a public collection. Maynard's acquisition soon became an object of pilgrimage for younger painters like Mark Gertler. Other pictures bought by the National Gallery – whose purchases were kept secret until the end of the War – included two other Ingres paintings, another Delacroix, the fragments of Manet's *Execution of Maximilien*, and a painting each by Forain, Ricard and Rousseau and drawings by David, Ingres and Delacroix.

This was the real beginning of Maynard's collection. Later purchases belong to his years of growing personal wealth, and behind most of them lay the advice of Duncan and Vanessa: a telephone call about a Derain for sale;

112. Duncan Grant,
Maynard Keynes and Clive
Bell in the garden at
Charleston, 1919

'We have seen two very fine Segonzacs – 1 landscape and 1 still life. What about them?'; a last-minute telegram from Duncan over a Seurat sketch for the *Grande Jatte*; a commanding letter from Vanessa. To have Maynard and his money there on the spot, to be able to persuade him to buy, these were the compensations for relative poverty. But Maynard fully appreciated the situation and was only too willing to concede. His respect for Vanessa and Duncan as creative artists, amounting it seems to a kind of humility, was all-embracing.

In April, all conscientious objection exemptions were withdrawn and the military had the power to call up the COs. It looked as if Duncan and Bunny would be among the first to feel the effects of this measure, although Vanessa believed that Duncan at any rate would be medically rejected. But Duncan meanwhile was engaged on a project of his own, namely to try for a commission to paint a picture under the War Artists scheme. It was a tantalising prospect but some of his friends had grave doubts about such a move. Would it not put his position as a CO in some danger? Was it worth becoming entangled with the authorities in this way, having so far successfully if painfully avoided them? He would be exchanging one kind of captivity for another. But his excitement at the idea of being free from agricultural work blurred these considerations. After an initial refusal, the Pelham Committee agreed to his release and Robert Ross, a member of the committee of the British War Memorials scheme whose recommendations secured the appointment of official war artists, informed Duncan that he would soon be painting for the Ministry of Information instead of hay harvesting that summer. The subject of the picture was of course important – Duncan and Ross met to discuss this in London:

> My dear Ross, It was such a pleasure to see you yesterday, and I fear I did not express any of the gratitude I feel to you for taking all these pains for me. I dare not dwell on the possibility of success, but in any case I shall always be grateful to you. I think if there is yet time I should not suggest the German prisoners. I do not think it's a very good subject – they only work in batches of 5 with a guard standing over them in a bare field. In fact any subject but this I should like. What about an aeroplane factory? Roger suggested this and I expect it is full of possibilities. But after all any subject you are likely to suggest, I am willing to do – but I would rather it was not, on second thoughts the German prisoners. . . .
> Yours sincerely Duncan Grant.[3]

In the event, the whole plan fell through due to the authorities thinking Duncan's proposed picture was pacifist in intention. And although Duncan then saw more clearly his friends' objections, the collapse of the plan brought a wave of anger and depression at yet another thwarted attempt to extricate himself from the stagnation of farm work.

At this time Vanessa found she was pregnant, the baby due in December. As Duncan was the father, Clive was informed and took the news in the best of spirits if somewhat alarmed at his own parents' reactions. Bunny was particularly uplifted by the news in this time of despair. Virginia was full of practical suggestions urging daily consumptions of milk and chocolate as 'the only way in which either of you will pull through without some temporary absence in one of those secluded houses where I'm such a brilliant success. Now, my dear Duncan, I appeal to you to carry this out, with immense confidence in your fund of masterly common sense. Milk is at your door; it is cheap; it is the only pure food left; there is nothing but a queer superstition in Nessa's mind derived I believe from Aunt Fisher against drinking it. You haven't this in your blood, I entreat you therefore drink milk twice a day, and each time think of me with tenderness.'

Roger, goaded perhaps by the circumstances of Vanessa's pregnancy, tried once more to regain some of the lost territory of his relationship with her. In June and part of July, he was staying at Bo Peep cottage in the Downs between Firle and Berwick villages, conveniently nearby. 'I lead a very retired and quiet existence here,' he wrote to his sister Margery[4] '– not quite hermit-like, for I'm near to Charleston where Vanessa Bell and D. Grant

113. *Portrait of Gabrielle
Soëne*, 1919, by Roger Fry.
50 × 30⅛ in. The
Metropolitan Museum of
Art, New York, Gift of Mrs
Pamela Diamand, 1959. A
French dressmaker, Mlle
Soëne helped at the Omega
and exhibited her costumes
there in November 1918.
Edward Wolfe painted her at
the same time as Fry, later
replacing the background
with a landscape

live, and go in occasionally. Tho' I don't ever really see her so. The only way is to get her out of her domestic hole – she's too absorbed in that to really notice one's existence, so that I get very little out of it.' In fact this was rather a restrained account of an experience which he later called 'that nightmare of a time at Bo Peep which nearly ended in a complete smash up of our friendship.'[5] He was profoundly depressed by the coolness of Vanessa's reception, the absence of any welcome so it seemed. His affair with Nina Hamnett had come to an end earlier in the year; he was lonely and miserable and physically unwell. In times like this, he looked to Vanessa for comfort and support, but she remained aloof. She was indifferent, she was callous – so Roger supposed – entirely taken up with Duncan and her household, determined to put an end to their friendship. Indeed it is difficult to discover Vanessa's attitude to Roger at this particular moment – over and above, that is, her deep admiration and love of him as a friend. Perhaps his proximity seemed to encroach on her private world at Charleston. Perhaps she felt Roger was unreasonably jealous of Duncan. But a reconciliation came about later in the summer. Roger was to love Vanessa for some time to come, although he was neither self-effacing in his attitude nor uncritical of it: 'I am myself again now, you know, after all these years of not being. All sorts of things I'd suppressed because they didn't meet with anything in you are coming back. It's a very queer stage. I don't like myself any better, but I'm no longer disgusted with it for not being exactly like you or what you like or admire.'[6]

The later mood of their friendship is suggested in another letter:

> There are moments when I have to stop myself from letting a lot of old feelings come to the top, but I can stop them now. Lord, it's taken me a time to get to it hasn't it, but now it seems a pity I shouldn't see a great deal of you as I can get so much pleasure and such rare moments of pain and I expect I can be nicer to you than I used.
>
> I think it's really the greatest compliment I could pay you to have thought it worth-while to go on through all those years to get to this, don't you? . . .[7]

This was not the only upset between friends that year. In the autumn Clive was involved in two quarrels – 'plots of the Ottoline type' as Vanessa called them. The first concerned the supposedly disparaging views held by Clive's friends towards Mary Hutchinson, and in the subsequent quarrel Virginia was branded as culprit, but on suspicion only. The second involved Clive and Maynard and the domestic arrangements of the house they now shared at 46 Gordon Square. There were accusations of financial dishonesty and an involved story concerning the misuse of Clive's spare bed. Some very nasty things were said. Clive felt Maynard was becoming too grand and behaving in a thoughtless, arrogant manner – a symptom of the bad effects of growing fame and influence. Clive had earlier struck out at Maynard in an unfavourable comparison with Lytton who at the time was basking in the astonishing success of *Eminent Victorians*, accepting every invitation with a mixture of amusement, flattery, bewilderment, and outright scorn. A publisher's

cheque would often come in the same post as some scented or coroneted envelope 'requesting the pleasure of . . .'.

'I gather Duncan does not go quite all the way with Maynard in thinking Lady Cunard the most intelligent, sensitive, disinterested and high-minded woman alive. How far does he go? I was pleased to notice that contact with the great seemed to have spun very few cobwebs in old Lytton's beard. I believe he still takes Margot [Asquith] for a vulgar and slightly disgusting woman,' wrote Clive in a letter to Vanessa in July 1918.

It was an old argument, this effect of fame, of brushing shoulders with the rich and the ensuing contamination. One rushed back from the squares of Mayfair, from dinners with dukes, parties with princesses, the loops and tendrils of titles catching at one's back, and sank into a chair in Gordon Square. Had one caught something, were spots already breaking out? One's friends gathered round probing and prodding and after some severe X-raying, would pronounce. Of course, when they did, one had already gone up to bed. The diagnosis was put away among the other record cards of one's character. There was Desmond frittering his days away with the Asquiths – how could he enjoy such a thing? And Maynard weekending at the Wharf or off to the McKennas (the Chancellor of the Exchequer and his wife). What could his motives be? More often than not at this time, it was Maynard who came under scrutiny. Not only was he culpable of snobbery as they thought, but it seemed likely that his important position at the Treasury would ruin his brain and corrupt his character as he fell into the unscrupulous arms of politicians. While Maynard was certainly irritated by his friends' criticisms of him, they had their effect. 'It was because his friends kept him aware of the danger that he might, for the sake of a brilliant official career, be a party to bringing about terrible evils, that he finally took the course he did in resigning his post rather than accept the reparations clauses of the Peace Treaty. That resignation led to the writing of *The Economic Consequences of the Peace* which was the foundation of his subsequent fame.'[8] Clive, in his memoir of Maynard Keynes written years later, took the same line: 'Cabinet Ministers and *The Times* might praise, but if he had an uneasy suspicion that Lytton Strachey, Duncan Grant, Virginia Woolf and Vanessa Bell did not share their enthusiasm, public flattery might appear something to be ashamed of.'[9]

While there was much talk of peace in September and October, most people remained sceptical: 'Julian says you had a fit at dinner on hearing about the Peace Proposals. Well it's all very exciting but I remain rather stunned and absolutely unresponsive, except to Sheppard's wild excitement and the general good humour which surrounds us. I don't really dare to think of Peace, it seems a joke,' Duncan wrote to Bunny from London where he was on holiday with Vanessa for a fortnight, decorating Maynard's sitting room. Maynard had given Duncan and Vanessa this commission in the summer and they had worked intermittently on designs for the large folding doors which were in the room that had once been Vanessa's studio. It was exhilarating to be in London, with Maynard arranging parties and outings, and visits to the Russian Ballet. There was an exciting rumour that Diaghilev was going to commission the Omega Workshops to design sets and costumes for a new ballet – Duncan to do the dresses, Roger and Edward Wolfe the sets. Then Clive said he had heard that Duncan alone was going to be asked. Wyndham Lewis had also heard this rumour and took the opportunity to spit at Duncan when they met in the street one day. But like the Peace Proposals, the project unfortunately 'fizzled out'.

The Russian Ballet had not appeared in London since 1914, Nijinski was gone but there were two new dancers, Massine and Lydia Lopokova.

The most popular of its [the Russian Ballet's] productions – and in consequence that given most often – was a ballet based on Goldoni's comedy of the same name, *The Good-Humoured Ladies*, danced to music arranged by Vincente Tommasini from some of the five hundred sonatas of Domenico Scarlatti's and given a simple Guardi-like setting by Léon Bakst. In this work it was the grace, pathos, entrancing cleverness, the true comic genius and liveliness of a dancer new to this country

Lydia Lopokova, which made the chief impression. . . . Her face too was appealing, inquisitive, bird-like, that of a mask of comedy, while, being an artist in everything, she comprehended exactly the span and the limits of her capacities: the personification of gaiety, of spontaneity, and of that particular pathos which is its complement, she had developed the movements of her hands and arms in a way that hitherto no dancer had attempted, thereby achieving a new step forward in technique.[10]

Lopokova was obviously delighted to be the centre of such admiration; at the numerous parties for the Russian Ballet her vivid response to the unexpected, her sense of fun, and her racy, imperfect English captivated all who met her, in particular Maynard Keynes whose wife she became in 1925. The party at which they first met was given by the three Sitwells in Osbert's house in Swan Walk, Chelsea, after a performance of *Schéhérazade*. 'Jack [St. John Hutchinson] kept telling us,' wrote Duncan to Bunny the following day, 'in a raucous whisper to stop talking, but I am getting so used to Society that even the worst social dilemmas pass me by only perceived with a bland smile. The smart set were there, terrible creatures all and exactly alike. And Ottoline really resplendent in her yellow Spanish gown with little Lopokhova in blue in tow.'[11] The food and drink were memorably good. Lopokova christened a stuffed canary 'Pimp' in deference to its less colourful companions in a glass case. Among the other guests were Edward Wolfe, 'Chile' Guevara – just back from painting in Cornwall where he had seen a ghost – the Hutchinsons and Clive 'who roared at the top of his voice to everyone.' Virginia was also present and at the centre of some plot against Ottoline, but it 'meant no more than that we withdrew to somebody's bedroom in great numbers and left Ottoline, got up to look precisely like the Spanish Armada in full sail, in possession of the drawing room.'[12]

Bloomsbury was very much involved with the Ballet this time and there were regular visits to the Coliseum. They were fascinated by the changes that had been made in the décor and choreography since its last London season. Roger started a correspondence with Larionov and Goncharova; he showed some of Larionov's marionette designs at the Omega in February 1919 and wrote a highly appreciative article about him for the *Burlington Magazine*. Clive wrote a graceful poem to Lopokova, Roger asked her to sit to him in costume; Duncan was visited by Massine in Fitzroy Street. (The dancer arrived at the top of the stairs still sweating and exhausted after a performance.) Lopokova's dressing room was besieged by admirers, usually taken there by Ottoline. Bunny went on one visit; on another, Ottoline took Aldous Huxley, Gertler and Dorothy Brett – 'we all went round to the back afterwards to see Lopokova, the première danseuse, who is ravishing – finding there no less a person than André Gide, who looks like a baboon with the voice, manners and education of Bloomsbury in French.'[13] Pre-War memories surfaced for a while with the gaiety of the Ballet. Its survival was immensely reassuring and its appearance an omen of Peace. When Duncan returned to Charleston, to thrashing and mangling, he felt refreshed in spirit.

115. *Dancers*, 1917, by
Duncan Grant. $18\frac{1}{2} \times 26\frac{1}{4}$
in. Victoria and Albert
Museum, London. A
decorative panel for the
Omega Workshops, possibly
suggested by a drawing of
Blake's

But there was plenty to do besides farm-work: new servants to deal with and the children to look after. Not least there was to be a show at the Omega and Roger was eager for new work to be dispatched.

It was not a large exhibition and was mainly devoted to the Omega artists but it attracted attention and had favourable reviews.[14] Roger showed a portrait of his new friend Gide (bought by Arnold Bennett) and a study of Charleston from the summer; Vanessa a still life; Duncan a *Flower Piece* which was singled out as 'the picture that comes nearest perhaps to complete expression than anything in the room'. There were works by Gertler, Benjamin Corea, Sickert, Gaudier-Brzeska, Edward Wolfe's portrait of Barclay Doone, watercolours by McKnight Kauffer, and a large solid portrait of a landlady by Nina Hamnett. A laudatory page was devoted to the show by John Salis writing in the *New Witness* (8 November 1918). Salis was a sympathetic and perceptive reviewer of work by younger painters such as Guevara, Wolfe and, above all, Nina Hamnett, but he pointed out that Wolfe 'may go in danger of being hypnotized by his own fluency'. He found the drawings by Gaudier-Brzeska and Sickert the most interesting things in the exhibition. He ended the review with praise for the Omega: 'It is a tribute to his [Fry's] talent that the Omega has managed to last through times so troublous and so polemic. That it has a message to English decoration and that the future of English decorative art will owe him a debt seem certain.' But 'the times so troublous and so polemic' had taken their toll and this in fact was the last show of paintings at the Workshops.

Then, very suddenly, after a rush of decisions and hasty ceasefires, the War was over. So quick was the end that people could hardly believe the news. The immediate relief was immense. Many have recorded the abandon and riotous joy of the crowds on that day, 11 November, as they swirled in the streets, drink flowing, strangers kissing, a bonfire scorching Nelson's column, the music, laughter and speed, the disregard of the steady and inevitable rain. Many of the people mentioned in this book gathered some time during that day at the collector Montague Shearman's elegant flat in the Adelphi. The news of the party spread like wildfire – 'Mary Hutchinson told us that everyone would be welcome at Monty Shearman's flat. . . .' Mary and St. John Hutchinson and Lytton had come up from the country that day. Shearman himself had been lunching at the Eiffel Tower in Percy Street. So had the Sitwell brothers, the Huxley brothers, and Carrington. He asked them all. He ran into Nina Hamnett and asked her (already the worse for wear after two bottles of champagne in Trafalgar Square). After the Ballet, Diaghilev, Massine and Lopokova arrived. There was Ottoline, the D. H. Lawrences, Gertler, Clive, Maynard, Duncan and Bunny. Lytton was observed dancing. And was it this night or later that 'Augustus John appeared, amid cheers, in his British officer's uniform, accompanied by some land-girls in leggings and breeches who brought a fresh feeling of the country into the overheated room'? Lawrence gloomily pronounced on the horrors to come, the uncertain but certainly terrible future. Later in the evening, Bloomsbury gathered at Gordon Square voicing similar sentiments.

When life returned to normal, the revelling over, and farm-work resumed until notice of discharge, it was naturally Vanessa's welfare that concerned her friends. On Christmas Day at two o'clock in the morning, a baby girl was born. 'It was very romantic that first Christmas of peace and a most lovely moonlit, frosty night. I remember waking up – the early morning after she had been born and hearing the farm men come up to work singing carols and realizing it was Christmas Day and it seemed rather extraordinary to have a baby then. . . .'[15] Maynard, Duncan and Bunny were in the house. At first, Susannah, as the child was temporarily called, seemed to be doing well. Then she started losing weight and the local dotard of a doctor administered medicines which only made her worse. Vanessa's milk was suspected. There were consultations and correspondences with doctors – Maurice Craig in London and Saxon Sydney Turner's father in Brighton. Eventually a wild wire to Noel Olivier, recently qualified as a doctor, turned up trumps in the shape of an enormous, genial and capable woman, Dr Marie Moralt, who arrived and installed herself. Moralt believed the local doctor was murdering the baby with carbolic but he was difficult to countermand, having a strong prejudice against lady doctors. But Moralt won, took charge of the case, brushing aside professional etiquette and the baby soon improved. Following this unpleasant experience came a series of those domestic crises which seemed to have dogged every Bloomsbury household at remorseless intervals. A thieving maid threw things at Vanessa and was dismissed. Julian and Quentin were shuttled from Asheham where they were too much for Virginia, to their father in Gordon Square. The cook left and no replacement

116. *Woman in Furs*, 1919, by Vanessa Bell. $26\frac{7}{8} \times 22\frac{3}{16}$ in. The Fitzwilliam Museum, Cambridge. A portrait of Dr Marie Moralt painted in May 1919 at Charleston. Duncan Grant's picture done at the same time is in a private collection, London

was to be had. Virginia sent her own cook Nelly for three weeks. Eventually the turmoil ceased; Vanessa was able to get up, though still weak from exhaustion and worry, Duncan began to paint, and the baby, now named Angelica, recovered. Marie Moralt came once more, however, and sat for her portrait to Duncan and Vanessa. 'She's simply wonderful to paint', wrote Vanessa to Roger, and her pleasure is evident in the witty picture which resulted (plate 116). Peace and leisure to work came at last to Charleston.

But in London the terrible epidemic of Spanish influenza had struck, carrying off, among many others, the painter Harold Gilman. Edward Wolfe also caught it, and only just recovered. 'The Omega is almost completely devasted with 'flu. Mr and Mrs Upton [the caretaker and his wife] both laid up – she's quite bad with bronchitis and today Paice [the accountant] says he thinks he's beginning it – poor Wolfe is dangerously ill with pneumonia and has to have a trained nurse. He can only take Brandy and milk. They could get none for him so I had to get a bottle from Richard, 30/–!! I hear from Paice that he's a little better this morning so I hope he will get thro' but I've been very worried.'[16]

Then of course the 'vile English' made the running of the Omega impossible: the accounts were a disaster, unknown debts turned up, nobody came to the Private View of Larionov and some children's drawings, Nina was gone, Wolfe ill, masses of furniture had to be painted. Roger was completely tired out and on top of everything was moving to a new house with his daughter Pamela and sister Margery.

[1] VB to RF, 22 February 1918.

[2] Sir Charles Holmes, director of the National Gallery, London. Sir Charles wrote his own account of the Degas Sale in his memoirs *Self and Partners*, Constable, 1936.

[3] *Robert Ross, Friend of Friends*, ed. M. Ross, 1952, p.328.

[4] 2 June 1918.

[5] RF to Pippa Strachey, 17 September 1918.

[6] RF to VB, 15 June 1916.

[7] RF to VB 28 August 1919.

[8] D. Garnett, *The Flowers of the Forest*, 1955, p.150.

[9] Clive Bell, *Old Friends*, 1956, p.50.

[10] Osbert Sitwell, *Laughter in the Next Room*, 1949, pp.13–14.

[11] DG to LS, 13 October 1918.

[12] VW to LS, 12 October.

[13] A. Huxley to Juliette Baillot, 14 September 1918, Collected Letters of A. Huxley.

[14] Simultaneously, on the ground floor of Fitzroy Square, was a small show of dresses designed by a young French girl, Gabrielle Soëne – 'an extremely subtle artist' – mainly using Omega fabrics.

[15] VB to M. K. Snowdon, 25 December 1923.

[16] RF to VB, 20 January 1919.

After what she called 'the most awful time I've ever had in my life' Vanessa gradually recovered and could report in February 1919 that she was 'sane and in fair health and the baby is getting fat quickly'. The domestic disasters seemed to resolve themselves but it was some time before she felt able to spend days in London. Her feelings about Charleston as a home were so mixed that at first it was difficult to see the house in the light of peacetime. It was heavy with War associations and it was two or three years before she became free of them. She had spent more time in the house than anyone and, inevitably, dealing with domestic practicalities during the War had darkened her initial enthusiasm. But with the possibility of visits to London – she had taken in 1919 Alix Sargent-Florence's flat at 36 Regent Square – and the renewed chance of travelling abroad, she began to see Charleston's advantages as a home for her children in the summer, and a place where she could be alone if she wished and paint for lengthy periods.

Flowerbeds soon appeared in the walled garden formerly given over to vegetables. The garden itself was minutely redesigned by Harry Norton, a mathematician's plans being preferred to the erratic calculations of Duncan and Vanessa. In the orchard beyond there was a large army hut which in 1920 was converted into a studio. 'We have had a skylight put in and white-washed it and it now makes a very good studio with a good North light and heaps of room for two or three painters. Also it's very nice being some way from the house, it's so quiet.'[1] The idea of painting there in the summer was appealing and Vanessa thought a group of painters might come – there was plenty of room. 'We had Wolfe here for the week-end. He was very nice and most appreciative of the paintings we showed him – lots and lots of old things he made us rake out.'[2] He came again in May with Osbert Sitwell (plate 117). 'Little Wolfe is here and he and Duncan want to try to paint some hats which is said to be the fashion now in London. D. has written to Gabrielle [Soëne] to ask her to choose some and if the Omega would buy them for us perhaps we could try about six and sell them to Mary, Mrs Jowitt etc. It's only a small experiment and I don't suppose it will come to much but possibly people's snobbery will induce them to buy a hat painted by Duncan.'[3] André Derain was another of the painters Vanessa hoped might come to paint at Charleston. He and Picasso were both in London during the summer.

It was Derain who made the strongest impression and who felt at home with the Bells, Roger and Duncan. He arrived in May to supervise the production of *La Boutique Fantasque* for which Diaghilev had commissioned him to do the sets and costumes. Roger took him in hand – 'He's perfectly charming – a great lazy giant, very intelligent and not at all "the great man" ' – and entertained him at Dalmeney Avenue, his new house in 'the wilds of Camden Town' and introduced him to several painters. Derain particularly admired Vanessa's *Nativity* which Roger owned and it was into Vanessa's Regent Square flat that Derain moved. His unaffected and humorous character and the authority he brought to bear on aesthetic problems, as well as more practical ones, impressed the English painters. At the London Group he praised Roger's work above all – without knowing he had painted the pictures – and even a Carrington was, he found, admirable. For some years his influence in England was strong, he became 'the hero of the hour in English circles'[4] and was nowhere more applauded than in Bloomsbury.[5] His décor for *La Boutique Fantasque* had an immediate impact on stage design and its qualities are discernible in Duncan and Vanessa's interior decorations (plate 126).

Picasso's visit had a different flavour. Whereas Derain was perfectly at home in Vanessa's flat off the Gray's Inn Road, Picasso and his wife Olga lived in grander style at the Savoy. The fastidious Olga had to be well accommodated and entertained. Picasso, in evening clothes, and she in glamorous 'haute couture' were seen at smart, fashionable parties. Picasso did however find time for dinner at Dalmeney Avenue and a visit to the Omega, shortly to close, where he was much intrigued by the methods used in the painting of furniture and pottery.

At the rehearsals of the Russian Ballet, Picasso made many drawings of the dancers including some of Lydia Lopokova who was rapidly becoming deeply involved with Maynard Keynes. For part of the time she took rooms in Maynard's house, 46 Gordon Square.[6] Clive was very active in these summer festivities and there were dinners and parties in his rooms. He saw

117. Charleston group, May 1919: Quentin Bell in the foreground and l. to r. Edward Wolfe, Osbert Sitwell and Duncan Grant

Picasso put the finishing touches to the act-drop for *Le Tricorne*, the much admired scene of Spaniards in a box watching a bullfight. A sudden distraction was Lopokova's inexplicable flight from London which astonished and disappointed. Her excuse was ill health. In fact she had fled from her husband, Randolfo Barocchi, the Ballet's administrator. They had married in 1916, supposedly at Diaghilev's instigation, and were divorced in 1922. Three years later she married Maynard Keynes and settled permanently in England.

In October Matisse came to London to discuss a new ballet *Le Chant du Rossignol* for which he was to carry out the décor. It was given in Paris early the following year. While in London there was a show of his recent paintings – 'lovely but for the most part rather slight sketches', Vanessa told Roger after visiting the Leicester Galleries. 'We have induced Maynard to buy one of the best, a small seated figure with bare arms, very sober in colour, for 175 gns.[7] All are sold. He's evidently a great success nowadays.' '*Ils sont foux – les Anglais!*' was the artist's amused but grateful exclamation. Charles Vildrac was another visitor. He was called over by Matisse to bring more pictures to supplement the exhibition. He spent an evening with Duncan and Vanessa at Regent Square telling them about the War 'which made it seem more real than anything else I had heard,' Vanessa commented. Vildrac had resumed the running of his gallery in Paris, a valuable contact for English painters, some of whose work he showed in the spring of 1920. Roger's and Vanessa's paintings were particularly admired and among appreciative visitors were Rouault, Derain, Larionov and Goncharova. French pictures came swiftly over to London during the next two or three years and a precedent was set when the Sitwell brothers in collaboration with the poet-dealer Zborowski, organized an exhibition of 'Modern French Art' at Heal's Mansard Gallery in August 1919. While its reception was not as devastating as the Post-Impressionist exhibitions, it was furiously abused by the public, and philistine invective enlivened the pages of various journals. Clive was in hot water for his favorable notice in the *Nation*. 'Ten years ago I should have felt inclined to argue with some of your correspondents,' he wrote to the Editor.[8] 'To-day it would be absurd. Even *The Times* now admits officially that the battle is won. . . .' Of the masters of the modern movement, Matisse, Derain and Picasso were unrepresented. There was work by Vlaminck, Marchand and Friesz, and by two painters, as yet hardly known in England, Utrillo and Modigliani. Bundles of drawings by the latter could be had, at a shilling each, from a basket in the gallery. Among the young artists showing few mean much to us over fifty years later save perhaps Halicka. In declaring that French art was still vital, Clive was relying too much on the impression made by the masters, the younger generation were left straggling behind, pleasant enough but in the main derivative. But at this time, Clive seemed more prepared to encourage a second-rate French painter than any English one and his often damning comments on English painting led to deep hostility.

After 1919, English exhibitions in London no longer had the easily accessible platform of the Omega, which had become too expensive and

118. *The Round Table*, 1920, by Roger Fry. $29\frac{3}{4} \times 27\frac{1}{4}$ in. The Mayor Gallery, London. Jean Marchand, Mme Marcel Gimond (with guitar) and Sonia Lewitska, the Polish painter and close friend of Marchand. Fry visited Marchand at Cagnes in 1919 and got to know the sculptor Gimond in 1920. A sketch for this painting (which includes Gimond) painted in Vence, spring 1920, is in a private collection, London

difficult to run. Roger was fast loosing money and felt he would soon be unable to pay the staff and the artists. A slight revival of sales in 1919 hardly compensated for increased costs. No new painters were coming along with fresh ideas; it could not exist on painted hats, and tastes were changing. Edward Wolfe wished to return to South Africa, Nina Hamnett was still eager for the cafés of Montparnasse, Winifred Gill and Gladys Hynes were no longer there. If Roger wanted to write a book, or paint, or go abroad for weeks on end, then he had to give up the Omega. In June a sale was organized and everything was sold off cheaply. It had been, in spite of all the vexations, an exciting and influential venture. It had produced some of the most interesting applied design of the century in England, and though after its closure the Omega was temporarily forgotten, the artists who had worked there continued painting pottery, designing fabrics, undertaking murals. Vanessa and Duncan became the leading modern interior decorators of the 1920s and inspired many younger painters to undertake such work. But with the dissolution of the Omega, which had provided a showroom and a business backing, most of their work was carried out in the houses of friends. And meanwhile, watered down, commercial designs flooded the shops, and in the late twenties there was a craze for very simple, unadorned pottery of the type Roger had pioneered fifteen years before, and for cubist-inspired wallpapers, fabrics, and linoleums which seemed to have little of the dynamic and immediate expressiveness of the Omega work in 1913 and 1914.

119. An exhibition of Omega products at Miller's Gallery, Lewes, Sussex, in 1946. In the centre, pottery by Fry and on the small table Gaudier-Brzeska's 'Sleeping Doe'. Painted silk hanging possibly by Doucet. To the right is Grant's 'Lily Pond' screen 1914. Two paintings by Doucet hang on the left and on the right Vanessa Bell's *Portrait of Henri Doucet* is above Etchells' *From an English Sporting Print*

So the Omega workshops closed down. The shades of the Post-Impressionists have gone now to join the other shades; no trace of them is now to be seen in Fitzroy Square. The giant ladies have been dismounted from the doorway and the rooms have other occupants. But some of the things he [Fry] made still remain – a painted table; a witty chair; a dinner service; a bowl or two of that turquoise blue that the man from the British Museum so much admired. And if by chance one of those broad deep plates is broken, or an accident befalls a blue dish, all the shops in London may be searched in vain for its fellow.[9]

By the autumn of 1919 many of the painters associated with the Omega were exhibiting members of the London Group. Duncan had automatically become a member from the start, being one of the Camden Town Group exhibitors, but he had not shown – doubtless because of pressure from Roger and Vanessa – and had to be re-elected. Shortly after his election to the Jury Roger was called upon to hang the exhibitions which he did admirably. But, as was inevitable in so miscellaneous a group, factions reared their heads and it was eventually agreed that the Jury should be drawn by lot. 'The result was that very incompetent people did the hanging and in two years the Group had no more funds. Then they asked me back,' wrote Roger.[10] In the twenties he worked tirelessly on the Group's behalf becoming, as one writer claimed, 'the spearhead of Bloomsbury penetration'.[11]

In 1918, the critic of *The Times* had written that 'the group as a whole begins to look dangerously academic'[12] and certainly the experimental wind had been taken out of its sails when the Vorticist wing defected. But an influx of new members in the post-War period ensured a generally high standard of painting in the bi-annual exhibitions – notably from Matthew Smith, Gertler, William Roberts, Sickert and Paul Nash. Many of the minor names in the London Group gave the shows a solid if sometimes dispiriting backbone. Numerous Provençal landscapes, tiresome Cézanne drapery in the stillest of still lifes, and discreet pattern-making which was passed off as construction, lent a depressing uniformity. Keith Baynes, Edward Wolfe and Frederick Porter, among the new members, were however still searching for expression and their capacity to experiment distinguished them from their more imitative colleagues. In the early thirties the Group was sufficiently lively and flourishing to attract the membership of such young artists as Hepworth, Moore, Coldstream, Pasmore and Moynihan.

Of the painters associated with Duncan and Vanessa at the London Group and elsewhere, Keith Baynes is perhaps the most prominent. He was born near Reigate in 1887, the son of a well-to-do clergyman. A career at Trinity College, Cambridge, was cut short by ill-health and he went to live at Annecy in France. In 1910, after a long stay in Jamaica, he returned to England and began to paint seriously. The following year, he spent the winter at St. Jean de Luz where he saw a collection of contemporary French paintings, among them a small Marquet landscape which made a strong impression on him. He also made a trip to Holland to see the Van Goghs before entering the Slade School in 1912. He took an interest in his contemporaries and profited more

120. *Mary, c.* 1926, by
Edward Wolfe. 30¼ × 26 in.
Private Collection. In its
simplicity of handling and
composition *Mary* is one of
Wolfe's most assured and
fluent portraits from this
period

from his study of recent French painting than from the teaching of Tonks
and Brown.[13] Unfit for military service, Baynes rather unhappily joined his
family in Somerset after leaving the Slade, making occasional visits to
London and going to see Sickert in Bath. He began to exhibit – sturdy,
thickly painted still lifes and landscapes, some of which are startlingly severe
in design. In 1919 he returned to London, renewing his Slade friendships –
with Iris Tree and Carrington for example – going to the Music Halls,
particularly the New Bedford and the Alhambra, Leicester Square. He was
taken to see Lydia Lopokova after a performance of *La Boutique Fantasque*
and found her lying on the floor, her legs in the air, to get back her breath. For

121. *Interior of Sickert's Studio*, 1920, by Keith Baynes. 30 × 20 in. Private Collection.
Shortly after this picture was painted, Duncan Grant took over the studio from Sickert

a short time in 1919 he painted in Sickert's studio at 8 Fitzroy Street (plate 121) and through David Garnett was introduced to Duncan, Vanessa and Roger, painters whose work he found sympathetic.

Keith Baynes soon became a frequent exhibitor in the post-War period. He was a sociable, easy-going character, quietly and modestly mannered, with a perky sense of humour, a sharp eye for local colour and a taste for a bawdy joke. His sociability led him into circles beyond Bloomsbury although he managed to steer clear of the rowdy Bohemianism of Fitzrovia. He went often to France where he knew several French painters including Friesz; later on he became Dufy's 'English disciple'. His love of France found a response in Bloomsbury as had his admiration of Sickert. But he was not overwhelmed by Bloomsbury and looked at them from a wry and detached angle. Maynard Keynes bought his work and in 1931 his one-man exhibition at the Reid and Lefevre Gallery was widely covered by the Press partly owing to Lydia Keynes's speech at the Private View. In the 1930s he was a familiar face at parties, a slight figure in a neat suit, round glasses magnifying his eyes. His dachshund George received almost as much attention from the newspapers as Keith himself.

Elected in 1919, with the help of Gilman, to the London Group, Keith Baynes became a conscientious member. While his painting has become steadily more personal and gradually more removed from Duncan's and Vanessa's (though they were always distinct) their alliance was fruitful and they regularly exhibited together beginning with group shows at the Independent Gallery and later at Agnew's.

In February 1920, Duncan held his first one-man exhibition at the Paterson Carfax Gallery, St. James's. He was thirty-five, considerably older than was usual for such exhibitions, although he was known as an established but 'difficult' painter. For those looking for further signs of audacity, the pictures were disappointing. The earliest painting was *The Tub* of 1916 (owned by Roger Fry until its destruction by fire) but the majority of exhibits were from 1918 and 1919 and included the *Juggler and Tightrope Walker*[14] the 1918 *Portrait of a Lady* (Vanessa Bell)[15] and the late 1919 *Venus and Adonis* (plates 122, 124).[16] Generally speaking, the earlier fauvist brilliance of colour has given way to sombre, richer harmonies; paint is applied more thickly; collage elements are absent and a rigorous interpretation of the third dimension replaces the flat composing and strong surface patterning of such paintings as *Man With Greyhound* or *The Tub* (1916), where there is no attempt to conceal the rough surface and hinge marks of the wood-panel support. No matter how exhilarating and fully resolved many pictures from c.1910 to 1916 appear to be, they are still to some extent explorations towards the style which emerged with the large interior of the Charleston dining room already discussed, and of which *The Hammock* (1923)[17] is a notable example. Both these paintings are complex in design and solidly painted. The contrast is particularly apparent in Duncan's still-life painting. For example, in a flower-piece of about 1915 (plate 95), the shapes of an arum lily, large

122. *Juggler and Tightrope Walker*, 1918, by Duncan Grant. 40¾ × 28½ in. Collection Mrs. Frances Partridge, London. A combination of decorative spontaneity and an ample delineation of volume, Grant's main preoccupation in this and the following year

poppies and straggling grasses are continued beyond their actual representation and spill out into the handling of the paint that surrounds them, the space of wall and table top. Echoes and cross-currents are set up throughout the picture surface – 'gay, vernal and lyrical'. In a still life of about 1920 each

123. *Portrait of Vanessa Bell*, *c.* 1915, by Duncan Grant. 36 × 24 in. Collection Mark Lancaster. An earlier version, with collage, of the 1918 painting in the National Portrait Gallery. Swift brushwork and kaleidoscopic colour contrast with the later version's more solid realization.

124. *Venus and Adonis*, 1919,
by Duncan Grant. 25½ ×
37½ in. The Tate Gallery,
London

constituent part is firmly modelled, the stress is less on the linear relationships, more on the compact relation of the parts to the underlying
structure. The fantastic, improvisatory element has gone.

Clive and Roger both wrote enthusiastic articles about the exhibition and
while Clive trumpeted unqualified praise – 'Duncan Grant is the best painter
in England' – Roger's appreciation contains a reservation about the new
direction of Duncan's work which Roger, for one, regretted though he was
deeply respectful of so conscious and deliberate a decision. 'Mr Grant has
this gift of spontaneous and inevitable self-revelation. But over and above
this the personality thus expressed is peculiarly charming. It reveals itself as
transparently sincere, well poised and serene.' It was the lack of some of that
power to enchant that Roger regretted. In 'Mr Grant's intense efforts to push
his art further, to amplify, solidify and deepen the expression of his vision,'
he had been forced 'to scrap some of his most distinctive qualities'. Two in
particular are evoked – his 'singularly sensitive and distinguished "handwriting" ' and 'his exquisite sense of colour; he has always been able to relate
colours in such a way that each constituent colour of the chord has its full
resonance and purity.' He contrasts the freedom and lightness of *The Tub*
with the *Juggler and Tightrope Walker*, where 'the relief is everywhere more
searchingly, more solidly established. Colour counts everywhere more as an
indication of the plasticity, less as a separate direct expression of the idea.'[18]
Over a considerable period, critics in general sympathetic to Duncan Grant's
painting, shared Fry's misgivings that Duncan had turned away from his
earlier mode. Of course, Duncan took no notice and went his own way,
wrestling with the problems of relief and disposition of form, a struggle
which was simultaneously engaging other artists such as Derain and

Marchand. His lyricism found expression in his decorative painting – in panels, in murals, in designs for textiles and for the theatre. They were not of course mutually exclusive – it all depended on the particular problem, the mood at the time. So the free-flowing paint and essentially linear conception of the *Nymph and Satyr*[19] with its delicate harmony of pinks and greens contrast strongly with the rounded, firm-fleshed studio nudes of the same period. Both are absolutely typical of his work. There is none of the pre-War eclecticism, the jumping about among borrowings from African art, from cubist Picasso, or from Matisse. This variety of personal response shows an inventiveness and curiosity beyond the range of most of his English contemporaries who by the twenties and thirties were entrenched in their particular styles, rarely going outside a narrow range. Such variety could also be disconcerting and a lack of passionate engagement reduces many pictures to superficial exercises. The formal inventiveness does not always find its match with the subject in hand, so that one wonders why so much invention was spent on a motif that appears empty or even trivial. Vanessa's observation 'that the most important general difference between French and English art was that the English seemed to be always thinking of the pictures they were producing and the French of something else, I suppose of something they were trying to express by means of the pictures which in themselves were unimportant to the painters,' could be applied to Duncan's less successful work, although it is doubtful whether she had him in mind when she made this distinction.[20]

The War years necessarily left a deep and unforgettable mark on Bloomsbury. After 1918 it was never quite the same and in 1920, with the inauguration of 'The Memoir Club', it already looked at itself historically, reminding itself of the past in the changed circumstances of post-War England. But it was not retrospectively complacent and among the papers read on the evenings when this group of middle-aged friends gathered after dinner – at the MacCarthys in Wellington Square, in Gordon Square or in the country perhaps – there were some trenchant and surprising re-evaluations. But to the public, Bloomsbury was only just born, for it was in the twenties and thirties that its name was most constantly heard, that it became notorious, stood for this or that, presenting a curiously solid phallanx in an era of mounting 'insecurity and barbarism'. It was progressive and it was played out; it courted success and it was absurdly unworldly. The contradictions and paradoxes eddied and multiplied until eventually all that was disliked or found unsavoury in contemporary cultural life could venomously be laid on the quiet doorsteps to the east of the Tottenham Court Road.

To some extent Bloomsbury deserved the invective it got. Indeed there was mutual admiration; there was an ostrich-like attitude to public affairs, an exclusiveness, a superiority, a tolerant contempt for new movements in art and literature – or so it seemed. All these criticisms apply and do not apply when, as we must, we see Bloomsbury as a group of friends rather than as some highly organized 'criminal association' knocking on the head any new manifestation of talent, with everyone wildly in love with each other and with each other's work, breathing a fetid and neurotic air of snobbery and self-congratulation.

It is perhaps too easy to defend Bloomsbury's attitudes and intellectual position in these later years by pointing to the fact that its hopes for civilization were a casualty of the 1914–18 War. Yet to a large extent we must; its pre-War optimism was severely crippled. 'Before the War' was a phrase that prefaced essays, paragraphs, conversations. It evoked a time that was progressive and healthy, denoting an entirely different way of thinking about the world. Anyone who had known life before 1914 shared this attitude, but to Bloomsbury the phrase seemed to have an added poignancy, a wistful regret which, while never running over into nostalgia, served as some kind of touchstone by which to measure the quality of life afterwards.

The quality of daily domestic life was certainly better, even if a rather sceptical eye was turned to the advances made in material comforts. There was for a start more money in the bank, though, with the exception of Maynard, no one in Bloomsbury could be called rich. But books and pictures sold; there were cars, houses in the country, a house in France for the Bells. Travel abroad was a constant annual feature. The benefits accruing from growing appreciation by the public were cautiously absorbed; bathrooms, telephones, studios, wine for dinner, all added to the comforts of life – though of course the plumbing went wrong, the telephone would ring, the cars brought unwelcome visitors or broke down on the Corniche, the studios were difficult to heat. With the painters especially there was a kind of ramshackle

125. Mural by Duncan Grant, *c.* 1927, in the sitting room at 37 Gordon Square. Variously coloured sponged and marbled papers had been a feature of Omega interiors and Grant used them also at 3 Heathcote Street, London, (destroyed) in the flat of Angus Davidson

improvisation. Vanessa had arrived at a way of life that seemed perfectly to suit her. Her children came first and she was with them as much as possible. Domestic problems and troubles continued to flare up now and again, but she found time to paint and to involve herself in a number of decorative schemes in private houses. Indeed her output was enormous. She was with Duncan a great deal, but left him relatively free to follow his own tastes, amusements and friends. 'As for Nessa and Duncan,' wrote Virginia in her Diary for 2 September 1930, 'I am persuaded nothing can be now destructive of that easy relationship, because it is based on Bohemianism.' Duncan's and Vanessa's way of life certainly had superficial resemblances to the Bohemian community they lived amongst in Fitzroy Street, but fundamentally their outlook was different. They never quite fitted in to the loose and easy life of studios and pubs as described for instance in the memoirs of Nina Hamnett or Augustus John.

> . . . Although Duncan Grant lived at the Whistler studio for a time, he was seldom there in spirit and if some rather pushing acquaintance tried to buttonhole him at a Fitzroy Street party he would listen politely for a few moments, then explain, 'excuse me, but I really must find Mrs Bell . . .' while he drifted away to his own more congenial atmosphere.[21]

For the generation starting to paint and exhibit in the twenties, Duncan and Vanessa were in a sense a glamorous pair. They had enviable friendships with some of the leading French painters, and their circle of friends in London included some of the most exciting new writers – T. S. Eliot, Virginia Woolf, Aldous Huxley. But they were not, as it were, residents of Fitzrovia, you could not be sure of finding them at the Eiffel Tower or Bertorelli's or in the Fitzroy Tavern. On the other hand, they were not reclusive and did much behind the scenes for their fellow artists, which culminated in their support of the Euston Road School. A new circle of painters gathered around them – Keith Baynes, Frederick J. Porter and Douglas Davidson for example, who, though they never formed a school as such, were associated together in the London Group and in the London Artists' Association – but Duncan and Vanessa generally tended to avoid the coteries of painters and the gossip of the studios, in London as much as in Paris. Of their pre-War fellow artists, Etchells had, after the Omega row, eventually given up painting for architecture, Gaudier-Brzeska was dead, Bomberg they never saw, Gertler moved in a very different circle, Nina Hamnett was often abroad, Lamb was only an intermittent acquaintance, and Roberts, while a fellow-exhibitor at the London Artists' Association, was never a friend. There was however an increasingly warm friendship with the doyen of Fitzroy Street, Sickert, and there were cordial and sympathetic relationships with Matthew Smith, John Nash rather than with his brother Paul, Frank Dobson and Bernard Adeney. While the Hogarth Press was host to the first books of Day Lewis, Isherwood and John Lehmann, to anthologies such as *New Signatures*, which included poetry by Spender, Auden, and Empsom – the thirties writers – the painters befriended the rising generation of artists some of whom were to form the short-lived Euston Road

126. A corner cupboard painted in *c.* 1924 by Duncan Grant for Angus Davidson

School. Julian Bell introduced John Lehmann and, through him, the younger poets, to the Hogarth Press, and his brother Quentin acted as go-between in some respects between Vanessa and Duncan and such younger artists as Robert Medley, Claude Rogers, Victor Pasmore and William Coldstream, who all exhibited initially with the London Artists' Association and worked in and around Fitzroy Street.

A walk today from Fitzroy Square down Fitzroy Street, into Charlotte Street, round to the left into Percy Street and out into the roar of traffic in the Tottenham Court Road, would be irksome and depressing to anyone who knew those streets in the twenties and thirties, since so much is gone. From the mid-eighteenth century the district had been favoured by painters and engravers. Among them were Constable and Richard Wilson and, in the nineteenth century, Daniel Maclise. Early this century the area became known for its foreign restaurants, small specialized shops and good pubs. Framers, lithographers, models and artists' colour suppliers added variety and completeness. Soon afterwards came an influx of young artists such as August John at 21 and 8 Fitzroy Street and his sister Gwen, living in a damp basement in nearby Howland Street.[22] With the meetings of the Fitzroy Street Group at number 19, Gilman and Bernard Adeney, among others, were recruited to the area, and Matthew Smith lived at one time in Fitzroy Street and later in Charlotte Street.[23] As for the street itself, Richard Buckle has given an amusing description of it:

> Considering what a mean and monotonous thoroughfare it is, Charlotte Street is surprisingly charged – for me at any rate – with history and significance. Like an adventuress, it keeps changing its name: originating humbly, though on a ducal estate, in the Euston Road, then making a surprisingly brilliant match into the Duke's family and becoming one side of Fitzroy Square; soon widowed, it becomes artistic but retains its noble surname down the two blocks of Fitzroy Street, where so many studios are; next, crossing Howland Street, it enters the domain of the Duke of Bedford, but marries the foreign chef and becomes Charlotte Street, famed for its exotic restaurants; then, with a right-left swerve – a serious operation which leaves it with a permanent kink – it enters on a dubious old age in Rathbone Place, and expires as it began, in trade, in Oxford Street.[24]

The Eiffel Tower restaurant at the bottom of Percy Street (it became the White Tower in 1938) was the best known restaurant of the area, patronized not only by the local community but by visiting writers and painters from France and America. The proprietor Stulik was as well known as his guests. 'Percy Street,' wrote Wyndham Lewis, '. . . is principally noted for Stulik. There are other people in it but he's the one who counts.' In 1914, Lewis lived at 4 Percy Street spending most of his time in bed writing his first novel *Tarr*. Later in the War he carried out decorations in the private dining room upstairs at the Eiffel Tower – 'Gay vorticist designs cover the walls and call from the table cloth.'[25] At various times, Augustus John, Derwent Lees and Victor Pasmore lived in rooms above.

The other great centre, much rowdier and more mixed, was the Fitzroy Tavern – still standing but without a vestige of its former atmosphere – 'the most celebrated meeting place of the demi-monde'. Nina Hamnett became a fixture in the late twenties and thirties and nearly every memoir of that time and place contains its thumbnail portrait of her. From the bracing company of Sickert and Fry she had fallen into other arms – pugilists, sailors, lower Bohemia, and alcoholism. With her cloche hat, thin legs, and stage-duchess voice, her anecdotes of a glamorous past with Gaudier-Brzeska and Modigliani, she soon reached the unenviable position of being 'a character', her former achievements unrecognized, her talent wasted, writing a few reviews for the *Licensed Victuallers' Gazette*. (She fell from the window of her room in Westbourne Terrace in 1956, either drunk or soberly determined – the circumstances of her death remain mysterious.)

In 1919 Duncan had used Roger's studio at 18 Fitzroy Street. After various fruitless attempts he at last found a studio early in 1920 which was to remain his until its destruction in 1940 – The Whistler. It was a studio we have already encountered, a huge room built out from the back of 8 Fitzroy Street where in 1908, when it was leased to Augustus John, the Bells had had their first meeting with Ottoline Morrell. From 1915 it had been occupied by Sickert until he moved to France after the War. At the top of the house lived the painter Frederick Porter, a New Zealander by birth who had studied at the Atelier Julian and moved to London soon afterwards. Mainly a still life and landscape painter, he held a show of his work at 8 Fitzroy Street in 1916. He was associated with Duncan and Vanessa in the London Group and was a founder member with them of the London Artists' Association.

The Whistler with its large windows and high, misted mirrors, its untouched eighteenth-century atmosphere of great fires and candlelight, opened out from a small entrance at the end of a labyrinthine journey from the street.[26] There was a dusty, undomesticated stone-flagged hall at the end of which was a flight of stairs to the half-landing but instead of the customary window there was a green glass door. Opening this one looked down a long iron-floored passage with a corrugated roof lit along the sides by panes of frosted glass. 'When you walked down it you made a noise like a stage thunder-storm', wrote Angelica Garnett. 'When Miss Mary Hogarth came to visit, she made such a noise that Nessa christened her "The Mother with the Wooden Tail", in memory of a particularly terrifying story that her governess used to tell her.'[27] Finally, there were some steps down and a door to another studio (which Vanessa took in 1928) but the passage continued left, down more steps, past a straw porter's chair with a hood to it,[28] and finally into the studio. The room had a large, east-facing window, an old gasfire with elaborate fireplace and a mirror above; and across from this, a round stove mounted on a hearth of decorated tiles.[29] Next to it was a small chest of drawers on which stood a stone head of Buddha and later a carved male torso.[30] There were plenty of chairs and tables, and a heavy sofa which, along with a large oval mirror, Sickert bequeathed to Duncan. For some time

Duncan's 1905 copy of Piero della Francesca's angels in *The Nativity* hung on the wall and there was a classical female head by the sculptor Marcel Gimond, which appears in some of Duncan's still lifes.

Sometimes Duncan slept at number 8 but more usually he found a bed at 46 Gordon Square, and from 1925 he and Vanessa had rooms at number 37. Vanessa took the slightly smaller studio next door and the two were made more domestic. A small kitchen was arranged in Vanessa's room and part of the space partitioned by big appliqué curtains to make a bedroom. Angelica Garnett has described the routine of these later years:

> Vanessa cooked both breakfast and lunch, but in the evening Flossie, tall and gaunt, presided over the kitchen. Vanessa shared her with Helen Anrep, for whom she cooked lunch. She arrived at number 8 at about 6 o'clock, carrying supplies in a basket, and proceeded to cook our supper. This we ate at an octagonal folding wooden table, covered with aluminium. It was made I think, to Vanessa's design, and intended for someone else but proved to be too heavy, so it remained in the studio as an emblem of modernity. In the evenings it reflected the blue of the wine-glasses and the light of the candles.[31]

Angelica generally stayed at the studio when on holiday from school. From there she could go to the theatre, be painted, or act in the charades and specially written plays that were a feature of life at Fitzroy Street.

One of those theatrical parties was given for Angelica's birthday. Her brother Julian wrote a skit featuring Duncan as Sir Frederick Leighton receiving Lady Ottoline Morrell (played by Angelica) who had come to have her portrait painted. But the sitting is constantly interrupted by telephone messages from the maid bringing extraordinary news of, and questions from, everyone in Bloomsbury, which mocked their foibles and eccentricities. Roger babbles of the 'dark star' and the 'black box'; Virginia comes and eats her lunch on the hall floor, the Keynes's offer a poisoned pig as a present, Leonard and Angus Davidson ask the time,[32] and Vanessa who has been abducted seeks to be rescued from the Isle of Dogs. In an epilogue Ottoline/Angelica brought the house down by chastising anyone who had been left out of the drama.[33]

This was one of many plays written by the Bell children, usually with the help of Virginia or Vanessa. Virginia's own notable effort 'Freshwater' was given at the studio in January 1935. It was based on the Isle of Wight life of Mrs Cameron, Watts, and Tennyson and others, with Angelica as Ellen Terry (plates 127, 128); Duncan played Watts and, unable to learn his lines, had them pinned to his canvas.

Duncan and Vanessa used Fitzroy Street as the London address from which they advertised themselves as interior decorators and muralists. The potter Phyllis Keyes would discuss paints and glazes there, the embroiderer Mary Hogarth, clomping along the corrugated passage, would come to be advised about wools, and Allan Walton to commission fabric designs.

A constant stream of models and sitters for portraits was another feature of life at Fitzroy Street. The young dancer Rupert Doone posed to Duncan for

127. Angelica Bell dressed as Ellen Terry for her part in Virginia Woolf's play 'Freshwater' produced in January 1935

128. *Angelica as Ellen Terry*, 1935, by Duncan Grant. $31\frac{3}{4} \times 21\frac{1}{4}$ in. Private Collection.
Between 1930 and 1935 Duncan Grant made a considerable number of large pastels which
include many male and female nudes and *Mme Dasté* (Collection Lord Clark) and *Mrs
Leslie Stephen* (Private Collection, London)

several drawings and portrait heads in the twenties.[34] Duncan also designed a *divertissement* for Doone and Lydia Lopokova at the Coliseum in 1924 and in 1932 he carried out the sets and costumes for *The Enchanted Grove* with choreography by Doone and music by Ravel and Debussy, given by the Camargo Ballet at Sadlers Wells. But Rupert Doone's really notable achievement, the idea for which came to him as early as 1925, was the Group Theatre where he produced the plays of Auden and Isherwood and Spender's *Trial of a Judge*. One of his collaborators in this venture was Robert Medley, a painter who had been encouraged by Vanessa and Duncan. He was a cousin of Francis Birrell and had from early days been a frequent visitor at the Strachey household in Gordon Square. He was generally better liked than Rupert Doone who could be overbearing and exigent. Vanessa was particularly fond of Robert Medley and entrusted Quentin to his care in Paris.

Among others who sat to Duncan and Vanessa during these years were Edward Sackville-West, seated at the studio piano, Aldous Huxley, whom Vanessa painted in 1929, several beautiful young women such as Jane Clark (later Lady Clark), Rosamund Lehmann and Dora Morris, and the latter's brother Peter, also a painter, who became a close friend. There was the painter George Bergen and a policeman friend of E. M. Forster's, Harry Daley, whose beat was conveniently nearby in the Tottenham Court Road.[35]

Among the most extraordinary sitters was Mrs Violet Hammersley. In her youth she had been painted by Steer and was a friend of painters and writers of that generation; she was musical, widely read, a devout Roman Catholic and a great entertainer. She was brought to Fitzroy Street by Rosamund Lehmann's husband Wogan Phillips. With her enormous black eyes and raven hair she was like some splendid witch, and wild rumours circulated about her private life. Had she killed her husband? Was she cruel to her three charming children? She first sat to Duncan in 1934 but the most finished portrait of her was done in 1937, a large sombre composition where she is seated at the piano. One seems to hear her deep, sepulchral voice saying to Duncan as she plays, 'Call me Violet' – the beginning of a life-long friendship.

[1] VB to RF, 15 August 1920.

[2] VB to RF, 29 November 1918.

[3] VB to RF, 18 May 1919.

[4] Denys Sutton, *Derain*, 1959.

[5] Osbert Sitwell in *Laughter in the Next Room*, 1950, p.146, maintained that even the cows at Garsington had caught the Derain fever and lowed 'Doë-rain, Doë-rain!' in the Oxfordshire fields.

[6] It was there that Maynard and Clive gave a memorable supper party. Derain, the Picassos, Massine and Ernest Ansermet were guests from the Ballet and Lytton, Duncan, Vanessa, Aldous Huxley and Drieu la Rochelle were among the painters and writers invited.

(7) *Woman in Armchair, c.* 1917, Keynes Collection.

(8) The *Nation*, 27 September 1919.

(9) Virginia Woolf, *Roger Fry*, 1969, p.218.

(10) RF to Marie Mauron, 23 November 1920.

(11) A. Forge in the catalogue foreword to the London Group Jubilee Exhibition, Arts Council 1964.

(12) 7 November.

(13) Among his fellow students was Sylvia Myers, the future wife of Harold Gilman, a painter who from 1915 to Gilman's death in 1919 meant much to Keith Baynes as friend and informal teacher.

(14) Originally in the collection of Sir Michael Sadler; now owned by Mrs Frances Partridge.

(15) The National Portrait Gallery, London.

(16) The Tate Gallery, London.

(17) The Laing Art Gallery, Newcastle.

(18) 'Mr Duncan Grant's pictures' by Roger Fry in the *New Statesman*, 21 February 1920.

(19) Collection Raymond Mortimer.

(20) VB to RF, June 1922.

(21) M. Lilly, *Sickert: The Painter and his Circle*, 1971.

(22) Nina Hamnett lived for several years in Thackeray House, Howland Street; the novelist had at one time lived there and describes the large studio in *The Newcombes*.

(23) Nearer our own times such artists as Robert Medley, Graham Bell, Claude Rogers and Victor Pasmore lived in the area, the last named taking Duncan Grant's studio until it was bombed in 1940.

(24) *Adventures of a Ballet Critic*, R. Buckle, 1953, p.151.

(25) *Colour*, April 1916. The article also mentions the Omega Workshops' decoration of the Cadena Café, Westbourne Grove, London, 1915.

(26) I am indebted here for certain details to *Sickert: The Painter and his Circle*, op. cit.

(27) Angelica Garnett, 'Number 8 Fitzroy Street', unpublished memoir, 1973.

(28) This chair was left to Duncan Grant by John Hope-Johnstone, a previous occupant of the building. There is a drawing of it by Sickert (Private Collection, London).

(29) See *The Pink Vase*, 1934, Leicester Museum and Art Gallery.

(30) See *The Stove; Fitzroy Street*, 1936, ill. 14 in *Duncan Grant* by Raymond Mortimer, 1944.

(31) Angelica Garnett, op. cit.

(32) See *Virginia Woolf* by Quentin Bell, Vol. II, 1972, pp.130–1.

(33) The fancy-dress of the audience had its surprises with Virginia as a voluptuous Sappho, Vita Sackville-West in a mask of herself gone to the bad, and Roger in his father's judicial wig.

(34) Examples are in the collections of Robert Medley and Mrs Barbara Bagenal.

(35) The portraits include *Edward Sackville-West at the Piano, c.* 1928, by Duncan Grant, private collection, London; *Aldous Huxley*, 1929, by Vanessa Bell, Collection J. Tayleur; *After the Opera: Mrs Clark*, 1935, by Duncan Grant, Collection Lord Clark; *Miss Dora Morris, c.* 1930, shown in 'Recent Paintings by Duncan Grant', the Cooling Galleries, 1931 (no. 9); *The Policeman*, 1934, by Duncan Grant, National Gallery of Sweden, Stockholm; *Mrs Hammersley*, 1937, by Duncan Grant, Collection C. R. Hammersley (a further portrait and a drawing (1937) of Mrs Hammersley are owned by the Art Gallery, Southampton); *Pour Vous*, 1930–7, a portrait of a Miss Holland, a relation of Oscar Wilde's and a professional model, was originally in the collection of the late Edward le Bas. Two head and shoulder portraits of Miss Holland (*c.* 1934) are owned by the artist.

With the publication of *The Economic Consequences of the Peace* in December 1919 Maynard Keynes became a celebrity in Europe as well as England. He had also suddenly become rather wealthy owing to his speculations on the fluctuating European exchanges, and was determined to take a really comfortable perhaps even extravagant holiday. Italy was decided upon and Duncan and Vanessa were the obvious companions. Arriving in Rome they took rooms in the old-fashioned Hotel de Russie in the Piazza del Popolo. There were no tourists, in fact very few travellers at all; the weather throughout April was gloriously sunny and every day Maynard pronounced that they were richer than the day before. They began to spend their money, buying enormous quantities of objects of every kind; in about a month they had spent over three hundred pounds. There were rush-bottom chairs and an inlaid table for Maynard; Vanessa bought pots, dresses, velvet buttons, seventeen pairs of gloves, and (for Roger) a large vase; Duncan bought twenty-two frames, a settee, an inkstand, a marionette, and a large anonymous still life. When not scavenging in the markets and shops or making excursions to the surrounding countryside, Duncan and Vanessa painted and Maynard read and wrote.[1] They rented a large studio in the Via Magutta and had plenty of models, who were much cheaper than in London. The studio belonged to a young lady from Bergamo who, as the studio was so big, thought that by an arrangement of curtains she as well as her English friends could use it at the same time. Each morning La Signorina would receive her visitors, mostly it seems young cavalry officers, behind the partition of curtains. Chatter and laughter went on continually, driving Maynard mad until he could no longer bear it. Knowing very little Italian he nevertheless beckoned the young woman and gave her such a talking to that the rest of their days were completely peaceful.

A projected visit by Maynard to the Berensens at I Tatti near Florence rather cast a cloud over the last days in Rome, for he insisted that the painters accompany him – in fact they had also been asked. In Rome life had been quiet and free, but at I Tatti Maynard would be treated as a celebrity with all the introductions, parties, and fuss that so exalted a state entailed. Nevertheless it was decided they must accompany him and all their purchases were crated up and sent by sea to England, and at the end of April they arrived at I Tatti. Vanessa and Duncan felt ill-at-ease at the villa, unable to express themselves freely, and all the time sensing that their host thought he knew exactly what they must feel about pictures (being friends of Fry).

Vanessa at lunch one day expressed admiration for Raphael. It became clear, as the atmosphere darkened, that they should not have looked at Raphael and (being friends of Fry) had done so surely without admiration. Vanessa reported the atmosphere in a letter to Roger, cursing 'the horrors' of life at I Tatti – in spite of the extreme comfort of the place, the Louis XV furniture, and exquisite breakfasts in bed. She decided she profoundly distrusted Berenson – one of those monolithic and irreversible decisions that Vanessa on occasion made. It was in this uneasy atmosphere that there occurred a most distressing event. The Loeser family and the Berensons had fallen out years before. The quarrel had recently been made up and a reconciliation party at the Loesers was planned. Maynard was naturally high on the celebrity list and the painters went along with him. Duncan was somewhat surprised to find himself being asked financial questions while Maynard and Vanessa were shown the Cézannes and other paintings for which the house was famous. But the party was pleasant, the people most friendly, and when it was time to go Duncan decided to walk back to Settignano across the hills from Florence. As he set off, a shout of 'Mr Keynes! one minute please Mr Keynes!' stopped him in his tracks. It was his host wishing to introduce the economist to Countess Serristori. Duncan, after a second's argument with his conscience, played along with his host's mistake and bowed deeply to La Serristori. Walking back Duncan felt he possessed a great secret which, though it would be disgraceful if found out, was exciting for that very reason. Later that evening at I Tatti he was perturbed to hear of a return party for the Loesers, twenty or thirty people for dinner and a concert afterwards by the Loeser Quartet. He told Maynard and Vanessa of the afternoon's mistake and wondered whether he should 'confess' to the Berensons. They were too amused to offer suggestions. Inevitably, Duncan's identity was revealed and he was in disfavour throughout the party. What really roused Duncan's indignation was that Vanessa was similarly treated. '*I pittori*' were in disgrace. It was with considerable difficulty that Duncan found a chair for Vanessa at the concert, just by the door. They were very glad to leave and made for Paris where everything was more familiar and infinitely more congenial. A visit to Picasso was the highlight of their brief stay, as Vanessa wrote to Roger on her return to Gordon Square:[2]

Duncan and I went to see Picasso, whom I like very much and find quite easy. He showed us quantities of his latest work and things he is actually at work on, nearly all more or less abstract designs though I suppose usually suggested by nature. Some were amazingly beautiful. I think all gave one very definite sensations and he was interested to find out whether they were the ones he wanted to produce. On the whole I think he was pleased by our likings. He also showed us an astonishing painting of two nudes most elaborately finished and rounded and more definite than any Ingres, fearfully good I thought. Also a very interesting beginning of a portrait group of the Emperor and Empress Eugénie and Prince Imperial done from a minute photograph. Also lots of tiny watercolours, many of them sketches for the curtain for his new ballet, all rejected by Diaghilev with whom he was furious. He says he will do no more ballets. [3]

While Duncan and Vanessa were in Rome, some of their paintings were on exhibition at the Vildrac Gallery in Paris. Vanessa was greatly pleased by compliments from the French passed on to her by Roger – 'especially as I had been getting very despairing about my painting. It's very cheering up at such times to think one has ever done anything worth looking at even if one isn't doing much at the moment.' Duncan's pictures were received less enthusiastically, mainly on account of the unrepresentative selection for there was little of his recent work. Roger's solid canvases – some recent paintings from Provence – were much admired giving him the encouragement that in England he never found forthcoming. This was emphasized by the comparative fiasco of his large exhibition in June and July at the new Independent Gallery in Grafton Street. Very little was sold, in spite of cheap prices, and the notices were generally cold though the *Burlington Magazine* was loyal and reproduced *Provençal Kitchen* and Clive was the soul of discretion in the *New Statesman:* '"A critic's painting": I shall not quarrel with the phrase, provided it be understood that the critic in question is perhaps the first in Europe on account of the depth and subtlety of his sense of art, and that what makes his criticism precious is precisely what gives a peculiar quality to his painting.' [4]

Percy Moore Turner who ran the Independent Gallery was sympathetic to contemporary English and French painting, and in November 1920 he asked Duncan and Vanessa to exhibit watercolours with the French painter Robert Lotiron. In May 1922 Vanessa held her first one-artist exhibition there; a group of paintings by Othon Friesz were on show in another room. [5] Vanessa wrote to Clive the day after the opening 'I am astonished that I have already sold seven pictures and drawings – so at any rate I shan't be out of pocket over it – Turner is very much pleased.' Vanessa was particularly gratified with Sickert's praise in the *Burlington Magazine:* 'Instinct and intelligence and a certain scholarly tact have made of her a good painter. The medium bends beneath her like a horse that knows its rider. In the canvas *The Frozen Pond* . . . the full resources of the medium in all its beauty have been called into requisition in a manner which is nothing less than masterly.' [6] In a review in the *New Statesman* [7] Roger commended her honesty, the absence of anything affected or elaborately clever, her grave absorption in the general theme of her painting and the very distinguished handling of colour. He found fault in her sometimes narrow conception of design and seems to suggest that the simplicity of her work prevents further formal discoveries. Her *Woman in Furs* (plate 116) he commends as 'perhaps the most brilliant thing in the exhibition'. Vanessa's excited description of Picasso's monumental nudes – 'most elaborately finished and rounded and more definite than any Ingres' – found some echo in her own treatment of the nude at this time as well as in certain large figure compositions. The Tate Gallery's *Nude* (plate 129) with its sculpted mounds of flesh bears some resemblance, but it has none of Picasso's stark, symbolic atmosphere. It is still very much a tired, studio model. More successful are the still lifes and interiors many of which were painted in St. Tropez in the winter of 1921–2. They formed the bulk of her exhibition.

While the painters at this time were not exactly unsociable – though Charleston increasingly became a refuge from the turmoil of Bloomsbury – Clive's sociability was leading him into circles beyond Gordon Square. He was an expert host, plump and jovial, a highbrow whom hostesses could ask to their houses without fear of his turning up in the wrong clothes and talking of the wrong pictures. Charm, wit and generosity flowed from him and the younger generation found in him an ally and were infected with his eager inquisitiveness. His letters to Vanessa – epigrammatic, observant, often intolerant, comic and solicitous – give an extraordinarily diverting and varied account of certain fashionable and intellectual circles in Paris and London. The new young writers and painters are examined, their progress followed and their characters analysed. One of Clive's new friends was Raymond Mortimer who in 1919 worked at the Foreign Office. He appeared one night with Aldous Huxley (another recurrent name) at the Eiffel Tower restaurant which Clive and Lytton were just about to leave. An after-dinner bottle of Madeira cemented their friendship and Raymond Mortimer soon became an intimate of the Bells, Duncan, the Woolfs and of the Strachey household. There are glimpses in Clive's letters of Virginia and Lytton: 'Lytton I hear crossed the channel – from Tilbury to Dunkirk too – in the greatest gale of the season for the pleasure of spending an evening with Norman Douglas.'[8] Unexpected figures appear: William Rothenstein, for example, 'surrounded by his wife and children, sitting like Socrates on a stool at the feet of his disciples from the civic department of South Kensington'. There are the young: the 'capable but not unamusing' Man Ray in Paris; Cyril Connolly, 'young, unprincipled but intelligent'; Iris Tree, who 'has had a baby by a Czechoslovakian who is six foot three high – Another little job for Lady Tree'; her sister Viola, met at a performance of a Strindberg play, saying her life with Alan Parsons (her husband) was indistinguishable from a Strindberg play.

Between the wars, Clive lived in Paris for weeks at a time, usually paying two annual visits there, in the spring and the late autumn. His letters describe countless parties and excursions, the latest exhibitions, theatrical and musical events, and meetings – with Derain and Mme Derain, Segonzac, Marchand, Kisling, Charles and Rose Vildrac, Friesz, Picasso, Cocteau, and a host of others including Satie and Poulenc. On one occasion Picasso made a drawing after lunch in his immaculate apartment in the rue la Boétie of Clive, Cocteau, Satie and Olga Picasso. On another, Clive was drawn by Nils de Dardel lovingly feeling the person of Isadora Duncan: '*Je ne suis pas une femme,*' she drawled at him, '*je suis un génie!*' One of the most celebrated 'banquets' of the time was that given in May 1922 by Mr and Mrs Sidney Schiff. Clive recounts the evening in a letter to Vanessa.[9] The party was given after a performance of the Russian Ballet and many of the guests were connected with it but Sidney Schiff's main purpose 'was to assemble at his

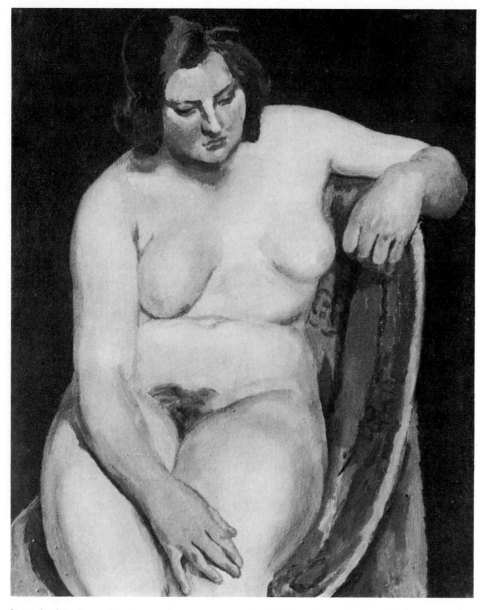

129. *Nude, c.* 1922–3, by Vanessa Bell. 32 × 25¾ in. The Tate Gallery, London. Vanessa Bell was deeply impressed by some of Picasso's female nudes which she saw in Paris in February 1922

hospitable board – in an upper room at the Majestic – the four living men he most admired.'

There were forty *couverts* at the Majestic and one had the opportunity of shaking hands with Marcel Proust, Stravinsky, Picasso and James Joyce. James Joyce was so much the great man that he arrived in the middle of supper – at two in the morning – not dressed; but as no one in the room except our host and hostess, Hilda Benick and myself, had ever heard of him, his entrée fell rather flat. And his entrée was all there was to it, for, whether he was drunk or shy I know not, but he said not one

130. *Portrait of Lydia Lopokova*, 1923, by Duncan Grant. 29 × 23½ in. Collection Lady Keynes. Lydia Lopokova dressed in the style of Ingres's *Mlle Rivière*. In 1922 Duncan Grant designed the sets and costumes for *Togo: or the Noble Savage* with music by Milhaud and choreography by Massine. Lopokova and Ninette de Valois (a distant relation of Grant's) were among the cast

word throughout the evening. There were a great many beauties English and French and a good many minor acolites e.g.: Marcelle Meyer, Olga Picasso, Mlle Channel, Lady Gibbon, Mrs Fellows – Auric, Poulenc, Larionoff, Satie, myself.

It was on this occasion that occurred the celebrated exchange between Proust and Stravinsky. 'Doubtless you admire Beethoven,' began the writer. 'I detest Beethoven,' was Stravinsky's reply. 'But, *cher maître*, those late sonatas and quartets . . . ?' '*Pires que les autres.*' [10]

Clive's observations from the South of France or Venice evoke the pain-

terly Bohemianism of the former and the quirky extravagance and social whirl of the latter. In January and February 1930 he stayed in Cannes in a flat belonging to Madge Garland (later Lady Ashton). With him was his constant companion during the early thirties, Benita Jagger (later Mrs John Armstrong). The previous occupants had left the flat in great disorder and 'like Madge herself the flat is not made for rough weather.' By February Clive was more comfortably settled and had established a routine, working in the morning in a pyjama suit with the sun coming in through the windows. After lunch there were letters to write, perhaps a siesta or a walk, and then more writing from five until eight o'clock. In the evening there was dinner and a little dancing at the 'Boeuf' where there were numerous companions such as Raymond Mortimer and Edward Sackville-West who 'appears to have been pitched out of the arms of a sailor into a cobbled court down several flights of stairs,'; however they all found the company at John Banting's house nearby too rowdy, with jazz all night, dancing, whores and sailors, black singers, painters, journalists, and any casual passer-by. Banting was a member of the London Group and since 1925 a resident of Fitzroy Street. While he is best known perhaps for his very personal contribution, a sinister gracefulness, to the 1936 International Surrealist Exhibition, he was also a decorator, gently blending a romantic fantasy with the geometric, orderly cubism of Gris and Braque. But his work as a decorator was on a small, private scale. 'It's a pity he thinks about nothing but drinking and fucking because I believe he has a talent – not for painting pictures – but for decorating. I shall be surprised if it comes to much,' wrote Clive.[11] With Banting's increasing Surrealist tendencies, his association with Bloomsbury diminished though he continued to

131. Francis Birrell, Raymond Mortimer and Clive Bell, Venice, September 1931. 'Alternately known as "I tre signori" and "The Three Musketeers", we seem to arouse some curiosity by the superficial differences of temperament which we present upon the Piazza, drinking our vermouths. Clive . . . looks glum, uncharacteristically, Franky is the spit of his father, and the third figure has, I fear, a worthless Black Sheep air.' (Raymond Mortimer to Vanessa Bell, 18 September 1931, on a postcard of the photograph)

132. Clive Bell's library at 50 Gordon Square decorated 1926 by Vanessa Bell and Duncan Grant. Fireplace and tiled hearth by Vanessa Bell. On the top cupboard door, a view of the pond at Charleston

execute book jackets of distinction for the Hogarth Press, such as that for Isherwood's early novel *The Memorial* and Henry Green's 1939 *Party Going*. Clive's sympathies on the whole were not with Surrealism though he held a grudging admiration for Miro and Masson and was generally more favourable to Surrealist writing than painting. His son Quentin's early flirtation with Surrealism was encouraged as a welcome emancipation from the Post-Impressionism of Charleston.

But there were drawbacks to Clive's cosmopolitan existence: 'In any new plans that may be forming I do beseech you not to leave me out entirely. I far prefer your society and Duncan's and "the Charleston atmosphere", to any other, and – strange as it may seem – in London and Paris I often feel terribly lonely – and also I can't write in either of the capitals.'[12]

Since his early days in Paris Clive had enjoyed the company of artists. Not only was their talk stimulating and unusual but their way of life was congenial. For so sociable a young man, the plunge into studio and café life had been refreshing after the agreeable but sometimes bleak society of which he had been a part in the Cambridge of G. E. Moore. To his credit, Clive never saw himself as an intrinsic element or active partner in the modern movement in painting. In fact he rather disliked the practical side of the painter's work, though the initial stimulus of being inside a studio always retained a certain glamour for him. When it came to writing about pictures, his criticism is informed with a measure of technical knowledge and an appreciation of a painter's immediate problems which save him from the inevitable errors of those ignorant of such things. Likewise, Roger Fry's experience as a painter is the origin of much that is acute and suggestive in his writings. As a regular art critic, Clive Bell's knowledge in this sphere gives credibility to some surprising assessments. He knows how a painter has come by such and such an effect, realizes the problems involved, and the effort of attempted solutions. Painters such as Derain or Segonzac appreciated not only his great personal amiability and well-nourished conversation, but his ability to go beyond a merely literary or descriptive understanding of what they had produced with paints, brushes and canvas.

Writing and reading and looking at pictures – 'this pathetic life of the intellect' to which 'I am eternally committed' – were the main occupations of his life. Although the majority of his books starting with *Art* (1914) concern painting and related subjects, his interests were wide; he was not afraid of expressing himself forcibly in print on controversial subjects of the day. We have already seen that his pacifist pamphlet *Peace at Once* was seized and destroyed. His 1939 *War Mongers* was an equally compelling polemic. *Since Cézanne* appeared in 1922 and was followed the next year by *On British Freedom*, an impassioned, neglected little book taking as its theme the 'genteel servitude which passes under the name of Anglo-Saxon civilization'. He begins with the proposition that 'in September 1922 an ordinary Englishman is on the whole, less free than a Roman slave in the time of Hadrian' and continues to let fly at intolerance, restrictions and censorship. It is of course an intolerant book but on the subject of censorship and sexual freedom it still has its pertinence. There followed the short study *Proust* (1928), the first book on that author in England, and the widely-read and much-abused *Civilization*. His essays, some subsequently collected, most dispersed in the back numbers of English, French and American periodicals include pungent, amusing appraisals of social and political topics, on public and civic decoration, on blood sports, conservation and censorship. They are the concerns of a man passionately interested in the quality of life, in the pleasures and pursuits open to his fellow beings, in those questions of opportunity and freedom and their expression, both public and private. His viewpoint as propounded in *Civilization* is one of tolerance and liberality, unmechanical and unsanctimonius. His 'sense of values' derives from a belief in the sacrifice of comfort and utility to beauty, and the cultivation of those means to good which include the elementary appreciation of sun and rain, wine and bread, and the more sophisticated ingredients of science, the arts, respect for the great tradition of thought, an unshockable acceptance of 'un- or ill-explored parts of human nature'. The conclusions he reaches on the value of the spiritual over the material are a compound of 'sweet reasonableness' and an infuriating élitism which can run to triviality and pretentiousness. At one point in *Civilization* a passionate digression on the fluctuating standards of restaurants seems enough to carry his case that we live in a barbarous age. As Virginia Woolf remarked after reading the book – which is elaborately dedicated to her – 'he has great fun in the opening chapters but in the end it turns out that Civilization is a lunch party at No. 50 Gordon Square.'[13]

'I dare not be profound,' he writes early on in *Civilization*. His intellect skims in provocative arabesques; received opinions topple like so many clay

PLATE V

PLATE VI

pigeons, reputations are knocked for six. He is never dull; dullness for Clive Bell was a besetting sin. His horror of boredom, of taking himself and the world too seriously makes his books a mixture of the very readable and the very silly. His prose, with its echoes of Voltaire and Swift and La Rochefoucauld, of the eighteenth-century fop and the bright contemporary man of letters won for him a reputation as a much-prized journalist. That proposed great book 'The New Renaissance' of which *Art* and *Civilization* are but two fragments, never materialized. Though he would not, one feels, have considered himself a failure, a continual underestimation of his gifts gives to his work an unmistakable poverty of conviction.

That others did not take him very seriously as a writer hardly worried him. 'I've got something to say about lots of different things and I mean to say it', he wrote to Molly MacCarthy,[14] who thought him simply a 'poseur'; and Leonard and Virginia were sceptical. 'Are you waiting for Clive's book [*Art*] to come out to know what to think on that and every other subject?' wrote Lytton to Duncan.[15] And Roger, though he saw Clive as his chief ally in the defence of Post-Impressionism in England, was in later years inclined to find him too easily swayed by the 'currents of avant-garde opinion' and criticized his judgements as snobbish and superficial. Clive's reviews of contemporary painting were often narrow but he was always eager to praise where he found merit, and was never dishonest about his own feelings. He wrote appreciatively of Kenneth Martin, John Tunnard, Edward Burra and William Scott. We can be sure that when early on he singled out Jackson Pollock and Francis Bacon for praise he was not, as Roger Fry must have thought, 'swayed' by advanced opinion. When Surrealism was fashionable in England in the thirties, he staunchly upheld his unfavourable view though he appreciated its liberating influence on some of the younger English painters like Trevelyan, Hillier and Sutherland. 'Bell is a most agreeable person, if you don't take him seriously, but a great waster of time if you do, or if you expect to get any profound knowledge or original thought out of him, and his Paris is a useless one.' So wrote T. S. Eliot to the American writer Robert McAlmon.[16] Eliot's 1910–11 stay in Paris does not appear to have aroused in him a curiosity for the visual arts and in this respect he was unlike many of the poets of his generation for whom Post-Impressionism and Cubism were a nourishing influence. In France poets and painters were inextricably linked in the modern movement – a similar pattern occurred in the late 1950s and early '60s in America. While Eliot knew and was painted by a number of artists in England, he was never associated with them in the way Pound, for example, was close to the Vorticist group. Eliot's friendship with Bloomsbury had literature as its basis so that talk of books with Clive Bell was more to his taste than talk of painting. For Eliot, Paris was the home of Joyce rather than Picasso.

Picasso was a welcoming friend to Clive though their meetings became less frequent with Picasso's phenomenal increase in fame in the 1930s and '40s: 'I lunched with Picasso, chez Lipp, and went to the studio, which is rather like a waiting-room at a station – full of people he seemed barely to know – two secretaries, answering the telephone and cataloguing. Little or nothing else to be seen. He spends a good part of each morning receiving people who come with sham Picassos hoping for the best.'[17]

But in the twenties, though a great figure in Paris, Picasso was more accessible and as we have seen Duncan and Vanessa visited him. They went again in 1922.

> Did I tell you we went to see Picasso? Some of his latest things are very fine. There are studies of his baby [Paulo] and large figure pieces, rather like those he showed us last year but better and more complete. Also lots of abstractions in stripes and lines. He was very anxious to see you when you're in Paris, he said. He seemed to be leading a very fashionable existence and had just been to a grand wedding that day.[18]

Another hint of the kind of life Picasso was leading with Olga at that time is suggested in a postcard to Clive in London asking the latter to bring over to Paris two new suits Picasso had ordered from an expensive tailor.

One of the longest visits Duncan and Vanessa paid to Paris was in 1924 when half Bloomsbury seemed to be there at one time or another.[19] Clive and St. John and Mary Hutchinson joined them one evening for dinner before going to a performance of a play by Tristan Tzara at the 'Cigale'. A party and dancing followed where Segonzac, Lydia Lopokova, Marc Allegret and Nancy Cunard were among the other guests. Another visit to the 'Cigale' was to see Derain's short ballet *Gigues*; and the following day there was lunch with Derain and Mary Hutchinson, joined later by Segonzac. In the evening Vanessa and Duncan met the poet Villeboeuf who on calling Vanessa a goddess was immediately asked to Charleston for the summer.

Their days were not given over entirely to social life or 'the whirl of Paris' as Vanessa called it – she was always more sociable in Paris than in London, 'a gadabout' Duncan called her – and there were long mornings looking and copying in the Louvre and visits to other exhibitions – Monticelli at Paul Guillaume's and Impressionists at Knoedler's. Then there were long conversations with Derain, teasingly insulting Picasso, dismissing Cubism, and saying how Corot was the greatest of all nineteenth-century painters, and that Pissaro's influence on Cézanne had put the latter off his real course of development for years. On another day there was an excursion with the Picassos to the Murphys, rich Americans living at St. Cloud, for a sleepy, sunny lunch *alfresco*. Afterwards in the garden they all listened to some Chinese music on a gramophone. Picasso was entranced and conjured up an image of the intricate manipulation of the feet of the Chinese dancers.

Duncan then left Paris for a fortnight to stay in Germany with a painter friend Franzi von Haas. However, Berlin was not to his taste and returning to Paris was a relief. There was a splendid evening at the Russian Ballet with Maynard and Lydia, where they saw *Parade* once more and *L'Amour Vainqueur* with sets by Gris, and *Le Train Bleu* – which was receiving its first performance (20 June) – Cocteau's ballet with Milhaud as composer, scenery by Channel, and a drop-curtain by Picasso. On the next day Duncan lunched with Rupert Doone in Montparnasse and then went to a Bonnard exhibition with Maynard and Lydia. Afterwards, there was another visit to Guillaume's to see work by Derain and Maillol and some negro sculpture. There was a meeting with Marchand and Sonia Lewitska, the Polish painter who had exhibited at the Second Post-Impressionist Exhibition and was described by Roger as a 'sort of wild rodent who rushes about like a squirrel in a cage'.[20] This Paris visit, though longer than most, was typical of many in its diversity and richness and the stimulation if afforded in contrast to the tame and provincial artistic life in London. Most of Duncan and Vanessa's painting associates spent profitable times in Paris: Frederick Porter, Keith Baynes, Nina Hamnett, Matthew Smith and Edward Wolfe. Clive indiscriminately recommended a good dose of Paris to young painters, and his francophilia aroused the distrust and animosity of those painters firmly entrenched in the English 'scene'. The English painters he did admire, however, were praised for having come through strong exposure to the French movement to find themselves securely within an English tradition – not the tradition of Palmer or Blake but that of the English landscapists – of Gainsborough, Cotman, Crome and Constable. They had 'jumped the Slade and Pre-Raphaelite puddles', nurseries of narrow provincialism where Augustus John and Stanley Spencer were dismissed as ringleaders. That group of English painters over whom Clive opened his critical wings to give them a too-insistent blessing, became in 1925 the London Artists' Association.

Maynard Keynes was instrumental in founding the Association – one of several organizations concerning painting and the ballet with which he was involved. This involvement was never dilatory or self-seeking; his well-known capacity for hard work, his attention to detail, his overall vision were together concentrated on whatever project was at hand. The London Artists' Association 'came into being towards the end of the year, 1925,' wrote Maynard,

> as the result of a meeting with a group of artists, who had found themselves without an efficient organization for dealing with their work and had consequently sold almost incredibly few pictures during the previous year or two. . . . The result of our conversation was to make us feel that a small organization formed on co-operative principles might, even if it had no great financial backing, at least do something to reduce the anxieties of promising painters and perhaps help to get a better market in the long run for their works. The idea was that an organization could be formed which, acting as agent to a group of artists, would allow them to work in greater freedom from continually pressing financial considerations by providing them with a small guaranteed income and taking upon itself the entire management of the business side of their affairs. Three friends who were interested in modern painting came forward and offered to join with me in guaranteeing a certain sum for this purpose – Mr Samuel Courtauld . . . Mr Hindley Smith and Mr L. H. Myers. . . .[21]

The Association held regular group and one-man exhibitions; it also sent shows to the provinces and made sure its artists were well represented abroad.[22] The opening exhibition in May 1926 was at the Leicester

228

133. *Portrait*, 1926, by Duncan Grant. 32 × 22 in. The Mayor Gallery, London. The sitter for this portrait was Bea Howe, a writer and friend of Clive Bell. Painted at 8 Fitzroy Street

Galleries, and in 1928 the Association found a permanent home through the hospitality of the Cooling Galleries at 92 New Bond Street. Fred Hoyland Mayor, whose gallery in Sackville Street had shown modern English and French painting until it closed in 1926, became the secretary. 'Frederick Mayor,' wrote Clive[23] '. . . by the charm and gaiety of his nature and his almost uncanny flair did much to put this Association "on the map".' Mayor later managed the Guillaume and Brandon Davis Gallery before opening his own gallery once more in 1933 with work from England, France, Germany and America.

Following Fred Mayor in 1929 came Angus Davidson, already a close friend of Bloomsbury. His brother Douglas was a painter much influenced by Duncan and Vanessa and he collaborated with them in interior decoration. Previously, Angus Davidson had worked at the Hogarth Press where for nearly five years he had patiently sacrificed literary ambitions to the monotony of tying up parcels and writing invoices. His charming, hesitant manner, agreeable looks and conscientious attitude made him an admirable secretary as did his uncomplaining acceptance of £15 pay a month – part of Maynard's ruthless cutting down of overheads. The artists themselves however were rarely out of pocket and some of the exhibitions – especially the low-priced Christmas ones – were tremendously successful until the slump of 1930. Financial disagreements were rare but arguments flared up from time to time about the over-exposure of some painters' work, and about certain sales going on behind the Association's back and the election of new members ('I got a fearful dressing down from Roger, and gather you've had one too for letting Paul Nash into the Association', wrote Maynard to Vanessa on 10 February 1927). The original nucleus was of fairly well established painters in the Post-Impressionist tradition – Grant, Baynes, Adeney, Vanessa Bell, Porter, Fry and the sculptor Dobson. But by the very nature of the organization, less tried and younger painters were attracted to it – Raymond Coxon, Robert Medley, William Coldstream, R. V. Pitchforth. Edward Wolfe and William Roberts were also members. In spite of Roberts' early association with Wyndham Lewis, he was welcomed and befriended by Maynard who not only bought many of his pictures but commissioned the large portrait of himself and Lydia Keynes in the latter's possession.[24] Allan Walton was a painter member, but he was better known as an interior decorator and co-founder with his brother of Walton Fabrics. Many artists in the Association were commissioned by him to design textiles, particularly Duncan and Vanessa, Cedric Morris, Adeney and Keith Baynes. Not only were paintings exhibited but fabrics, painted trays, boxes and screens and stools in embroidery and cross-stitch. There were sculptures by Dobson, Elizabeth Muntz and Stephen Tomlin. Tomlin's best-known work is the bust of Virginia Woolf of 1931. There are also busts by him of Duncan, Lytton Strachey and David Garnett and his painted ceramic heads had considerable success. But his work rarely equalled his ambitions; he was intelligent, charming, with a fertile imagination and a love of discussion which even Bloomsbury sometimes found exhausting. Lytton records tottering to bed at two in the morning at Charleston after a wide-ranging

conversation on aesthetics. 'It's all this awful question of the content of a work of art' wrote Vanessa to Roger [25] of the same occasion, when Lytton and Tommy (as Tomlin was known) were guests. He could be melancholy and neurotic and was constantly unsure about his work. His love affairs with men and women were very often unhappy. He was married to Julia Strachey, the writer and niece of Lytton, and died in 1937.

134. *The Open Door*, 1929, by Duncan Grant. 35 × 31 in. Arts Council Collection. A view into the garden at Charleston from the painter's studio. The theme of interior-exterior is even more common to Vanessa Bell – compare *Charleston Garden* (plate 151)

Another painter in the Association was Ivon Hitchens whom Maynard particularly admired. He became a probationary member in 1929 and continued to benefit from sales inspired by Maynard. Early in the Second World War, Hitchens was bombed out of his Hampstead studio and went to live in considerable discomfort in a caravan near Petworth, Sussex. Maynard encouragingly bought two paintings, one of which went through the Contemporary Art Society to the Tate Gallery.

In July 1931 the Association received the resignations of Keith Baynes, Vanessa and Duncan. All three, through the influence of Baynes' friend Lewis Hoare, had decided to take up an offer from Agnew's to deal in their work. It was a surprising move coming from so august a firm but the offer was generous and all three were beginning to feel the restrictions of the Association. Maynard was naturally piqued, feeling Agnew's could not possibly succeed in getting more for their paintings than had the Association. He became indignant and overbearing and there was a resulting coolness. The move to Agnew's in fact gave the three painters a greater freedom to exhibit elsewhere and their work appears in exhibitions at many London galleries in the thirties, especially at the Lefevre Gallery where Vanessa and Duncan both had extremely successful one-artist exhibitions in 1934.

By the time of their abandonment of the London Artists' Association, Duncan and Vanessa were among the most widely known painters in England, but no longer could they be thought of as among the country's leading innovators. The young, while often grateful for practical support and friendly interest, could be understandably dismissive. To many of them Duncan and Vanessa's innovatory work of twenty and more years before was completely unknown. The abstract paintings, the collages, Duncan's kinetic scroll of 1914 and his Vorticist exhibits, Vanessa's authoritative work in the fauvist idiom, were stored away at Fitzroy Street and Charleston.[26] They were almost a source of embarrassment and in Vanessa's later rare allusions to them she seems surprised at their relative audacity. But she realized also that they were the inevitable results of the various ways of tackling the pictorial problems which had confronted herself and Duncan at that time.

135. Duncan Grant and Vanessa Bell at 'La Bergère', Cassis, 1930

[1] Duncan Grant's *Irises, Lilies and Pear*, exhibited at the Tate Gallery (1959, no. 44), dates from this Italian holiday.

[2] 17 May 1920.

[3] The ballet was *Pulchinella* with Massine's choreography and Stravinsky's music; it was in fact the last of Picasso's sets and costumes to be done for the Russian Ballet though *Le Train Bleu* had as a curtain an enlargement of a smaller, earlier painting by Picasso.

[4] 19 June 1920.

[5] Othon Friesz (1879–1949) was among the best known and most acceptable contemporary French painters in England in the 1920s, along with Kisling, Segonzac and Jean Marchand. Clive Bell saw Friesz often in Paris and wrote favourably of his work; later he conceded that a dangerous professionalism had spoilt his talent as it had Kisling's. His hopes for Friesz as a great decorator came to nothing. See 'Othon Friesz' in *Since Cézanne*, 1922.

(6) *Burlington Magazine*, July 1922.

(7) 'Vanessa Bell and Othon Friesz', 3 June 1922.

(8) CB to VB, 9 February 1928.

(9) 22 May 1922.

(10) Clive Bell, *Old Friends*, 1956, p.180.

(11) CB to VB, 6 March 1930.

(12) CB to VB, 20 June 1928.

(13) See Quentin Bell, *Virginia Woolf*, Vol. II, 1972, p.137

(14) 17 January 1913.

(15) 15 January 1914.

(16) 2 May 1921. See Robert McAlmon, *Being Geniuses Together*, 1970.

(17) CB to VB, 22 May 1947.

(18) VB to RF, 24 February 1922.

(19) Quentin Bell was also in Paris, staying with the Pinaults, a French family with whom a few years later Julian Bell was to stay before going up to Cambridge in 1928.

(20) RF to Margery Fry, 4 May 1920.

(21) J. M. Keynes, 'The London Artists' Association', in *The Studio*, June 1925. From 1925 to 1931 Duncan Grant earned an average of over £1,900 a year from the Association.

(22) Venice and Dresden, 1926; Marie Sterner Galleries, New York, 1928.

(23) Catalogue note to an exhibition by members of the LAA, Ferens Art Gallery, Hull, 1953.

(24) After the liquidation of the Association (1935) Roberts along with Wolfe continued to benefit financially by a special arrangement with Maynard who also organized shows for them at the Reid and Lefevre Gallery. The variety of members in the thirties was considerable and included many of the later Euston Road artists – Pasmore, Coldstream and Claude Rogers. Cedric Morris and Sickert's third wife, Thérèse Lessore, were also elected.

(25) VB to RF, 23 September 1926.

(26) 'We have been turning out a lot of rolled up pictures from our stores here. I think both Duncan and I have changed extraordinarily during the last ten years or so – I hope for the better. But also it seemed to me there was a great deal of excitement about colour then – seven or ten years ago – which perhaps has rather quietened down now. I suppose it was the result of trying first to change everything into colour. It certainly made me inclined also to destroy the solidity of objects but I wonder whether now one couldn't get more of that sort of intensity of colour without losing solidity of objects and space' (VB to RF, from Charleston, *c.* 1925).

In any account of modern design between the Wars in England certain names and works stand out: McKnight Kauffer's posters and murals, the geometric carpets of Marion Dorn and Evelyn Wyld, textiles by Dorothy Larcher, Phyllis Baron, Edward Bawden and designs by Duncan Grant and Vanessa Bell. Their output was phenomenal but little now remains. Much was destroyed, by accident and by bombing in the last War. The murals in Leonard and Virginia Woolf's home at Tavistock Square and at Ethel Sands' house in Chelsea were lost in this way. Happily, however, the decorations for Raymond Mortimer's flat and for a large dining-room at Penns-in-the-Rocks in Sussex – a commission from Lady Dorothy Wellesley – were saved as the painters had worked on detachable panels or board.

One of the earliest of Duncan and Vanessa's collaborations with Roger Fry was at Fry's house Durbins where each painter executed an enormous figure in bright colours on a wall of the hallway (winter 1913–14). The Omega awakened new possibilities of total decoration – murals, fabrics and furnishings. The painters tended to favour what might be called the Florentine or 'architectural' approach to decoration, which aimed at the clarification of a room's structure or, in the case of an interior without distinctive features, to create an architectural scheme on the walls by painted spaces, panels, divisions, etc. The other style of decoration, which included Byzantine and Eastern forms of mural, was more pictorial, where the structure was not necessarily defined. In England when the Omega started, the mural as picture was the dominating style and the Florentine mode was practically lost. Of course these definitions are loose and elements are interchangeable. Duncan and Vanessa's later decorations tend to make use of both styles where pictorial features are at the same time framed by and form part of a whole structural programme. Thus to see one panel from Penns-in-the-Rocks isolated from its intended surroundings gives little idea of the powerful decorative unity envisaged by the painters. So much has been destroyed or dismantled that it is difficult to recapture from a handful of photographs the extraordinary distinction of these rooms. Quite apart from aesthetic considerations, it is unfortunate that there is no complete interior to evoke for us that particular way of life, a reflection of the values of what Duncan's and Vanessa's friends called 'civilized' life.

From the original simplicity of Omega interiors with their bands and panels of pure colour, Duncan and Vanessa's decoration became richer and more elaborate, charged with a recognizable calligraphy and an inventive

burgeoning of motifs they made peculiarly their own. In a curious way some
of the later schemes in the thirties, such as the Music Room (plate 143), were
almost caricatures of their style, so excessive is the patterning, so rounded
and full-blown are the repeated features of their decorative language. It was a
language both personal and modern and yet replete with references to the
past – to eighteenth-century France, to Venice and Florence, to Byzantine
mosaics and to the architecture of Greece. It was a style particularly suited to
the colourful transformation of eighteenth-century London rooms with their
sash-windows and panelling, the plasterwork of ceiling and fireplace and
alcove. Duncan and Vanessa's great virtue was their respect for the individuality of a room, its scale and corresponding proportions. Not for them
the crashingly obvious allusions to the character of the room's owner. Their
iconography was of a civilized generality, a harmonious background to lives
that were comfortable, informal, conversational, and for people familiar with
the fruit and flowers of Provence, with Italian gardens, Greek myths, the
Commedia del 'Arte, and the decorative conventions of the past. Only in that
sense was their work psychological in appeal. To those without knowledge of
these conventions, it appears empty and tame. To others their decorations
are more remarkable and original than their easel paintings.

One of their first mural projects after the War was a commission from
Maynard for his rooms in Webb's Court at King's College, Cambridge.
Duncan's previous mural there on one part of the wall (which was divided by
a central door) had remained unfinished. The new paintings were to go either
side of the door from ceiling to the top of the dado (plate 137). Duncan and
Vanessa began work in August 1920 using the new studio in the Charleston
garden. Quentin, aged ten, painted pictures on the studio doors with infectious enthusiasm. On 26 August Vanessa reported their progress to Roger:

> I have tried to sketch some of the figures I have been doing for you – but
> I have only room for three. There are eight altogether, four by Duncan
> and four by me. They are supposed to represent law, science, history
> etc. though you mightn't think it – in fact we're always changing their
> arts and their sciences. They're about 5ft high and 2½ft wide and so it's
> rather an undertaking. The backgrounds are marbled, half in burnt
> umber and black, the other half in Venetian red and Indian red. They
> have yellow ochre bands round; the male figures are nude mostly in pure
> naples yellow. The females have dull green, vermilion, prussian blue
> and white dresses. But they're not nearly finished yet though we want to
> do them rather quickly and directly. The hut makes a splendid studio
> and there are eight divisions all along one side which just take the
> panels, so it's a perfect place to do them in. Of course we haven't done
> very much else as we want to get this finished while we're here.

In fact the room was not completed until 1922. Besides the eight panels,
various features of the room were picked out in plain colours and for the large
windows at either end Vanessa made huge appliqué curtains. Some of the
furniture included spoils from their visit to Rome. The elongated rather
melancholy figures are perfectly suited to the space they occupy and the

austere proportions of the room. While immensely dignified and sombre in colour they are painted so solidly and emphatically that the vitality which the initial sketches contained seems lost. Even the background marbling is stiff and unaccented. That balance between the image as a self-contained, pictorial unit and as part of a total decorative scene has not been fully realized; the panels are too much like large pictures, in spite of the uniformity of treatment and subject.

In London, there were decorations in Adrian and Karin Stephen's rooms in Gordon Square (February 1921), tiles and a carpet for Beatrice Mayor in Campden Hill Gardens, fireplaces for Margaret Bulley (1926), and decorations and painted furniture for Clive's flat at 50 Gordon Square (plates 132, 136). On a cupboard door in the latter a bowl of fruit stands on the ledge of a window opening onto a landscape – the pond at Charleston. Series of circles and squares, dots and dashes, marbling, hatching, and *écriture* appear on doors, fireplace, mouldings, and the large bookcases. There was a tiled hearth and painted lampshades. Other commissions in the 1920s (including drawing-room panels and specially designed furniture) came from Angus Davidson (plate 126), Raymond Mortimer (plate 138), Leonard and Virginia Woolf, and from L. A. Harrison a painter of the older generation and a friend of Steer and Sargent. An unusual feature of this last project (1925) at Harrison's country home Moon Hall, Gomshall, Surrey, was Duncan's painting directly onto the cement of the porch. In 1927 there was a commission from Mary Hutchinson for the decoration of her drawing room at 3 Albert Gate, Regent's Park, where she had moved from her house in Hammersmith (which also contained painted doors and decorative features begun by Duncan and Vanessa in 1917, through the Omega, and finished in 1919).

136. Cupboards and bookshelves decorated by Duncan Grant and Vanessa Bell, 1926, in Clive Bell's flat, 50 Gordon Square. The painting above is by Juan Gris, *Les Oeufs* (1912) owned by Bell and now in Stuttgart

In July 1927 a further commission took Duncan and Vanessa to France. They had been asked to decorate a summer loggia at the Château d'Auppegard near Offranville in Normandy. The house belonged to Ethel Sands, a wealthy spinster of American parentage, a friend of Henry James and other writers, and a talented pupil of Sickert's from the days of the Rowlandson House School. Before the War her house at Newington near Oxford had seen gatherings of painters and writers similar to the ones at Garsington. Through Sickert and Lady Ottoline Morrell, Ethel Sands became friendly with a younger generation of painters; her own work, much influenced by Sickert and the French Impressionists, was as delicate and refined as the rooms she created. From Newington she had moved, with her constant companion the painter Nan Hudson, also American, who had studied under Carrière and was a member of the London Group, to Chelsea and the Château d'Auppegard. The Chelsea house contained extraordinary mosaics by Boris Anrep which continued up the walls making the hall seem like a street, with splashing fountains, and windows from which faces peer, including the bearded, bespectacled Lytton Strachey. From Normandy Vanessa wrote to Roger of their stay. The food was heavenly, there was music and reading aloud. Duncan's old teacher Jacques-Emile Blanche came over one day for tea expressing his admiration for Roger and for Virginia's writing – Virginia herself appeared for a short visit. But there were drawbacks. 'Please send us a glimpse of ordinary, rough and tumble, dusty, everyday existence,' Vanessa wrote to Roger,

> I am beginning to be in danger of collapse from rarefication here. The strain to keep clean is beginning to tell. Duncan shaves daily. I wash my hands at least five times a day – but in spite of all I know I'm not up to the mark. The extraordinary thing is that it's not only the house but also the garden that's in such spotless order. It's almost impossible to find a place into which one can throw a cigarette end without its becoming a flaring eyesore. Ethel goes out at night and hunts snails till there are practically none left. Old men come in to polish the floors, women come and cut the grass, others come and wash. Nan makes muslin covers to receive the flies' excrements (I don't believe Nan and Ethel have any – they never go to the W.).

'I think it is fair to say that the modern movement in textile design began with the establishment of the Omega Workshops,' wrote Paul Nash.[1] Nash's association with the Omega was short-lived but he was infected by Roger Fry's efforts to alter the face of contemporary design through the direct intervention of the artist. In fact he went further than Fry in his more accommodating response to the use of the machine and the severities of inter-War design as exemplified by the Bauhaus, and by Le Corbusier and Djo Bourgeois. His own work outside painting was a large and distinguished contribution to applied art – fabrics, posters, interior design and book illustration. He differed from the Omega artists in that he discounted the conception of the artist/decorator as a painter transforming interiors with

137. Two figures by Duncan Grant, two of eight panels by Grant and Vanessa Bell executed 1919–21 for Maynard Keynes's rooms in Webb's Court, King's College, Cambridge

brushes and paints. He preferred to think of the artist as a composer of interiors whose sensitivity to colour and texture should be exercised in conjunction with the architect. He had a horror, shared by Fry and his associates, of the professional interior decorator, 'a kind of hybrid, possibly possessed of some taste, a smattering of knowledge and a good deal of commercial acumen'.[2] Like Fry he realized that there was an antagonism between mechanization on a large scale and the vitality and sensibility of an artist's hand, particularly in pottery and textiles. That artists were needed to design was without question; otherwise one came across, to give Nash's example, the textile firm's manager proudly showing off his 'modernist line . . . feeble or garish designs, unhappy travesties of a modern idiom, unintelligently conceived and executed in bad taste.'[3]

One of the important figures between the Wars who showed himself sensitive to the problems involved in textile production and yet was determined to make use of a variety of painters he admired was Allan Walton. He was a painter himself, a member of the London Group and the London Artists' Association, and as an interior decorator worked much along the lines of Duncan and Vanessa, painting panels and designing carpets. His brother ran a textile firm where the cloth was woven in Yorkshire and printed in Manchester. As well as designing himself, Walton commissioned designs from other painters, supervised their production, and organized their exhibition and sale to the shops. The designs were in a variety of colour schemes, printed on both cotton and silk. The artists he commissioned between 1931 and 1939 included Bernard Adeney, Keith Baynes, Cedric Morris, Paul Nash, Duncan Grant, Vanessa Bell and Frank Dobson.[4] One of the most prolific of the younger designers was Edward Bawden, whose murals with Ravilious and Charles Mahoney at Morley College, a scheme reminiscent of the 1911 Borough Polytechnic paintings, were unfortunately destroyed in the last War. There were Alice-in-Wonderland surrealist decorations for the International Building Club in Park Lane and wallpapers and fabrics for 'Modern Textiles' run by Elspeth Little, a designer herself. While such painters as Bawden and Ravilious were not stylistically affiliated to Duncan and Vanessa they were part of the whole movement away from the austere interiors and pastel shades that were conspicuous in the late twenties.

Perhaps the most complete interior carried out by Duncan and Vanessa was a proposed Music Room installed upstairs at the Lefevre Gallery and opened in December 1932 (plates 143, 144, 145). Flower pieces on six panels, seven feet by five, with circular mirrors above, and framed at the top and bottom by painted scalloped drapery, set the colour scheme and floral motif for the decoration. One end was occupied by a large curtained window and a sofa, furnished in Walton fabrics, Duncan's 'Grapes' being used on both with especially designed flounces and pelmet. Two small chairs were similarly covered. On another wall was a fireplace with a tiled hearth and a mirror above, with small circular mirrors let in down either side of the painted frame. There were wicker chairs with oval embroidered panels on the back, a small screen painted by Vanessa, a gramophone, and a grand piano decorated by Duncan. A carpet and a smaller rug were perhaps the most distinguished

features of the room though a duet stool worked in cross-stitch by Duncan's mother remains a splendid object. Cushions, lampshades and vases completed the scheme.

The opening of the room was a great social occasion where Bloomsbury mingled with Mayfair at a party given by Virginia and Vanessa – hailed by the popular press as 'shining stars in the literary and artistic world and uncrowned queens of Bloomsbury'. Blue and green cocktails were served with goldleaf floating on the surface. 'At the inauguration,' wrote the young Cyril Connolly,[5] 'the room vibrated to a Debussy solo on the harp, and the music, with its seasonal elegiac, seemed to blend with the surrounding patterns of the flowers and falling leaves in a rare union of intellect and imagination, colour and sound, which produced in the listener a momentary apprehension of the life of the spirit, that lonely and un-English credo.' But Cyril Connolly went on to blot his copybook: 'The whole is a fine sight for the connoisseur who enjoys discriminating between the work of the two painters, one so much better than the other. . . .' His relations with Bloomsbury were thereafter, though happily not permanently, strained. Among the guests, Roger was heard to ask plaintively why sculpture was so much more interesting than painting. Virginia was observed lighting a cigarette in a manner 'unhurried, airy and medieval – a kind of Borgia deliberateness'. And in the midst of the crowd was 'Mr Duncan Grant,' who, 'felt like making abstract designs of the minds of various people he talked to.'

The room was generally well received though one paper complained that the colour was bilious and another that the whole was a riot of bad taste. It was certainly a long way from the savagery and severity of the Omega. Though patently a show-piece, crowded and over-insistent in its constant

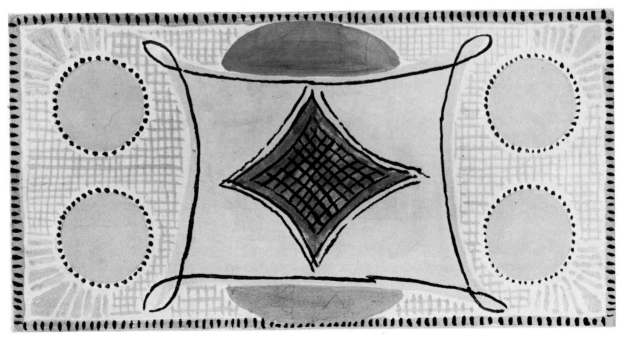

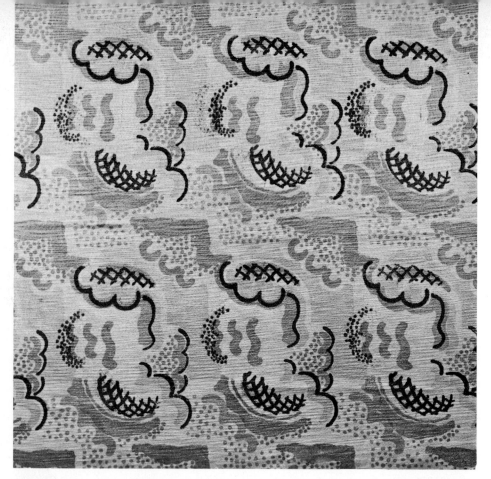

141. Textiles by Duncan
Grant for Allan Walton Ltd.
An eight colour spun satin
design of 1932 and
142. 'The Little Urn'
designed in four colours on
spun satin, c. 1932

143. 'Music Room', 1932, installed at the Lefevre Gallery. A complete interior decorated and furnished by Vanessa Bell and Duncan Grant. Photo Lefevre Gallery

144. Rug by Vanessa Bell made for the Music Room, 1932

patterning, the colour scheme held the various elements together, suggesting
'a great canvas of autumn', wrote Cyril Connolly. The artists had 'joined to
their natural grace and measure a riotous sense of colour, a romantic splen-
dour which was the one element lacking in their former distinction.'

Virginia had commissioned a carpet to be designed by Duncan for 52
Tavistock Square and it arrived at her house on 1 December as the Music
Room was being finished. From the Music Room she bought the screen by
Vanessa and the large mirror over the fireplace. But the carpet inspired an
ecstatic letter to Duncan:

> I must seize my pen, though I am reeling with excitement, to tell you
> that we have just unrolled your carpet and it's perfectly *magnificent*. (I
> seldom underline a word, but on this occasion I must.) It seems to me a
> triumphant and superb work of art, and produces in me the sensation of
> being a tropical fish afloat in warm waves over submerged forests of
> emerald and ruby. You may well ask what sort of forest that is – I reply it
> is the sort of fish I am. As you know, it is the dream of my life to be a
> tropical fish swimming in a submerged forest; and now that is per-
> manently gratified – with what effects on my morals, my art, my
> religion, my politics, my whole attitude to reality, God only knows. . . .
> Further, I feel perfectly sure that I am not paying you a penny or even a
> halfpenny for all this subdued but gorgeous riot (the forest that is) – you

146. *Seated Woman*, 1929, by
Duncan Grant: 23½ × 18 in.
Private Collection. Pastel
and charcoal drawings such
as this are prominent among
Duncan Grant's work at this
time. They were invariably
studies for his large
decorative compositions

have made me a tropical fish gratis and for nothing – so that no expression of mine can really convey adequately my gratitude, which must
remain as a lump of entire emerald (I said it would get into my style –
thank God, my article on Sir Leslie is finished) until death us parts. I've
just had a paean of praise of the room from Ott: everyone seemed
enthusiastic. I hope some cash will result. Now I am going to swim in
my forest. V.W.

Dorothy Wellesley (later the Duchess of Wellington) was a great admirer
of Virginia's novels and through her friendship with the Woolfs became the
editor of the Hogarth Press series 'Hogarth Living Poets'. Volumes of her
own poems were published alongside her contemporaries – Vita Sackville-
West, F. L. Lucas, Frances Cornford. The series made a notable contribution to the modern movement when several thirties' poets appeared in
Cambridge Poetry (1929, and a second volume in 1930) and with individual
books by C. Day Lewis, William Plomer and John Lehmann. Dorothy
Wellesley herself is best known for her correspondence with W. B. Yeats
which she edited for publication in 1940.[6]
   Penns-in-the-Rocks at Wythiham, Sussex, was the Wellesleys' country
home, a late seventeenth-century brick house among lawns and gardens and
close to a fantastic, ancient group of rocks and boulders shaded by trees,
oddly contrasting with the civilized order of the house. It was for the dining
room of Penns that Dorothy Wellesley commissioned decorations and furnishings from Duncan and Vanessa early in 1929 (plates 147, 148). Painted

147. The dining room,
Penns-in-the-Rocks, Sussex,
by Vanessa Bell and Duncan
Grant, 1930. The six painted
panels (three by each artist)
were painted mainly in
Cassis in 1929 and the
furnishings were ready by
the following year. Lady
Dorothy Wellesley, who
commissioned the room, also
bought several paintings by
the artists at this time

panels established the luminous, poetic atmosphere of the room, three principal ones along one wall having Duncan's grandly composed *Toilet of Venus* as their centrepiece. Single figures and a tall still life by Vanessa completed the decorations around the room. Pale grey ceiling and green-grey walls with borders of white circles and pastel hatching provided the setting for the panels. An octagonal table and cane-backed chairs were specially designed to occupy the centre of the room; semi-circular tables and a sideboard on the perimeter were also made. An unusual feature were the ground glass lights with small octagonal mirrors above, set on the walls between the decorations. Later additions to the room included a large carpet, a tiled hearth, and small tiled tables. In November 1930 Dorothy Wellesley invited several friends for a weekend party to inaugurate the room. Hugh Walpole (a voracious collector of pictures by Duncan and Vanessa), Ethel Sands, Vita Sackville-West and Leigh Ashton (later Sir Leigh Ashton, Director of the Victoria and Albert Museum) joined the artists shortly after the huge sequined appliqué curtains designed by Duncan and made by Vanessa had been finished and hung. Vanessa enjoyed the practical side of these decorative ventures more than did Duncan, though once his imagination was fired – he carried out odd measurements with bits of string and contributed wildly inaccurate plans – he and Vanessa worked together in extraordinary harmony.

In December 1930 Vanessa won third prize and £25 in a competition promoted by the *Architectural Review* for a scheme called 'Lord Benbow's Apartment'. Competitors were asked to design a modern yet discreet apartment for a wealthy, sporting widower. Raymond McGrath collaborating with McKnight Kauffer, Edward Bawden and Paul Nash won the first prize; Nash himself with Edward Wadsworth, the second. Vanessa Bell, wrote the judges, 'has shown a still greater contempt for the plan provided by Lord Benbow, and one feels that with very little alteration, the same scheme could be carried out in almost any room. At the same time, there is a largeness of conception about it which cannot be ignored and the scheme of colour is superb and puts it in a class apart.' Robert Medley was responsible for the furniture and light fittings; there were to be sculptures by John Skeaping, rugs by Vanessa and Humphrey Slater, and painted panels by Duncan and Vanessa which included decorative representations of hunting, horse-racing, cards, cricket and fishing. She did not go so far as Paul Nash in emphasizing the tastes of the client; Nash made his doors look like goal-posts, covered chairs in cricket-pads, and had yachting flags flying from the cocktail cabinet.

Commissions for posters came from Jack Beddington of Shell-Mex, Ltd.[7] who were, wrote Clive in a review of the posters shown at the New Burlington Galleries in June 1934, 'likely to do more for English art in a dozen years than the Royal Academy has done in a hundred.' Vanessa chose Alfriston, a village near Charleston in the Sussux downs, as her motif. Duncan chose St. Ives, the small town near Hilton village in Cambridgeshire where David Garnett lived.

Painted pottery and tiles were popular at the London Artists' Christmas exhibitions. Duncan and Vanessa usually went to a pottery in the East End to paint them before they were fired. Tiled tables – generally square and rather

148. *Bacchanale*, 1929–30, decorative panel by Vanessa Bell. 84 × 54 in. Southampton Art
Gallery. This right-hand panel flanked Grant's *Toilet of Venus* (also in Southampton Art
Gallery). The completed room received much attention and praise in the press and was greatly
admired by W. B. Yeats, a constant visitor to Penns-in-the-Rocks

low – were made up such as one for Mrs Grant in 1929 and one for Leonard and Virginia the following year. They made the acquaintance of Phyllis Keyes, a prominent figure over the next few years in Duncan's and Vanessa's lives.[8] Miss Keyes set up her own kiln and workshop in Warren Street in 1933. Her later pottery in Clipstone Street was bombed in the last War. Although she threw pots herself she often took old Italian or Spanish jugs and plates and re-cast them to be painted. At one time her assistant was Stephen Tomlin who made several ceramic heads there. The South African painter Graham Bell was also apprenticed to her for a while. But Miss Keyes had a disturbing habit of falling in love with the men who worked for her and this propensity made apprenticeship under her a risky business. Nevertheless she managed to produce a large body of work and had some influence on younger potters. She also persuaded manufacturers to employ well-known painters to design for them.[9]

A private commission for an elaborate dinner service came from Kenneth Clark and his wife Jane, who bought several pictures by Duncan and Vanessa in the thirties. In 1933 Kenneth Clark had written an enthusiastic forward to an exhibition of drawings by Duncan at Agnew's and had bought two pastel studies of the female nude, *The Orange Bandeau* and *Stooping Nude*;[10] and in 1935 Duncan painted Mrs Clark in Fitzroy Street. While Clark's personal taste inclined him to admire the 'intoxicating blend of grace and fantasy' found in Duncan's decorative studies and compositions, he particularly praised those drawings showing a grave 'respect for natural appearances', and those where solid realization had not ousted Duncan's 'natural charm of colour and handling'. The dinner service commissioned by the Clarks in 1932 portrayed various famous women of history including Marie Antoinette, Queen Alexandra, Ellen Terry, Emily Brontë and Elizabeth I.[11]

The Clarks were frequently at Fitzroy Street and Gordon Square in the thirties and Kenneth Clark's appointment as Keeper of the National Gallery in 1933 was warmly supported in Bloomsbury. During the 'Clark boom', as he was later to term this period, he and his wife lived for a time in great style surrounded by a splendid collection of pictures which included many Cézanne drawings and watercolours. Young painters, particularly of the Euston Road School, found practical support and encouragement from Kenneth Clark, especially in the War years. Victor Pasmore[12] and Graham Bell both benefited from his patronage and after Bell's death in the War, Kenneth Clark wrote an introduction to a book of reproductions, lamenting the loss of a painter only just beginning to realize himself. Graham Bell had early on come under the spell of Duncan's painting – 'an intoxicating infatuation' he called it; similar admiration for Duncan's work came from Coldstream and Claude Rogers. Duncan and Vanessa were tireless in their support of this younger generation, helping in many practical ways, introducing patrons and placing their work in exhibitions. Clive wrote favourable reviews and a monograph on Pasmore's work.[13] Duncan and Vanessa lent their names to the Euston Road teaching staff (1938), and the year before included work by Rogers and Pasmore in the 'Coronation Exhibition' at Agnew's, a large show of Contemporary British Painting chosen by them and

Keith Baynes. While the influence of the Euston Road School (all have since developed along their distinctive lines) is still debated, they certainly formed an ordered antidote to the decline of the École de Paris.

Another artist associated with the decorative work of Duncan and Vanessa was Mary Hogarth. Her early work in oils under Sickert's guidance made way later for drawings and watercolours of an economical line and grace, mainly of towns in Greece and Spain, particularly of Granada. She was often in Spain with the painter Wyndham Tryon to whom she was devoted and with whom she worked on designs for cross-stitch embroidery. It was as a needlewoman of great skill and taste that Duncan and Vanessa knew her. 'Hog', as she was called, was a perfectionist and while she often worried the designers with endless questions of execution, she served them superbly. In October 1925, an exhibition was held at the Independent Gallery of embroideries, cross-stitch and more specialized needlework. The designs were by Roger, Vanessa, Duncan and Wyndham Tryon.[14] There were chair seats and backs, a fender stool designed by Vanessa and worked by Mrs Elinor Rendel (the eldest of the Strachey children), and a handsome, low-keyed music stool designed by Duncan and executed by his mother (plate 149).[15] The exhibition was extremely successful and encouraging to other workers and Mary Hogarth continued to carry out the painters' designs until her death in 1934.

149. Music stool, 1924, designed by Duncan Grant and carried out in cross-stitch by Mrs. Ethel Grant. Charleston, Sussex

150. A bedroom cupboard, *c.* 1930, decorated by Duncan Grant. Decorations at Charleston date from all periods and include a bedroom by Angelica Bell and, in the garden, sculpture by Quentin Bell

Duncan's largest commission and one of his few public ones came in 1935 from the Cunard-White Star Company to decorate a lounge with three large panels for the R.M.S. Queen Mary. The largest panel, inspired by the Spanish dance *Seguidilla*, contains six figures dancing or playing instruments. The two smaller panels each contain two female figures, *The Flower Gatherers* and *The Sheaf*. In April 1935 Duncan decided to go to Rome to work on studies for the decorations as well as paint in the city and surrounding country.

In early May Vanessa arrived with Angelica.[16] They had driven from London in great luxury in a chauffeured car owned by Vita Sackville-West. Models in Rome were cheap and numerous and Duncan began large half-sized studies for his panels, as well as painting still lifes on rainy days, and landscapes in the gardens and further afield on trips to the Campagna, especially Frascati. Vanessa had also been asked to do 'panels, stuffs, carpets and everything for what they call the 18th class drawing-room' on the Queen Mary. She made studies for a large painting of figures grouped about a fountain. At the end of May Leonard and Virginia arrived, Virginia increasingly disliking Vanessa's absences abroad. Clive was another welcome visitor coming on from Sicily and going on to Paris to see Derain, Picasso and Cocteau and hear Segonzac praise Vanessa as easily the best painter in England and make extravagant and flattering personal remarks which Clive eagerly passed on.

Once back in England, the really strenuous work on the Queen Mary panels began, not helped by the Company's altering their dimensions at exasperatingly regular intervals. By November Duncan's three panels were all in progress and Vanessa was working at hers from ten in the morning until four in the afternoon. In February the largest panel and one of the smaller ones by Duncan was put up in place in the Queen Mary lounge and visited by Sir Percy Bates, the Company's Chairman. He said he had always been against decorations in the lounge and took it upon himself to refuse them. Duncan was informed but it was his friends who seemed outraged and a fine uproar ensued; there were letters in the newspapers condemning Sir Percy's action, demands from Leonard that £10,000 compensation should be paid above the agreed fee for the work; Kenneth Clark, Raymond Mortimer, Samuel Courtauld and Clive forcibly expressed their scandalized feelings. One of the reasons given by Cunard for the refusal was that the decorations were not suitable for the kind of clientele who would be travelling on the liner. The *Standard* and *The Times* reported the whole story in detail. Some compensation was arranged and there was a show at Agnew's of the panels and all the studies in 1937, which was widely acclaimed, but Duncan's reputation, for which he of course cared nothing, was damaged in the eyes of those people who knew little of the whole affair beyond the fact that the panels had been refused. Soon after the storm broke in the newspapers, Duncan slipped away for a few weeks in Spain, jangled and exhausted by the fuss. During the Second World War the decorations were hung in the canteen of the National Gallery. The two smaller ones were exhibited again by Agnew's in 1972 and entered a private collection. A reviewer in *Country*

Life[17] wrote of the refusal: 'One cannot regret the decision, for they are obviously far too good for the decoration of a luxury liner, and ought to find a permanent home where their qualities would be better appreciated.' Raymond Mortimer later came to a balanced view of the whole incident, deciding that he saw good reason for the refusal of the panels. 'They would have contrasted violently with the style of decoration in which the rest of the ship was lavishly embellished. Moreover, they would certainly not have appealed to the film-stars, opera-singers, oil-magnates and other Big Business tycoons who before the war were bound to be the most valuable patrons of a luxury liner. It would perhaps have been better if the Company had thought of this before commissioning so distinguished and so inappropriate an artist.'[18]

151. *Charleston Garden*, 1933, by Vanessa Bell. 30 × 25 in. Private Collection, London. A view from Duncan Grant's studio at Charleston with Angela Bell sewing

152. *Miss Holland, c.* 1933–34, by Duncan Grant. 30 × 22 in. Thos. Agnew & Sons, London. A portrait study (one of a pair) notable for its fluent, painterly qualities typical of Grant's work at that time. Miss Holland, a model and relation of Oscar Wilde, posed for Grant on several occasions, particularly for *Pour Vous* formerly in the collection of Edward le Bas

An essential element in any account of the life Duncan and Vanessa led between the Wars is the small house La Bergère just outside Cassis in the South of France. La Bergère was built for the Bells on land belonging to a Colonel Teed, retired from the Bengal Lancers and cultivating his vineyard 'Fontcreuse'. He was extremely generous to Vanessa, a charming, amiable landlord who, while never pressing in his attentions, readily exerted himself to make the Bells comfortable, helping over the construction of the house and giving them vines to plant in the garden.

Vanessa's acquaintance with Cassis, at that time a quiet, small fishing village with a café in the Place and a hotel, the Cendrillon, for the English visitors, came about when Duncan fell victim to an attack of pneumonia in 1925 when staying with his mother and Aunt Daisy in Roland Penrose's rented villa 'Les Mimosas'. It was reported to Vanessa in London that Duncan had typhoid, and, deeply alarmed, she set off at once with Angelica and her nurse Grace who had become very much part of the Bell family.[19] She found Duncan thin and feeble but gradually recovering amidst the attentions of his mother, aunt, and their elderly female companion Metta Elwes. Vanessa was immediately taken with the area. Virginia's description of it after her visit with Leonard in 1925 had not been exaggerated.

At Cassis, Vanessa, with her family about her, experienced great happiness and told Roger: 'I always feel the greatest possible relief when anyone (except possibly you and Virginia?) goes away.'[20] Maynard and Lytton would

153. *South of France*, 1922, by Duncan Grant. $25\frac{1}{2} \times 31\frac{3}{4}$ in. The Tate Gallery, London. One of several landscapes painted at St. Tropez and among Grant's most lyrical evocations of Provence

complain, as did Virginia, that 'the painters' had retired to Cassis, so long were they away on some occasions. Vanessa relied for news from England on her correspondents – mainly Clive, Virginia and Roger (when he was not at Cassis himself). After a more than usually full and gossipy post she wrote to Clive that 'I feel once more in touch with old Bloomsbury which seems to be going on unchanged and peculiar as ever.' Maynard too would write with detailed accounts of the London Artists' Association, the latest news from Cambridge and such tempting morsels as: 'We had Leonard and Virginia to dinner a fortnight ago and enjoyed ourselves outrageously with four hours of

154. *Window, South of France*, 1928, by Duncan Grant. $38\frac{3}{4} \times 31\frac{1}{4}$ in. Manchester City Art Galleries. A view from 'La Bergère' looking towards Cassis and the Mediterranean. Painted during Grant's first stay at this 'second Charleston in France', as Vanessa Bell called it

malicious gossip – no one escaped.'[21] The society they saw in Cassis was very different from London though it had its intrigues and scandals and its flamboyant characters, such as the Greek painter Yanko Varda with his numerous mistresses and house full of artists and Bohemian hangers-on. At various times Braque, Miro and the English painter Julian Trevelyan were visitors.[22] There were colonels and spinsters, Wyndham Tryon and the Roumanian painter Grigoresco who wanted to marry the pretty young Grace (as did the chief pastry-cook of Cassis). Roland Penrose and his new wife Lee Miller provided a different kind of society and a little further down the coast, at Bandol, lived Aldous and Maria Huxley. Clive in the early thirties was on close terms with Aldous Huxley – 'he is one of the human beings I have got to know really well in the last few years and for whom I am truly thankful.'[23] Luckily the inhabitants of La Bergère got on well with the Cassidians and had two devoted women, Gabrielle and Elise, to cook for them and look after the house.

La Bergère itself was a compact house with two studio-bedrooms, a small room each for Angelica and Grace, a bathroom and a kitchen. Meals were usually taken outside on the terrace which with its vines and plants became almost another room. If the mistral made out-of-doors life impossible there was a small dining room inside. Naturally there were decorated doors and an odd assortment of furniture from the second-hand shops of Marseilles and Toulon, and pottery from Aix and Aubagne. One pottery at Aubagne still used its original eighteenth-century moulds. Its ware was often in demand and cases of it were despatched to England, including a whole dinner service which Virginia had bought on one visit. Such places were discovered or visited on the short excursions that were possible from La Bergère. One excursion with the Woolfs took them to Les Baux ('this is where Dante got his idea of Hell, said Duncan' wrote Virginia in her diary, 17 April 1928) and on to the asylum at St. Rémy where Van Gogh had stayed. Its peacefulness and pretty old garden pleased Virginia so much that she hoped the next time she went 'cracked' she could go and stay there. In his last years Roger stayed at the Mas d'Angirany, a Provençal farmhouse on the outskirts of St. Rémy, surrounded by olives and vines with the Alpilles rising in the background. Other regular visitors to Cassis included Angus Davidson, Raymond Mortimer and Clive's brother Cory Bell.

One of the major advantages of these years at Cassis was that it enabled Vanessa and more particularly Duncan to escape from the inevitable trappings of success. In the thirties they were extremely well-known in England, though attempts to invade their private lives by newspapers and interviewers were met with an icy refusal from Vanessa or a mumbled apology from Duncan who was 'just leaving' for France, or the country, or anywhere. This refusal to be drawn led to some stinging attacks and accusations of superiority. By that time 'Bloomsbury' was in use more as a term of abuse, a label for anything repressive, reactionary, and morally shady. In reviews of exhibitions critics would write about Bloomsbury rather than of the paintings – a trait which survives even now. 'Judging from an extraordinary article in *Drawing and Design* by Mr Reitlinger, it [Bloomsbury] is still able to rouse

155. Duncan Grant, Cassis, *c.* 1930

156. Vanessa Bell, Cassis, *c.* 1930

157. Raymond Mortimer,
Julian Bell, Vanessa Bell,
Quentin Bell at Charleston,
1928

158. *Julian Bell and Roger
Fry Playing Chess*, c. 1930–1,
by Vanessa Bell. $11\frac{1}{2} \times 21$ in.
Exhibited 1967, Folio Fine
Art, London. Present
location unknown. A
pencil study drawn at
Charleston for the oil
painting at King's College,
Cambridge. Fry was devoted
to Vanessa Bell's children
and Julian Bell helped him
with his translations of
Mallarmé

159. Vanessa Bell at
Charleston in 1932

160. Roger Fry at
Charleston in 1932

outsiders to fury – I have never read such an amazing piece of sour-graped rage – almost libellous about our co-habitations, only no name is actually mentioned,' wrote Vanessa to Clive from La Bergère.[24] On another occasion Vanessa was described as 'Mrs Duncan Grant' in the *Daily Telegraph* and she considered sueing for damages. Bloomsbury was indeed under attack – from Wyndham Lewis most directly, and from F. R. Leavis and I. A. Richards on literary and aesthetic grounds. Lytton's reputation after his death in 1932 sank astonishingly and Roger's posthumous name was not free from incrimination. Duncan and Vanessa cared nothing for such things except when distortion and personal allusions entered the critical arena. They had no professional jealousies and as we have seen were eager to help younger painters including those who maintained different aesthetic aims. In matters of politics the two painters were similarly inclined to the left, distinctly anti-fascist, and staunchly pacifist. But the idea of meetings and rallies, of accepting someone else's lead, was antipathetic; they did, however, help organizations through their painting. In 1939 both were on the committee of the Artists International Association, along with Moore, Gill, John, Paul Nash and Lucien Pissarro. In that year the Association held a large and varied fourth annual exhibition at the Whitechapel Gallery to demonstrate their solidarity for the 'Unity of Artists for Peace, Democracy and Cultural Development'. The impact of European events was evident in the theatre, in films, in poetry and novels. Painting was a different matter though Duncan and Vanessa had been among the first people to see and appreciate Picasso's *Guernica*. In Paris in the spring of 1937 they ran across Picasso at the Deux Magots and he invited them to his new rooms in the rue des Augustins. He had rented two top floors in a large seventeenth-century house and at one end of an empty room was the unfinished canvas *Guernica*, entirely in greys, black and white. After a while Vanessa commented '*C'est un peu terrible*', which pleased Picasso. '*Oui, c'est un peu pour m'expliquer sur les choses que se passent la bas.*' Quentin, who had accompanied them, asked Picasso to sit on the platform at the Albert Hall during a meeting in aid of the Basque children. Picasso instantly agreed to do so though in fact he did not attend.

A few months afterwards Julian Bell was killed in Spain while driving an ambulance for the Republicans. His death was a symbol of the growing horror of the decade and for Vanessa the end of all real happiness. For some months after the arrival of the telegram telling of Julian's death, she was confined to bed at Charleston. She was solaced by visits from Virginia and by the presence of Duncan, Quentin and Angelica. Painting only very gradually became possible again, small canvases of flowers and still lifes, and studies of the garden. From that time onwards she clung more fiercely to her family circle and she and Duncan spent more and more time at Charleston. Visitors were not always welcome; new friends of Duncan's were often subjected to a scrutiny which left them with an impression of a forbidding, silently masterful, rather terrifying lady. But those within the circle still experienced her mordant humour, her mischievousness, the sudden incisive remark, her pleasure at the pecularities of her friends, or at a bawdy joke which made her dissolve into laughter. To outsiders she was 'that stately lady' we see in

PLATE VII

PLATE VIII

161. *Self Portrait*, 1958, by Vanessa Bell. 19 × 15½ in. Collection Lord Clark

Duncan's wartime portrait of her, eyes gazing out at the spectator, aloof, aristocratic, isolated in a world which she viewed with uncompromising honesty and a courage born of humour.

[1] 'Modern English Textiles', in *Artwork*, January–March 1926.

[2] 'The Artist in the House', in the *Listener*, 16 March 1932.

[3] 'Modern English Textiles II', in the *Listener*, 15 June 1932.

[4] They were widely exhibited in London with an initial showing at the Cooling Galleries. In April 1932 some were seen at Zwemmer's bookshop, Charing Cross Road, alongside Chermayeff furniture and Kauffer rugs. In the following month more examples appeared at Keebles in Carlisle Street, Soho, where Osbert Sitwell opened an exhibition of mural designs by such younger painters as Burra, Ravilious and John Armstrong.

[5] The *Architectural Review*, February 1933.

[6] In a subsequent edition, Kathleen Raine wrote in the introduction: 'In Dorothy Wellesley Yeats found at once a symbol and a charming embodiment of the traditional aristocratic culture he admired. . . . At Penns in the Rocks he found again a house, where, as once at Coole Park, "all's accustomed, ceremonious".'

[7] Other painters working for Shell included Paul Nash, Clive Gardiner, Tristram Hillier, John Armstrong and du Plessis.

[8] She was also an important influence for Quentin Bell when making pots became his leading activity. Quentin lived for a time near Stoke-on-Trent to learn about painting and glazing pottery under the eye of T. A. Fennemore who, though a very different figure, did in a smaller way for pottery what Allan Walton achieved with textile design.

[9] One firm in particular put this into practice – Messrs E. Brain, makers of Foley China, who commissioned designs for tableware from a group of widely differing artists. There was some lugubrious work from Frank Brangwyn, Dame Laura Knight, and Dod and Ernest Procter. Barbara Hepworth, John Armstrong, Graham Sutherland and Ben Nicholson also contributed alongside Paul Nash, Duncan Grant and Vanessa Bell.

[10] Both reproduced in R. Mortimer, *Duncan Grant*, op. cit., plates 20 and 21; a further picture *After Zurbaran*, owned by Lord Clark, is reproduced, plate 15, and the superb *Figure in a Glass Case*, plate 11, was given by Lord Clark to the Birmingham City Art Gallery.

[11] Duncan's passionate interest in great actresses resulted in a plate graced by Eleanora Duse whom he had seen perform in Italy. About this time he gave a drawing of the French actress Mme Réjane to Lydia Keynes to celebrate the latter's performance as Norah in *The Doll's House*, 1934. Another actress who came to Fitzroy Street was Marie-Hélène Dasté, daughter of Duncan's old friend Copeau; a large pastel resulted which is also in Lord Clark's collection.

[12] Kenneth Clark was responsible for Pasmore's release from the Public Health Department, County Hall, thus enabling him to paint full time.

[13] Penguin Books, 1944.

[14] Tryon was not a decorator in the sense that the others were and his Spanish landscape worked on the back of a chair by Mary Hogarth was 'neither more nor less than a needlework copy of one of Mr Tryon's most characteristic landscapes.' R. R. Tatlock in the *Burlington Magazine*, October 1925.

[15] The stool is at Charleston, Sussex, and a large watercolour design is in a private collection, Berkshire.

[16] Angelica Bell had recently left Langford Grove School, Essex. She went on to the Michel St. Denis School of Acting and continued to paint, attending the Euston Road School. A tea service decorated by her was produced by Foley China. In 1942 she married David Garnett.

[17] 20 November 1937.

[18] See *Duncan Grant* by R. Mortimer, op. cit., where *The Flower Gatherers* is reproduced, pl. 18. *The Sheaf* forms the catalogue frontispiece to *Twentieth Century British Art*, Thos. Agnew's, November–December 1972.

[19] Grace Higgens was employed by Vanessa from 1921 and eventually became the housekeeper and cook at Charleston until she retired in 1971.

[20] 10 May 1928.

[21] JMK to VB, 2 June 1930.

[22] For an amusing account of Varda, see Trevelyan's *Indigo Days*, 1957, pp.59–63.

[23] CB to VB, Cannes, 25 February 1930.

[24] 6 February 1928.

Chronologies

VANESSA BELL

1879   *30 May* Vanessa Stephen born at 22 Hyde Park Gate, London.
Educated privately.

1882–94   Annual summer visits to Talland House, St. Ives.

1894   With her sister Virginia stays with G. F. Watts in Guildford, Surrey.

1896–1900   Studies under Sir Arthur Cope, R.A., at his school in Kensington.

1901   Submits drawing to the Royal Academy Schools and is accepted for September.
Taught by J. S. Sargent.

1902   *April* Visits Rome and Florence with her half-brother George Duckworth.
Her portrait is painted by C. W. Furse and exhibited at the New English Art Club.

1903   *March* Visits Watts.

1904   After the death of her father in February and a holiday in Italy (Venice and Florence), moves with Virginia and her brothers Thoby and Adrian to 46 Gordon Square, Bloomsbury.
Leaves the Royal Academy Schools.
Autumn Brief attendance at the Slade School.

1905   *February* Beginning of the Stephens' 'Thursday Evenings' at Gordon Square.
Her first commission, *Portrait of Lady Robert Cecil*, exhibited at the Summer Exhibition, New Gallery (400).
Summer Organizes the Friday Club for annual exhibitions, discussions, and lectures on art. First exhibition in November.
Friendship with Henry Lamb begins.
First meeting with Duncan Grant.

1906   *April* Painting Lord Robert Cecil.
31 July Refuses marriage proposal from Clive Bell.
September-October With Adrian, Virginia, Thoby and Violet Dickinson in Greece.

1907   *7 February* Marries Clive Bell.
April Honeymoon in Paris.

1908   *4 February* Birth of her son Julian Bell.
June-July Exhibits three paintings at Friday Club Exhibition, Baillie Gallery, London.
July Exhibits *Portrait* (1421) at the Allied Artists' Association, Albert Hall, London.
September In Italy with Clive and Virginia, staying in Siena and Perugia and visiting Assisi and Pavia. In Paris last week of September.

1909   *April-May* With Clive in Florence. Paints Rezia Corsini, a family friend.
Summer Exhibits *Iceland Poppies* (146) at the New English Art Club (N.E.A.C.) summer exhibition. Encouragement from Sickert.
September-October At Studland Bay, Dorset.

1910   *March-April* At Studland Bay, Dorset.
Exhibits *London Morning* (219), a nude study, at N.E.A.C. summer exhibition.
June Exhibits two still lifes at the Friday Club Exhibition, Alpine Club Gallery.
19 August Birth of her second son, Quentin Bell.
September At Studland Bay, Dorset.

1911   *February* Exhibits *Apples* (138) and other works at the Friday Club, Alpine Club Gallery.
At Firle, Sussex, with Virginia.
April Visits Turkey with Clive, Roger Fry and H. T. J. Norton.
September Mainly at Millmead Cottage, Guildford (near Roger Fry).
September At Studland Bay, Dorset.
October Visits Paris with Clive.

1912   *January* In the Isle of Wight with Roger Fry.
February Exhibits four pictures (including *Design for screen*) at the Friday Club, Alpine Club Gallery.
At Asheham House painting landscapes.
May In Italy with Clive and Roger Fry.
July Exhibits *Monte Oliveto* (800) at Allied Artists' Association, Albert Hall, London.
Represented by six paintings at 'Exposition de Quelques Indépendants Anglais', Galerie Barbazanges, Paris.
August Sells *The Spanish Model* to the Contemporary Art Society (C.A.S.) for five guineas.
Attends the Cologne 'Sonderbund' exhibition with Clive and Roger Fry.
Summer At Asheham House.
October-December Exhibits four paintings in the English section of the Second Post-Impressionist Exhibition, Grafton Galleries, London.

1913   *January-February* At Asheham House painting and designing for the Omega Workshops opening exhibition.

Exhibits at first 'Grafton Group' exhibition, Alpine Club Gallery.

May In Italy with Clive, Roger Fry and Duncan Grant; visits Rome, Viterbo, Ravenna and Venice. Returns via Paris.

July 8 Opening of the Omega Workshops at 33 Fitzroy Square, London.

August Summer camp at Brandon, Thetford, Norfolk, with Roger Fry, Maynard Keynes, Duncan Grant and others.

September-October Painting at Asheham House, including *Portrait of Lytton Strachey*.

1914 *January* Five paintings and a screen exhibited at the second 'Grafton Group' exhibition, Alpine Club Gallery. Retires from membership of the Friday Club.

May In Paris with Duncan Grant.

May-June Five pictures in 'Twentieth Century Art', Whitechapel Gallery, London, including *Childhood of Thisbe*.

August-September At Asheham House.

1915 *Spring* Takes the Hutchinsons' house Eleanor, West Wittering, Sussex.

Exhibition of costumes at the Omega Workshops.

August At The Grange, Bosham, Sussex, with Duncan Grant and Maynard Keynes.

1916 *February* Exhibition of paintings at the Omega Workshops.

At Wissett Lodge, Halesworth, Suffolk, with her children and Duncan Grant and David Garnett.

October Moves to Charleston, Firle, Sussex.

1917 *May* Sends five copies to the Omega Workshops 'Copies' exhibition.

September-October Eight paintings in the 'New Movement in Art', Mansard Gallery, Heal & Sons (shown previously at the Royal Birmingham Society of Artists).

November Exhibits with others at the Omega Workshops.

1918 *8-28 August* Six pictures in 'Englische Moderne Malerei' at the Kunsthaus, Zurich.

September-October With Duncan Grant decorates sitting room for Maynard Keynes at 46 Gordon Square.

November Woodcuts for *Kew Gardens* by Virginia Woolf, published by the Hogarth Press.

Exhibits with others at the Omega Workshops.

25 December Birth of daughter Angelica at Charleston.

1919 *March* Takes Alix Sargent-Florence's flat at 36 Regent Square, London, for one year.

Summer Meetings with Picasso and Derain in London. With Duncan Grant decorates Keynes's rooms at Webb's Court, King's College, Cambridge (finished 1922).

November Exhibits with the 'London Group' (and almost annually until her death).

1920 *May* In Rome with Keynes and Duncan Grant. Visits Picasso in Paris.

Moves to 50 Gordon Square.

Spring Exhibits with others at the Vildrac Gallery, Paris.

November Exhibits 16 water colours at the Independent Gallery, an exhibition shared with Duncan Grant and Robert Lotiron.

1921 *February* Decorates Adrian and Karin Stephen's rooms at 40 Gordon Square with Duncan Grant.

March Represented in 'Some Contemporary English Artists' at the Independent Gallery.

May Visits Paris meeting Derain, Picasso, Satie, Braque and Kisling.

October To La Maison Blanche, St. Tropez, with Duncan Grant.

1922 *February* Takes a studio in Paris for a month.

Moves to 46 Gordon Square.

June First one-artist exhibition held at the Independent Gallery.

1923 *May* In Spain with Roger Fry and Duncan Grant.

1924 *May-June* In Paris with Duncan Grant. Meetings with Picasso, Derain, Matthew Smith and Segonzac.

1925 Moves to 37 Gordon Square.

January Decorations with Duncan Grant for Peter Harrison at Moon Hall, Gomshall, Surrey.

May In Paris. Visits the Pellerin Collection of Cézannes with Duncan Grant and Roger Fry.

March-April Decorations with Duncan Grant for Raymond Mortimer's flat, 6 Gordon Place, London.

Summer at Charleston.

October Contributes to 'Modern Designs in Needlework', Independent Gallery.

1926 *May-June* First London exhibition of the 'London Artists' Association' (L.A.A.) at the Leicester Galleries, London.

May-June In Italy with Duncan Grant; visits Venice, Ravenna, Padua and Ferrara.

October With Duncan Grant decorates Clive Bell's flat at 50 Gordon Square.

Represented in L.A.A. exhibitions in Berlin, New York and Pittsburg.

1927 *January-May* Takes the Villa Corsica in Cassis, France.

August With Duncan Grant decorates the garden room at Ethel Sands and Nan Hudson's house Château d'Auppegard, near Dieppe.

1928 *January-May* First visit to her house La Bergère, Fontcreuse, Cassis.

Takes studio at 8 Fitzroy Street, adjoining Duncan Grant's.

October To Cassis, returning via Paris. Meetings with Picasso, Segonzac and Marchand.

November Represented at the Marie Sterner Galleries, New York, in exhibition of Modern English Pictures (L.A.A.).

1929 *January-February* To Germany, Austria and Prague with Duncan Grant.

May-June At La Bergère.

November Commission from Lady Dorothy Wellesley to decorate with Duncan Grant the dining room of Penns-in-the-Rocks, Withyham, Sussex (finished 1931).

1930 *February–March* Exhibition at the Cooling Galleries, 92 New Bond Street, London, with catalogue introduction by Virginia Woolf.
Autumn At La Bergère.
December Wins third prize for interior design for 'Lord Benbow's Apartment', a competition set by the *Architectural Review*. Collaborators: John Skeaping, Humphrey Slater, Robert Medley and Duncan Grant.

1931 *December* Included in exhibition of Allan Walton textiles at the Cooling Galleries.

1932 *December–January* At La Bergère.
Décor for *High Yellow* given by the Camargo Ballet, with choreography by Ashton and Bradley, music by Spike Hughes, costumes by William Chappell.
June–July 'Recent Paintings by Duncan Grant, Vanessa Bell and Keith Baynes', Agnew & Sons, London.
December Opening of a 'Music Room' decorated and furnished by Vanessa Bell and Duncan Grant, installed at the Lefevre Galleries, 1a King Street, London.

1933 *January* Décor and costumes for the Sadlers Wells Ballet production of *Pomona*, with choreography by Ashton, music by Constant Lambert.

1934 Décor for Ethel Smyth's ballet *Fête Galante*, with choreography by Dolin.
March Exhibition at the Lefevre Galleries.
October Pottery for Foley China exhibited at Harrods, London, in 'Modern Art for the Table'.

1935 Executed decorations for R.M.S. Queen Mary.
May–June In Rome with her family and Duncan Grant.

1936 In Paris with Duncan Grant, early summer.

1937 *January–February* Included in 'British Contemporary Art', Rosenberg & Helft, Ltd., 31 Bruton Street, London.
Spring At La Bergère.
May In Paris with Duncan Grant. Visits Picasso working on *Guernica*.
June–July 'Contemporary British Artists', Coronation Exhibition at Agnew & Sons, chosen by Vanessa Bell, Duncan Grant and Keith Baynes.
18 July Exhibition at the Lefevre Galleries.
Julian Bell killed in Spain.

1938 Carries out decorations for Ethel Sands' house with Duncan Grant, in Chelsea Square, London.
Teaching at the Euston Road School.
Autumn At La Bergère.

1939 *September* Last visit to La Bergère.

1939–45 Living at Charleston.

1941 *June–July* Exhibition, shared with Frank Dobson and Algernon Newton, at the Leicester Galleries.

1943 *June* Represented in 'Robert Colquhoun and Notable British Artists' at the Lefevre Galleries.

1943 *October* Ceremony to mark the completion of murals at

Berwick Church, Sussex; painted at Charleston (1940–2) in collaboration with Duncan Grant and Quentin Bell.

1944 Decorations with Duncan Grant for the Children's Restaurant, Devonshire Hill School, Tottenham, on the story of Cinderella.

1946 In Dieppe with Duncan Grant and Edward Le Bas.

1948 Venice and Lucca.

1949–55 Living at 26a Canonbury Square, Islington.
September Lucca.

1950 Member of the Society of Mural Painters. First Exhibition, Arts Council of Great Britain.
Venice.

1952 Lucca and Perugia.

1953 *Autumn* Auxerre.
Exhibition by past Members of L.A.A., Ferens Art Gallery, Hull.

1955 Takes a flat at 28 Percy Street, London, with Duncan Grant.

1956 In Asolo with Duncan Grant, Edward le Bas and Eardley Knollys.
February Exhibition at the Adams Gallery.

1957 In Venice, Lucca and Cortona.

1959 At Menton.

1961 *7 April* Dies at Charleston.
October Memorial Exhibition at the Adams Gallery, with catalogue foreword by Segonzac.

1964 *March* Memorial Exhibition at the Arts Council Gallery, London.

1966 'Paintings by Duncan Grant and Vanessa Bell,' Royal West of England Academy, Bristol.

1967 *November* 'Drawings and Designs', Folio Fine Art Ltd, London.

1973 *November–December* 'Paintings and Drawings', Anthony d'Offay Gallery, London.

DUNCAN GRANT

1885 *21 January* Duncan James Corrowr Grant born at The Doune, Inverness-shire, Scotland.
Early years in Burma and India.

1894–9 Attends Hillbrow Preparatory School, Rugby.

1899–1902 Attends St. Paul's School, London. Living with the Strachey family at 69 Lancaster Gate, London.

1899–1900 *Winter* With his parents in Bruges.

1900 Visits Malta where his father is stationed.

1901 Summer at Rothiemurchus.

1902 Summer at Streatley-on-Thames.

1902 *September* Attends Westminster School of Art.

1903 *Whitsun* Introduced to Clive Bell and Thoby Stephen at Cambridge.
Summer At Streatley-on-Thames and in the Hebrides.
Painting holiday in Holland.

1904–5 *Winter* In Florence with his mother. Copies Masaccio and Piero della Francesca. Visits Arezzo, Siena and Rome.

1905 Leaves Westminster School.
Summer In France and Wales.
Autumn Lives with his parents, now permanently in England, at 143 Fellows Road, Hampstead.
Takes a studio in Upper Baker Street.
Attends a meeting of the Friday Club and meets Vanessa Stephen for the first time.

1906 *February* Attends Jacques-Emile Blanche's school La Palette in Paris.
Summer Painting holiday at Rothiemurchus with Arthur Hobhouse.

1907 *January* Returns to La Palette in Paris, living at 22 rue Delambre.
February First meeting with Wyndham Lewis.
March Introduced to Augustus John by Henry Lamb. Visits Salon des Indépendants.
April Moves to Atelier 45, rue Campagne Première, Montparnasse.
June Leaves La Palette. In Florence and Certaldo, near Siena.
Summer At Rothiemurchus painting John Peter Grant.
November–December Exhibits two pictures at United Arts Club, Grafton Galleries: *South Porch, Chartres* and *Walnut Trees*.

1908 Summer term at the Slade School.
August–September In the Orkneys with Maynard Keynes who sits for his portrait.
October At Rothiemurchus.
December Takes a studio near Belsize Park Gardens, London. Paints Pernel Strachey.

1909 *April* With Keynes in Paris and Versailles. Visits Salon des Indépendants and meets Gertrude Stein.
Visits Matisse at Issy-les-Moulineaux, Paris.
Summer Painting at Burford, near Oxford.
September–October Shares rooms with Keynes in Belgrave Road, St. John's Wood, London
Exhibits two pictures at the Winter Exhibition of the New English Art Club, one of them a *Portrait of James Strachey*.
November Takes rooms with Keynes at 21 Fitzroy Square.

1910 *10 February* Takes part in the 'Dreadnought Hoax' with Adrian and Virginia Stephen, Horace Cole, and others.
April Visits Greece and Turkey with Keynes.
June Three pictures, including *The Lemon Gatherers*, at the Friday Club exhibition.
Summer At Burford.
Exhibits *Study* (350) at Winter Exhibition, New English Art Club.

1910–11 Murals for Keynes's rooms at Webb's Court, King's College, Cambridge.

1911 *February* Exhibits *Idyll* at the Friday Club.

April In Sicily and Tunis with Keynes; returns via Florence.
Summer Working on *Bathing* and *Football* murals for the Borough Polytechnic, London.
Painting holiday at Granchester with Jacques Raverat and Rupert Brooke.
October In France with Roger Fry and Clive Bell.
Moves with Keynes to 38 Brunswick Square, a house shared with Adrian and Virginia Stephen, Gerald Shove and Leonard Woolf.
December Exhibits *Parrot Tulips* at the Second Camden Town Group Exhibition, Carfax Gallery. Bought by Edward Marsh.

1912 *December–January Idyll* and *Lemon Gatherers* in exhibition of Contemporary Paintings organized by the Contemporary Art Society (C.A.S.) at City Art Gallery, Manchester.
February Exhibits *The Red Seal – decoration* and *Still Life* at the Friday Club.
July Represented in 'Exposition de Quelques Indépendants Anglais', Galerie Barbazanges, Paris.
Summer At Everleigh, Marlborough, and Asheham House, Sussex.
October–December Six pictures in the English section of the Second Post-Impressionist Exhibition, Grafton Galleries.
Commissioned by H. Granville-Barker to design a production of *Macbeth* – a project abandoned in 1913.

1913 *March* Exhibits at first Grafton Group Exhibition, Alpine Club, Gallery.
April Italy with Clive and Vanessa Bell and Roger Fry.
8 July Opening of the Omega Workshops Ltd., 33 Fitzroy Square, London.
September At Asheham House.
October In Paris to see Jacques Copeau who had commissioned costumes and scenery for *Twelfth Night*, to be produced at the Théâtre du Vieux Colombier. Visits Picasso.
15 November Attends founding meeting of the London Group.

1914 *January* Exhibits at second Grafton Group Exhibition, including *Adam and Eve*, commissioned by the C.A.S.
January–February In the South of France and Tunis.
February–March Included in exhibition of modern painting at the Sandon Society, Bluecoat Chambers, Liverpool (C.A.S.).
May In Paris with Vanessa Bell for the première of *Twelfth Night*.
May–June Four pictures in 'Twentieth Century Art', Whitechapel Gallery, London.
August–September At Asheham House.
Autumn Leaves Brunswick Square and takes a room in the Bells' house at 46 Gordon Square; studio at 22 Fitzroy Street.

1915 *February* Makes marionettes for a performance of Racine's *Bérènice* at the Omega Workshops.

Spring With the Bells and David Garnett at Eleanor, West Wittering, Sussex.

June Exhibits three pictures by invitation at the Vorticist Exhibition, Doré Galleries, London.

August In Dorset and at The Grange, Bosham, Sussex. Christmas and New Year at Asheham House.

1916 *March* Agricultural work in Suffolk, living at Wissett Lodge, Halesworth, with David Garnett and Vanessa Bell and family.

May As conscientious objector receives exemption from combatant service and undertakes farm-work for the rest of the war.

October Moves with Vanessa Bell and David Garnett to Charleston, Firle, Sussex.

1917 *May* Four copies at the Omega Workshops 'Copies' exhibition.

Summer Designs costumes for Copeau's production of Maeterlinck's *Pélleas et Mélisande*.

September-October Nine paintings in the 'New Movement in Art', Mansard Gallery, Heal & Sons (shown previously at the Royal Birmingham Society of Artists).

November Exhibits with others at the Omega Workshops, including *The Kitchen* and *The Tub* (1916).

1918 *Pélleas et Mélisande* performed in New York; also *Twelfth Night* with additional scenery by Grant.

8-28 August Six pictures in 'Englische Moderne Malerei' at the Kunsthaus, Zurich, an exhibition organized by the C.A.S.

September-October With Vanessa Bell decorates sitting room for Keynes at 46 Gordon Square.

November Exhibits with others at the Omega Workshops.

Released from farm-work. Continues living at Charleston and uses Fry's studio at 18 Fitzroy Street.

1919 With Vanessa Bell decorates Keynes's rooms at Webb's Court, King's College, Cambridge (finished 1922), replacing earlier decoration.

November Exhibits with the London Group (and continues to do so almost annually until the late 1950s).

1920 Takes a studio at 8 Fitzroy Street (until 1940).

February First one-man exhibition at the Carfax Gallery, St. James's, London.

May In Rome with Keynes and Vanessa Bell; visits Picasso in Paris.

Spring Exhibits with others at the Vildrac Gallery, Paris.

November Exhibits 20 watercolours at the Independent Gallery, Grafton Street, London, an exhibition shared with Vanessa Bell and Robert Lotiron.

1921 *February* Decorates Adrian and Karin Stephen's rooms, 40 Gordon Square, with Vanessa Bell.

March Represented in 'Some Contemporary English Artists' at the Independent Gallery.

May In Paris; meetings with Derain, Picasso, Satie, Braque and Kisling.

October At La Maison Blanche, St. Tropez, with Vanessa Bell and her family.

1922 *February* To Paris from St. Tropez. Takes a studio for a month.

1923 Designs costumes for *Togo or the Noble Savage*, music by Milhaud, choreography by Massine, with Lopokova, Massine and Sokolova among the dancers, for a Cochran review at the Royal Opera House, Covent Garden.

May In Spain with Vanessa Bell and Roger Fry.

June 'Recent Paintings and Drawings' at the Independent Gallery.

1924 Costumes for Lopokova and Rupert Doone in a Coliseum divertissement.

May-June In Paris with Vanessa Bell. Two weeks in Germany.

29 June Scenery for *The Pleasure Garden* by Beatrice Mayor, produced by the Incorporated Stage Society at the Regent Theatre.

Winter In France.

1925 *January* Decorations and fresco for Peter Harrison, Moon Hall, Gomshall, Surrey.

March-April Large mural and decorations with Vanessa Bell for Raymond Mortimer's flat at 6 Gordon Place, London.

May In Paris. Visits Pellerin Collection of Cézannes with Fry and Vanessa Bell.

Designs décor for ballet *The Postman* at the Coliseum with Lopokova and Woizikowski.

July Designs sets and costumes for *The Son of Heaven* by Lytton Strachey, première on 12 July at the Scala Theatre, London.

Summer at Charleston.

October Exhibition of 'Modern Designs in Needlework', Independent Gallery. Designs by Grant, Fry, Vanessa Bell and Wyndham Tryon, worked by Mary Hogarth, Mrs Bartle Grant and Mrs J. M. Rendel.

1926 *May* First London Exhibition of the London Artists' Association (L.A.A.) at the Leicester Galleries – Grant, Bell, Fry, Baynes, Porter, Adeney, Dobson.

May-June Represented at the XV Venice Biennale (L.A.A. consignment).

In Italy with Vanessa Bell –Venice, Ravenna, Padua, Ferrara.

October With Vanessa Bell decorates Clive Bell's flat at 50 Gordon Square, London.

Represented in L.A.A. exhibitions in Berlin, New York and Pittsburg.

1927 *December-May* At Cassis.

April-May 'Paintings by Duncan Grant' at the L.A.A., 163 New Bond Street, London.

August With Vanessa Bell at Ethel Sands and Nan Hudson's house, Château d'Auppegard, near Dieppe, decorating the 'Garden Room'.

October To Cassis with David Garnett.

1928 *January-May* At La Bergère, Fontcreuse, Cassis.

Summer at Charleston.

October To Cassis, returning via Paris. Visits Picasso, Segonzac and Marchand.

November Scenery for George Rylands' production of Milton's *Comus*, first given at the A.D.C. Theatre, Cambridge, and later at 46 Gordon Square, with Michael Redgrave and Lydia Lopokova.

Represented at the Marie Sterner Galleries, New York, in exhibition of Modern English Pictures (L.A.A.).

1929 *January-February* To Germany, Austria and Prague.

February-March Retrospective Exhibition (1910–29) at Paul Guillaume, Brandon Davis Ltd., 73 Grosvenor Street, London.

May-June At La Bergère and St. Raphael.

October 'Recent Work' at the L.A.A., Cooling Galleries.

November Commission from Lady Dorothy Wellesley to decorate with Vanessa Bell the dining room of Penns-in-the-Rocks, Withyham, Sussex (finished 1931).

1930 *February-March* Included in exhibition of paintings at Paul Guillaume, Brandon Davis Ltd., with John, Sickert, Smith and P. Nash.

September 'Eight Modern English Painters', Arthur Tooth & Sons, 155 New Bond Street, London. John, Sickert, Smith, Steer, Grant, P. Nash, Gore and Innes.

Autumn At La Bergère with the Bells, George Bergen and Roger Fry.

1931 *May-June* In Rome with Vincent Sheean at the Palazzo Lovatelli.

June-July 'Recent Paintings by Duncan Grant', L.A.A., Cooling Galleries.

December Exhibition of Allan Walton textiles at the Cooling Galleries. Fabrics designed by Grant, Vanessa Bell, Baynes, Morris, Dobson, Walton, Gifford and H. J. Bull. Also tiles, pottery and furniture painted by Grant, Vanessa Bell, Douglas Davidson and Raymond Coxon.

December-January At La Bergère.

1932 *March* Scenery and costumes for *The Enchanted Grove* produced originally for Camargo Ballet, given by the Vic-Wells Ballet, London. Choreography by Rupert Doone, music by Ravel and Debussy.

June Scenery and costumes for the second act of *Swan Lake*, Camargo Ballet, with choreography after Petipa and Ivanov. Scenery adapted from designs by Inigo Jones.

June-July 'Recent Paintings by Duncan Grant, Vanessa Bell and Keith Baynes', Agnew & Sons.

Represented at the XVIII Venice Biennale.

1933 *December-January* Opening of a 'Music Room' decorated and furnished by Grant and Vanessa Bell, installed at the Lefevre Galleries, 1a King Street, London.

May-June Included in 'Pictures for Collectors', Arthur Tooth & Sons, London.

June 'Drawings by Duncan Grant', Agnew & Sons.

1934 *May* Recent Paintings at the Lefevre Galleries.

October Pottery for Foley China exhibited at Harrods, London, in 'Modern Art for the Table'.

November-December 'Gainsborough to Grant', Agnew & Sons.

1935 Three decorative panels commissioned by the Cunard Steamship Company for R.M.S. Queen Mary.

May-June In Rome (33 Via Magutta) working on the 'Queen Mary' decorations. Joined by Vanessa and Angelica Bell in late May.

1936 *February* 'Queen Mary' decorations rejected.

April In Spain.

Early summer, visits Paris with Vanessa Bell.

1937 *January-February* Included in 'British Contemporary Art', Rosenberg & Helft Ltd., 31 Bruton Street, London.

Spring At La Bergère, painting in Toulon.

May In Paris with Vanessa Bell. Visits Picasso working on *Guernica*.

June-July 'Contemporary British Artists', Coronation Exhibition at Agnew & Sons, chosen by Grant, Vanessa Bell and Keith Baynes.

Wins Medal of Merit at the Paris International Exhibition, for Walton textile 'Apollo and Daphne'.

November-December 'Recent Works by Duncan Grant', Agnew & Sons, including murals and studies for the 'Queen Mary' decorations.

1938 With Vanessa Bell carries out decorations for Ethel Sands' house in Chelsea Square, London.

Teaching at the Euston Road School.

Autumn At La Bergère.

1939 *January-February* Member of Advisory Committee of Artists' International Association for 'Unity of Artists for Peace, Democracy and Cultural Development'. Contributes to fourth annual exhibition, Whitechapel Art Gallery, London.

September At La Begère, his last visit.

Represented in 'Contemporary British Art', World's Fair, New York.

November Included in group exhibition, Agnew & Sons.

Gives up studio at 8 Fitzroy Street which is destroyed by fire in 1940. Moves to Charleston where he is a member of the local Home Guard.

1940 *May* Included in 'Nine Painters' exhibition, Lefevre Galleries.

'Drawings and Sketches by Duncan Grant', Calmann Gallery, 42 St. James's Place, London.

Thirty-nine paintings chosen for the XXII Venice Biennale. The consignment was not sent owing to the War and was instead shown in London at the Wallace Collection.

May-June Living and painting in Plymouth as official war artist.

1942 Elected to the Art Advisory Panel of the Council for the Encouragement of Music and the Arts (later the Arts Council of Great Britain).

1943 *June* Represented in 'Robert Colquhoun and Notable British Artists', Lefevre Galleries.
October Ceremony to mark the completion of murals at Berwick Church, Sussex, by Grant, Vanessa Bell and Quentin Bell, painted at Charleston (1940–2).

1944 Decorations with Vanessa Bell for the Children's Restaurant, Devonshire Hill School, Tottenham, on the story of Cinderella.

1945 *June-July* 'Recent Paintings by Duncan Grant', Leicester Galleries.

1946 With Vanessa Bell and Edward le Bas, painting in Dieppe.
June In Denmark and Sweden.

1946–8 Takes a room in Marjorie Strachey's flat in Taviton Street, London.

1948 In Venice and Lucca.

1949–55 Takes a flat with Vanessa Bell at 26a Canonbury Square, Islington, London.

1949 *September* Lucca.

1950 Member of the Society of Mural Painters. First Exhibition, Arts Council of Great Britain.
Venice.

1952 Peregia and Lucca.

1953 *Autumn* Auxerre.
Exhibition by past members of the L.A.A., Ferens Art Gallery, Hull.

1955 With Vanessa Bell takes a flat at 28 Percy Street, London.

1956 In Asolo with Vanessa Bell, Edward le Bas and Eardley Knollys. Designs scenery and costumes for John Blow's *Venus and Adonis*, first given at the Aldeburgh Festival on 15 June, and in September and October at the Scala Theatre, London. Production by the English Opera Group with Margaret Lensky and Heather Harper.

1957 *May* Forty new paintings exhibited at the Leicester Galleries; exhibition shared with Anne Dunn.
Venice, Lucca and Cortona.

1958–9 Murals for the Russell Chantry Chapel, Lincoln Cathedral.

1959 *May-June* 'Duncan Grant: a retrospective exhibition', Tate Gallery, London.
With the Bussys at Menton.

1961 Menton.
Moves to 24 Victoria Square, London.

1962 Spain.

1963 *April* Retrospective Exhibition at the Minories, Colchester.
Spain.

1964 *November* 'Duncan Grant and his World', Wildenstein & Co. Ltd.

1965 *May-June* Morocco.

1966 *April-May* 'Paintings by Duncan Grant and Vanessa Bell', Royal West of England Academy, Bristol.
Visit to America.

1967 *June-August* Twenty-seven works in 'Artists of Bloomsbury', Rye Art Gallery, Sussex.
Greece.

1968 *Summer* Takes a studio in Fez, Morocco, for two months.

1969 *November* 'Portraits by Duncan Grant', Arts Council Exhibition, Cambridge and Newcastle, Hull and Nottingham.

1970 Moves to Park Square West, London.
Spring Cyprus.
Duncan Grant at Charleston, film by Christopher Mason.
Awarded Honorary Doctor of Letters, Royal College of Art, London.

1972 *January-February* Portugal.
April-May 'Drawings and Watercolours', Anthony d'Offay Gallery, London.

1973 *Autumn* Turkey.

1974 *Autumn* Scotland.

1975 *January-February* 'Recent Paintings', Anthony d'Offay Gallery.
February 'Paintings and Drawings by Duncan Grant', Southover Gallery, Lewes, Sussex.
February-March Ninetieth Birthday Exhibition, Tate Gallery.
'Early Paintings', Anthony d'Offay Gallery.

Selected Bibliography

ASKWITH, BETTY:
  Two Victorian Families, Chatto & Windus, 1971
BARON, WENDY:
  Sickert, Phaidon, 1973
BATES, H. E.:
  Edward Garnett, Max Parrish, 1950
BELL, CLIVE:
  Art, Chatto & Windus, 1914
  'peace at Once', National Labour Press, Manchester and London, 1916
  Pot-Boilers, Chatto & Windus, 1918
  Since Cézanne, Chatto & Windus, 1922
  The Legend of Monte Della Sibilla, Hogarth Press, 1923
  On British Freedom, Chatto & Windus, 1923
  Civilization, an Essay, Chatto & Windus, 1928
  Proust, Hogarth Press, 1928
  Victor Pasmore (Penguin Modern Painters), Penguin Books, 1945
  Old Friends: Personal Recollections, Chatto & Windus, 1956
BELL, JULIAN:
  We Did Not Fight, (ed.), Cobden-Sanderson, 1935
  Essays, Poems and Letters, edited by Quentin Bell, Hogarth Press, 1938
BELL, QUENTIN:
  'Roger Fry', An Inaugural Lecture, Leeds University Press, 1964
  Virginia Woolf, A Biography, 2 vols., 1972
  Bloomsbury, An Omega Book, Futura Publications, 1974 (1st edn, 1968)
BENNETT, ARNOLD:
  The Pretty Lady, Richards Press, 1950
  The Journals, Penguin Books, 1971
BERTRAM, ANTHONY:
  Paul Nash, The Portrait of an Artist, Faber, 1955
BLANCHE, JACQUES-ÉMILE:
  Portraits of a Lifetime (trans. by Walter Clement), Dent, 1937
BROWN, OLIVER:
  Exhibition, The Memoirs of Oliver Brown, Evelyn, Adams & Mackay, 1968
BROWSE, LILLIAN, and R. H. WILENSKI:
  Sickert, Faber, 1943
BOULTON, DAVID:
  Objection Overruled, McGibbon & Kee, 1967

CARRINGTON, DORA:
  Letters and Extracts from her Diary, edited by David Garnett, Cape, 1970
CHAPMAN, RONALD:
  The Laurel and The Thorn, a study of G. F. Watts, Faber, 1945
CLARKE, MARY:
  The Sadler's Wells Ballet, Adam & Charles Black, 1955
COOPER, DIANA:
  The Rainbow Comes and Goes, Hart-Davis, 1958
DAINTREY, ADRIAN:
  I Must Say, Chatto & Windus, 1963
EDE, H. S.:
  Savage Messiah, Heinemann, 1931
EDEL, LEON:
  Literary Biography, Hart-Davis, 1959
EMMONS, ROBERT:
  The Life and Opinions of Walter Richard Sickert, Faber, 1941
ESCHOLIER, RAYMOND:
  Henri Matisse, Librairie Floury, Paris, 1937
FORSTER, E. M.:
  Goldsworthy Lowes Dickinson, Arnold, 1934
  Abinger Harvest, Arnold, 1936
  Two Cheers for Democracy, Arnold, 1951
FRY, ROGER:
  Vision and Design, Chatto & Windus, 1920
  Duncan Grant, Hogarth Press, 1923 (new edition 1930)
  Transformations, Chatto & Windus, 1926
  Cézanne, Hogarth Press, 1927
  Last Lectures (introduction by Kenneth Clark), Cambridge University Press, 1939
  Letters of Roger Fry, edited by Denys Sutton, 2 vols., Chatto & Windus, 1972
GARLAND, MADGE:
  The Indecisive Decade, Macdonald, 1968
GARNETT, DAVID:
  The Golden Echo, Chatto & Windus, 1954
  The Flowers of the Forest, Chatto & Windus, 1956
  The Familiar Faces, Chatto & Windus, 1962
GERTLER, MARK:
  Selected Letters, edited by Noel Carrington (introduction by Quentin Bell), Hart-Davis, 1965
GIBSON, ASHLEY:
  Postscript to Adventure, Dent, 1930

GLENAVY, BEATRICE:
Today We Will Only Gossip, Constable, 1964
GRANT, ELIZABETH:
Memoirs of a Highland Lady, edited by Lady Strachey, 1898
(rev. edn by Angus Davidson, John Murray, 1950)
GRANT, BARTLE (ED.):
The Receip Book of Elizabeth Raper, with Portions of Her Cipher Journal. Portrait and Decorations by Duncan Grant, Nonesuch Press, 1924
GRIGORIEV, S. L.:
The Diaghilev Ballet 1909–29 (trans. by Vera Bowen), Constable, 1953
GUIGUET, JEAN:
Virginia Woolf and Her Works (trans. by J. Stewart), Hogarth Press, 1965
HAMNETT, NINA:
Laughing Torso, Constable, 1932
Is She a Lady?, Allan Wingate, 1955
HANNAY, HOWARD:
Roger Fry and Other Essays, Allen & Unwin, 1937
HARROD, ROY:
The Life of John Maynard Keynes, Macmillan, 1951
HART-DAVIS, RUPERT:
Hugh Walpole, Hart-Davis, 1952
HASSALL, CHRISTOPHER:
Rupert Brooke, Faber, 1964
HIND, C. LEWIS:
The Post Impressionists, Methuen, 1911
HOLMAN HUNT, DIANA:
Latin Among Lions, Alvaro Guevara, Michael Joseph, 1974
HOLROYD, MICHAEL:
Lytton Strachey, A Critical Biography, Heinemann, vol. 1 1967, vol. 2, 1968
HOMBERGER, ERIC, et al:
The Cambridge Mind, Cape, 1970
HUXLEY, JULIAN (ed.):
Aldous Huxley, A Memorial Volume, Chatto & Windus, 1965
HYNES, SAMUEL:
The Edwardian Turn of Mind, Oxford University Press, 1968
JOHNSTONE, J. K.:
The Bloomsbury Group, Secker & Warburg, 1954
KEYNES, JOHN MAYNARD:
Two Memoirs (introduction by David Garnett), Hart-Davis, 1949
KEYNES, MILO (ed.):
Essays on John Maynard Keynes, Cambridge University Press, 1975
LEHMANN, JOHN:
The Whispering Gallery, Longmans, 1955
I Am My Brother, Longmans, 1960
Virginia Woolf and Her World, Thames & Hudson, 1975
LEWIS, WYNDHAM:
Blasting and Bombadiering, Calder & Boyars, 1967
LILLY, MARJORIE:
Sickert: The Painter and His Circle, Elek Books, 1971

MacCARTHY, DESMOND:
Memoirs, MacGibbon & Kee, 1953
MAITLAND, F. W.:
The Life and Letters of Leslie Stephen, Duckworth, 1906
MARSH, EDWARD:
A Number of People, Heinemann with Hamish Hamilton, 1939
MAURON, CHARLES:
Aesthetics and Psychology, (trans. by Roger Fry and Katherine John), Hogarth Press, 1935
MORRELL, OTTOLINE:
Ottoline, The Early Memoirs of Lady Ottoline Morrell, edited by Robert Gathorne-Hardy, Faber, 1963
Ottoline at Garsington, Memoirs of Lady Ottoline Morrell, edited by Robert Gathorne-Hardy, Faber, 1974
MORTIMER, RAYMOND:
Duncan Grant (Penguin Modern Painters), Penguin Books, 1944
Channel Packet, Hogarth Press, 1948
The New Interior Decoration – see TODD, DOROTHY.
NOBLE, JOAN RUSSELL (ed.):
Recollections of Virginia Woolf by her Contemporaries, Peter Owen, 1972
PENROSE, ROLAND:
Picasso: His Life and Work, Gollancz, 1958
PLOMER, WILLIAM:
At Home, Cape, 1958
ROBERTSON, DAVID:
George Mallory, Faber, 1969
ROSS, ROBERT:
Friend of Friends, edited by Margery Ross, Cape, 1952
ROTHENSTEIN, JOHN:
Modern English Painters: Sickert to Grant, Innes to Moore, 2 vols., Grey Arrow Books, 1962
ROTHENSTEIN, WILLIAM:
Men and Memoirs 1872–1900, Faber, 1931
Men and Memoirs 1900–1922, Faber, 1932
Since Fifty, Faber, 1939
ROWDON, JOHN:
Duncan Grant, with a letter from Duncan Grant, 1934
SANDERS, CHARLES R.:
The Strachey Family 1558–1932, Durham, N.C., Duke, University Press, 1953
Lytton Strachey: His Mind and Art, New Haven, Yale University Press, 1957
SETAN-KARR, W. S.:
Grant of Rothiemurchus, A Memoir of Sir John Peter Grant, John Murray, 1899
SICKERT, WALTER:
A Free House, edited by Osbert Sitwell, Macmillan, 1947
SITWELL, OSBERT:
Great Morning, Reprint Society, 1949
Laughter in the Next Room, Reprint Society, 1950
SPENDER, STEPHEN:
World Within World, Hamish Hamilton, 1951
SPROTT, W. J. H.:
Human Groups, Penguin Books, 1958

STANSKY, PETER, and ABRAHAMS, WILLIAM:
Journey to the Frontier: Julian Bell and John Cornford, their lives and the 1930s, Constable, 1966

STEIN, GERTRUDE:
Picasso, Librarie Floury, Paris, 1938

STRACHEY, LYTTON:
Lytton Strachey by Himself: A Self-Portrait, edited by Michael Holroyd, Heinemann, 1971

SUTTON, DENYS:
André Derain, Phaidon, 1959

TAYLOR, A. J. P.
English History 1914–45, Penguin Books, 1973

TODD, DOROTHY, and MORTIMER, RAYMOND:
The New Interior Decoration, Batsford, 1929

WOOLF, LEONARD:
After the Deluge, Hogarth Press, 1931
Sowing 1880–1904, Hogarth Press, 1960
Beginning Again 1911–1918, Hogarth Press, 1964
Downhill All the Way 1919–1939, Hogarth Press, 1967

WOOLF, VIRGINIA:
The Voyage Out, Duckworth, 1915
To the Lighthouse, Hogarth Press, 1927
Walter Sickert: A Conversation, Hogarth Press, 1934
Roger Fry: A Biography, Hogarth Press, 1940
The Moment and Other Essays, Hogarth Press, 1947
A Writer's Diary, edited by Leonard Woolf, Hogarth Press, 1953
Letters of V. Woolf and L. Strachey, edited by L. Woolf and J. Strachey, Hogarth Press and Chatto & Windus, 1956

Selected catalogues

BAYNES, KEITH:
Fifty Years of Painting, with an introduction by William Townshend. The Minories, Colchester, 1969
Retrospective (1912–1972), with an introduction by John Woodeson. Gallery Edward Harvane, London, 1973
Watercolours and Drawings, with an introduction by Richard Shone. Pembroke Street Gallery, Cambridge, 1976

BELL, CLIVE:
Clive Bell at Charleston, with an introduction by Quentin Bell. Gallery Edward Harvane, London, 1972

BELL, VANESSA:
Memorial Exhibition, with an introduction by André Dunoyer de Segonzac. Adams Gallery, London, 1962
Memorial Retrospective, with an introduction by Ronald Pickvance. Arts Council, London, 1964
Drawings and Designs, with a preface by Richard Morphet. Folio Fine Art, London, 1967
Paintings and Drawings, with an introduction by Richard Morphet. Anthony d'Offay Gallery, London, 1970
Recent Paintings, with a foreword by Virginia Woolf. The Cooling Galleries, London, 1930

FRY, ROGER:
Memorial Exhibition, Museum and Art Gallery, Bristol, 1935. Opening address by Virginia Woolf, reprinted in 'The Moment', Hogarth Press, 1947
Paintings and Drawings, with an introductory essay by Sir Desmond MacCarthy. Arts Council, London, 1952
Paintings, Watercolours and Drawings, with a preface by Pamela Diamand. The Minories, Colchester, 1959
Vision and Design – The Life, work and influence of Roger Fry, with essays by Quentin Bell and Philip Troutman. Arts Council, London, 1966

GERTLER, MARK:
Retrospective, with a survey by John Woodeson. The Minories, Colchester, 1971

GRANT, DUNCAN:
Recent Paintings, with a foreword by David Garnett. The Cooling Galleries, London, 1931
Drawings, with a foreword by Kenneth Clark. Thos. Agnew & Sons, London, 1933
Retrospective Exhibition, with an introductory essay by Alan Clutton-Brock. The Tate Gallery, London, 1959
Duncan Grant and His World, with an introduction by Denys Sutton. Wildenstein & Co. Ltd, London, 1964
Paintings (with Vanessa Bell), with a preface by Denys Sutton. Royal West of England Academy, Bristol, 1966
The Murals, Berwick Church, a short history by Richard Shone. Published by the Towner Art Gallery, Eastbourne for the exhibition of Berwick Church Paintings, 1969
Portraits, with an introduction by Richard Shone. Arts Council, Cambridge Gallery, 1969
Watercolours and Drawings, with a note by Stephen Spender. Anthony d'Offay Gallery, London, 1972
Ninetieth Birthday Exhibition, with an introduction by David Brown, National Gallery of Modern Art, Edinburgh, 1975
Duncan Grant and Bloomsbury, with an introduction by Richard Shone. The Fine Art Society, Edinburgh, 1975
Ninetieth Birthday Display, with notes by Richard Morphet. The Tate Gallery, 1975
Watercolours, drawings and designs. Davis & Long, New York, 1975

HAMNETT, NINA:
Paintings and Drawings, with a preface by Walter Sickert. The Eldar Gallery, London, 1918

Paintings and Drawings. The Claridge Gallery, London, 1926

LONDON ARTISTS' ASSOCIATION:

Exhibition of Modern English Pictures, with a preface by Clive Bell. Marie Sterner Galleries, New York, 1928

Exhibition, with a foreword by Clive Bell. Ferens Art Gallery, Hull, 1953

SICKERT, WALTER:

Sickert, with a biography and notes by Wendy Baron. The Fine Art Society, London, 1973

WOLFE, EDWARD:

Exhibition, with a foreword by R. B. Cunningham-Grahame. The Cooling Galleries, London, 1930

Retrospective, with an essay by Bryan Robertson and a note on the artist by Richard Hughes. The Arts Council, London, 1967

Exhibition, with notes on the artist. The Mayor Gallery, London, 1973

GENERAL:

Artists of Bloomsbury. The Rye Art Gallery, 1967

Fitzrovia and the Road to the York Minster, with a memoir by Ruthven Todd. The Parkin Gallery, London, 1973

Vorticism and its Allies, with an introduction and notes by Richard Cork. The Arts Council, Hayward Gallery, London, 1974

Note on unpublished sources

The following letters, of which I have made extensive use, are among the Charleston Papers in the Library of King's College, Cambridge.

Vanessa Bell to Roger Fry (454 letters from 1911 to 1934).
Vanessa Bell to Clive Bell (over 300 letters from 1902 to 1960).
Vanessa Bell to Maynard Keynes (92 letters from 1908 to 1935).
Vanessa Bell to Thoby Stephen (24 letters from 1897 to 1901).
Vanessa Bell to Margery Snowdon (40 letters from 1902 to 1925).
Clive Bell to Vanessa Bell (393 letters from 1916 to 1958).
Clive Bell to Molly MacCarthy (38 letters from 1912 to 1915).
Roger Fry to Vanessa Bell (502 letters from 1910 to 1934).
Roger Fry to Duncan Grant (12 letters from 1910 to 1914).
Roger Fry to Clive Bell (21 letters from 1910 to 1934).
Maynard Keynes to Vanessa Bell (83 letters from 1916 to 1945).
Thoby Stephen to Clive Bell (59 letters from 1902 to 1906).
Walter Lamb to Clive Bell (71 letters from 1901 to 1911).
Virginia Stephen to Thoby Stephen (17 letters from 1897 to 1904).

Clive Bell to Saxon Sydney Turner (20 letters from 1905 to 1915).
Molly MacCarthy to Clive Bell (42 letters from 1912 to 1933).
Duncan Grant to Lytton Strachey (87 letters from 1902 to 1931).

A group of miscellaneous letters to Maynard Keynes of which the most considerable are groups from Clive Bell, David Garnett, Lady Ottoline Morrell, Virginia Woolf. Other correspondents include Barbara Bagenal, Katherine Cox, Frederick Etchells, Molly MacCarthy, H. O. Meredith, G. E. Moore and others. All these are among the Keynes Papers, King's College, Cambridge. In the same collection I have consulted Keynes's correspondence concerning sales, the Contemporary Art Society, the Council for Encouragement of Music and the Arts and the London Artists' Association.

In the Charleston Papers I have made extensive use of Duncan Grant's two part memoir 'Paris', a paper read to the Memoir Club.

In Duncan Grant's possession I also consulted letters addressed to him from Miss Winifred Gill of the Omega Workshops, copies of which are in the Libraries of the Tate Gallery and the Victoria and Albert Museum.

Index